The Windows XP Professional Cram Sheet

This Cram Sheet contains the distilled, key facts about Windows XP Professional. Review this information as the last thing you do before you enter the testing center, paying special attention to those areas where you feel that you need the most review. You can transfer any of these facts from your head onto a blank sheet of paper immediately before you begin the exam.

INSTALLATION AND DEPLOYMENT

1. Know the differences between ACPI and APM when installing the OS, as well as the ramifications if the wrong one is in place after installation.
2. Know all the following processes for unattended and Remote Installation Service (RIS) installations:
    - *winnt.sif*—Used to automate CD-ROM-based installs.
    - *sysprep.inf*—The answer file for System Preparation (Sysprep) installs.
    - *winnt.exe with the /u, /s, and /udf switches*—Used for unattended installations.
    - *winnt32.exe and unattend.txt*—Automate an upgrade to Windows XP.
    - *Requirements for RIS are* Active Directory, DNS, and DHCP.
3. **winnt32.exe** with the checkupgradeonly switch are used to verify hardware and software compatibility before installation.
4. **rbfg.exe** is used to create remote boot disks for RIS clients if computers don't have network adapters with Pre-boot Execution Environment (PXE) boot ROM.
5. **riprep.exe** is used to create images of Windows XP Professional and applications for an RIS server.
6. **risetup.exe** is used to configure RIS.
7. **update.exe /s** is used to apply a service pack to a distribution share in slipstream mode.
8. Know how to convert to NTFS file system after installation, as well as how to stop the conversion after it has been initialized.
9. Remember that you can rollback to the old OS after Windows XP is installed in some circumstances, but never when upgrading from Windows 2000.
10. Know the details surrounding dynamic update for installation as well as the critical switches: **dudisable**, **dushare**, and **duprepare**.
11. Understand the sysprep tool and the essential switches that are available: **clean**, **factory**, **nosidgen**, and **reseal**.
12. Know the two important commands used with the User State Migration Tool: **scanstate** and **loadstate**.
13. Know the different "updates" that are available:
    - *Dynamic Update*—Used with installation to install the critical fixes and drivers.
    - *Automatic Updates*—Used with the Windows update feature and Web site to automatically download and offer critical fixes and drivers for the OS.
    - *Windows Update*—Built in service that helps control the critical fixes and drivers for the OS.

CONFIGURING AND MANAGING RESOURCES

14. The default for new shares is Everyone, Allow, Full Control. If share permissions conflict with NTFS permissions, the *most restrictive* permissions take precedence.
15. When you combine NTFS permissions based on users and their group memberships, the *least restrictive* permissions take precedence. However, Deny entries *always override* Allow entries.
16. By default, NTFS permissions are inherited from the parent folder. Permissions that are not inherited are referred to as *explicit.* Explicit permissions always override inherited

54. Auto Private IP Addressing (APIPA) takes effect on Windows XP Professional computers if no DHCP server can be contacted. APIPA assigns the computer an IP address within the range of 169.254.0.0 through 169.254.255.254 with a subnet mask of 255.255.0.0.
55. Remote Assistance is the built in service which allows another user, typically a help desk or IT employee, to remotely help the end user with an issue that they are experiencing on their Windows XP Professional computer.
56. Remote Desktop is the built in service that allows you to access a session that is running on your computer while you are sitting at another computer.

TROUBLESHOOTING, MONITORING, AND SYSTEM RECOVERY

57. You can back up and restore files and directories with Windows Backup. You can launch this from the Accessories|System Tools Program group, the **ntbackup** command, or the properties sheet of any drive volume. Users can back up files to which they have at least the Read permission, and they can restore files to which they have at least the Write permission. To back up or restore other files, users need to be members of the Backup Operators group or the Administrators group.
58. Backing up the system state allows you to back up the registry, COM+ objects, and system startup files.
59. Know the following options for troubleshooting a system:
    - System Restore is the easiest way to return your computer to a previous state. Automatic restore points are set every 24 hours by default. You can also set your own manual restore points. Configure System Restore settings from the System Restore tab on the System Properties dialog box.
    - The Recovery Console is a special command prompt only mode you must boot the system into using the bootable Windows XP CD-ROM or by running **winnt32 /cmdcons** *before* a failure.
    - Safe Mode is generally the most useful troubleshooting mode because it starts the operating system with minimal services and drivers. It is best for removing services or drivers that are causing Stop Errors (aka "blue screens of death").
    - Last Known Good Configuration starts the system with the ControlSet (a portion of the registry) that was used the last time the system booted successfully and instantiated the Windows Explorer shell (desktop). If you install a driver or service that crashes *before you restart and log on again successfully*, you can restart the machine and select Last Known Good Configuration. Doing so effectively removes the driver or service from the active registry.
    - The Automated System Recovery (ASR) process is your *last resort* to recover the Windows XP operating system, the startup environment, and the registry. To use it, boot a system with the Windows XP Professional CD-ROM and choose the Repair option. You also need your most recent ASR floppy disk and your most recent ASR backup media set. The Windows Backup program (**ntbackup.exe**) is required for creating and restoring ASR backup media sets. .
60. Task Manager allows you to monitor particular performance metrics and to set the priority of applications. You should not select Realtime priority, which can interfere with other applications. Task Manager is also used to set processor (CPU) affinity for applications, but only on dual-CPU systems.
61. Use the Performance Console to monitor system performance and to establish baselines.
62. Logical disk counters for monitoring system performance do *not* need to be enabled using the **diskperf** command.

DIAL-UP AND RAS

63. IPSec negotiates encryption settings between the client and server to encrypt both passwords and data before an L2TP session is created.
64. EAP is an extension of Point-to-Point Protocol (PPP) for dial-up connections, and L2TP and PPTP clients. EAP supports several authentication protocols:
    - Message Digest 5 Challenge Handshake Authentication Protocol (MD5-CHAP)
    - Generic token cards
    - Transport Layer Security (TLS) for use with smart cards
65. Know well the default configurations for both dial-up and VPN connections with regard to the authentication, security, and encryption settings.
66. Internet Connection Sharing (ICS) uses the DHCP Allocator service to assign dynamic IP addresses to clients on the LAN within the range of 192.168.0.2 through 192.168.0.254. In addition, the DNS Proxy service becomes enabled when you implement ICS.
67. Internet Connection Firewall (ICF) is the service that monitors all aspects of the traffic that crosses the network interface, which includes inspecting the source and destination addresses, for further control. Typically port 80 (Web/HTTP), as well as ports 20 and 21 (FTP) are controlled.

HARDWARE AND DEVICE DRIVERS

37. Windows XP can control whether users can install signed or unsigned drivers, or both, for a chosen device. The selection for this is called Driver Signing and is made as a Group Policy Object (GPO) settings for the Local Computer or as a Computer Configuration setting for a Windows Domain. The three choices for Unsigned Driver Installation Behavior are: Silently Succeed, Warn But Allow Installation, or Do Not Allow Installation. From the GUI, the choices are labeled Ignore, Warn, or Block.
38. To restore a device driver back to its previously installed version, open Device Manager, right-click the device you are having trouble with, and select Properties. Click the Driver tab and then click the Roll Back Driver button.
39. Power Options in Control Panel lets you customize your power scheme settings. Standby does not save your desktop state to disk; if a power failure occurs while the computer is on standby, you can lose unsaved information. The hibernate feature saves everything in memory to disk, turns off your monitor and hard disk, and then turns off your computer.
40. Windows XP Professional supports a maximum of 2 processors (CPUs).

DISK DRIVES, VOLUMES, AND FILE SYSTEMS

41. A Windows XP basic disk is a physical disk with primary and extended partitions. You can create up to three primary partitions and one extended partition with logical drives on a basic disk, or just four primary partitions. You cannot extend a basic disk.
42. A Windows XP dynamic disk is a physical disk that does not use partitions or logical drives. Instead, it has only dynamic volumes that you create using the Disk Management console. You can extend a volume on a dynamic disk. Dynamic disks can contain an unlimited number of volumes. Only Windows XP Professional (and Windows 2000) computers can directly access local dynamic volumes. However, computers that are not running Windows XP can access shared folders on dynamic volumes over the network.
43. You can convert a dynamic disk with volumes back to a basic disk, but you'll lose all your data. If you find yourself needing to do this, first backup your data, convert the disk to basic, and then restore your data.
44. Mounted drives, also known as mount points or mounted volumes, are useful for increasing a drive's "size" without disturbing it. Mount points also enable you to access multiple local storage devices through empty NTFS folders so that you don't have to assign drive letters. Drive paths are available only on empty folders on NTFS volumes. The NTFS volumes can be basic or dynamic.
45. Windows XP offers FAT (also known as FAT16) and FAT32 file system support with the following conditions or specifications:
    - Pre-existing FAT32 partitions up to 2 Terabytes are supported in Windows XP.
    - Windows XP allows you to create new FAT32 volumes of only 32GB or less.
46. Disk quotas track and control disk usage on a per-user, per-volume basis. You can apply disk quotas only to Windows XP NTFS volumes. Disk quotas do not use compression to measure disk space usage, so users cannot obtain or use more space simply by compressing their own data. To enable disk quotas, open the Properties dialog box for a disk, select the Quota tab, and configure the options.
47. To convert a volume from FAT or FAT32 to NTFS use **convert d: /fs:ntfs**. This command is one way and is not reversible. After the conversion, NTFS folder and file permissions for the root of drive volumes are set to Allow Read and Execute for the Everyone group.
48. Encrypted files that are moved or copied to another NTFS folder remain encrypted. Encrypted files that are moved or copied to a FAT or FAT32 drive volume become decrypted. If users (other than the one who encrypted the file or a user with shared access) attempt to move an encrypted file to a different NTFS volume, or to a FAT or FAT32 drive volume, they receive an Access Is Denied error message. If users other than the one who encrypted the file attempt to move the encrypted file to a different folder located on the *same* NTFS volume, the file is moved.

NETWORK PROTOCOLS AND SERVICES

49. TCP/IP is the default protocol suite. Its default setting is to obtain an IP address automatically. All IP addresses must have a subnet mask.
50. DHCP runs on Windows NT and Windows 2000 and .NET Server computers to automatically lease out dynamic IP addresses to client computers.
51. DNS is required for Active Directory. DNS provides name resolution by mapping host names to IP addresses and vice versa.
52. WINS is not required for Active Directory. WINS offers name resolution by mapping NetBIOS computer names to IP addresses and vice versa.
53. To troubleshoot TCP/IP connectivity problems, use the **ipconfig** and **ping** command-line utilities. The **ipconfig** tool displays the local computer's IP configuration; **ping** tests connectivity to remote computers and can test the local configuration by pinging the loopback address of 127.0.0.1.

permissions—an explicit Allow will even override an inherited Deny permission.

17. To change NTFS permissions on a file or folder, you must be the owner, or have the Change Permissions permission, which itself is part of Full Control. NTFS permissions are *retained* from the source folder whenever you *move* subfolders or files to another folder on the *same* NTFS volume. NTFS permissions are inherited from the destination folder in all other move and copy operations.
18. NTFS for Windows XP supports both file compression and data encryption. Encryption is implemented via the Encrypting File System (EFS). You can compress or encrypt a file, but not both.
19. Windows XP Professional and Windows 2000 computers can connect to printers that are attached to Windows XP, Windows 2000, and Windows .NET Server print servers through a Web browser. This feature uses the Internet Printing Protocol (IPP). IIS must be running on the machine you want to connect to. You can enter one of the following URLs into your Web browser:

    http://print_server_name/printers

    http://print_server_name/printer_share_name

SECURITY ACCOUNTS AND POLICIES

20. Local user and group accounts can be granted privileges and permissions to resources on the same system only. They cannot access resources on other systems.
21. Local user accounts can belong to local groups on the same system only. Domain user accounts can belong to global groups, universal groups, domain local groups, and machine local groups.
22. Renaming an account maintains all group memberships, permissions, and privileges of the account. Copying a user account maintains group memberships, permissions, and privileges assigned to its groups, but doing so does not retain permissions associated with the original user account. Deleting and re-creating an account with the same name loses all group memberships and permissions.
23. The most powerful group on a system is its local Administrators group. The Power Users group is an excellent group for most users that need to control the computer's resources, but not the computer's administration.
24. Organizational Units (OUs) in Active Directory create a hierarchical structure of containers for other objects, such as users, groups, and computers. Objects inherit attributes of their parent objects.
25. The Resulting Set of Policies (RSoP) is the final set of policies that is applied to the user and computer. The **gpresult** tool can help determine this RSoP, as can the **RSoP MMC snap-in**. The **gpupdate** tool can help "refresh" the policies to ensure the correct policies are applied.

MANAGING USER AND DESKTOP SETTINGS

26. Know the purpose and configuration of all the accessibility features: StickyKeys, FilterKeys Narrator, Magnifier, and On-Screen Keyboard.
27. Use the MSCONFIG utility to change system startup settings, enable and disable services, and modify BOOT.ini file settings.
28. The Regional And Language Options applet in Control Panel specifies user and input locales. It can also be used to add new input languages. Use this applet to pair input locales with a specific keyboard layout when a user needs to work with different languages.
29. Transfer data files and program settings from pre-Windows XP computers using either the User State Migration Tool (USMT) or the File Settings And Transfer (FAST) Wizard.
30. Applications can be deployed to users via a Group Policy. Applications can be either published or assigned. Install published applications via the Add and Remove Programs applet. Assigned applications have shortcuts in the Start menu, which will launch the installation program for an assigned application upon first use.
31. Typically, only applications compiled as an .msi file can be deployed via a Group Policy. However, non-.msi applications can use a ZAP file to tell Group Policy how to install the application.
32. To enable roaming profiles, enter the UNC path to the user's profile in the user's account properties.
33. To configure mandatory profiles, rename ntuser.dat to ntuser.man.
34. The Offline Files feature caches copies of network files locally. It is enabled by default on the client. On the server side, Manual Caching Of Documents is the default setting for shared folders. You can choose to Encrypt Offline Files To Secure Data from the Offline Files tab of the Folder Options dialog box.
35. Dualview is an advanced display option that enables a mobile computer to extend the Windows XP desktop onto both its built-in LCD display and onto an external monitor. It also supports desktop PCs that have on video adapter installed with 2 video output ports. You enable Dualview via the Display applet in Control panel.
36. Use the Program Compatibility wizard to run legacy applications in Compatibility Mode for Windows 95, Windows 98/Me, Windows NT 4 SP5, or Windows 2000. No other modes are available.

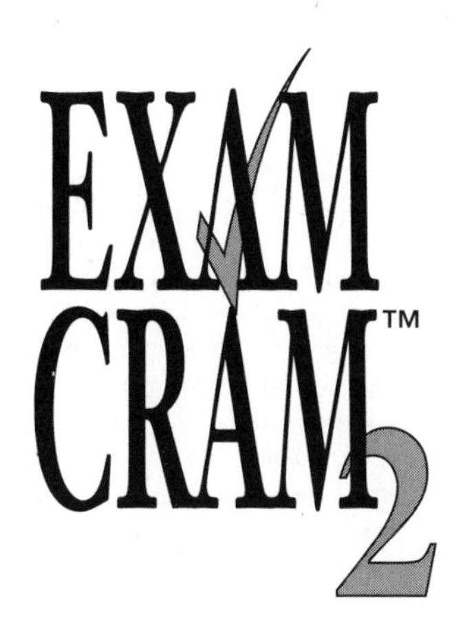

Windows® XP Professional

Practice Questions

Vic Picinich

Windows® XP Professional Practice Questions Exam Cram 2 (MCSE 70-270)

International Standard Book Number: 0-7897-3107-x

Library of Congress Catalog Card Number: 2003113761

Printed in the United States of America

First Printing: April 2004

07 06 05 8 7 6 5 4

Trademarks

Warning and Disclaimer

Bulk Sales

Que Publishing offers excellent discounts on this book when ordered in quantity for bulk purchases or special sales. For more information, please contact

U.S. Corporate and Government Sales
1-800-382-3419
corpsales@pearsontechgroup.com

For sales outside the U.S., please contact

International Sales
international@pearsoned.com

Publisher
Paul Boger

Executive Editor
Jeff Riley

Acquisitions Editor
Jeff Riley

Development Editor
Steve Rowe

Managing Editor
Charlotte Clapp

Project Editor
Tonya Simpson

Copy Editor
Mike Henry

Proofreader
Jessica McCarty

Technical Editor
Marc Savage

Publishing Coordinator
Pamalee Nelson

Multimedia Developer
Dan Scherf

Interior Designer
Anne Jones

Cover Designer
Anne Jones

Page Layout
Brad Chinn

Que Certification • 800 East 96th Street • Indianapolis, Indiana 46240

A Note from Series Editor Ed Tittel

You know better than to trust your certification preparation to just anybody. That's why you, and more than two million others, have purchased an Exam Cram book. As Series Editor for the new and improved Exam Cram 2 series, I have worked with the staff at Que Certification to ensure you won't be disappointed. That's why we've taken the world's best-selling certification product—a finalist for "Best Study Guide" in a CertCities reader poll in 2002—and made it even better.

As a two-time finalist for the "Favorite Study Guide Author" award as selected by CertCities readers, I know the value of good books. You'll be impressed with Que Certification's stringent review process, which ensures the books are high-quality, relevant, and technically accurate.

We've also added MeasureUp a powerful, full-featured test engine, which is trusted by certification students throughout the world.

As a 20-year-plus veteran of the computing industry and the original creator and editor of the Exam Cram series, I've brought my IT experience to bear on these books. During my tenure at Novell from 1989 to 1994, I worked with and around its excellent education and certification department. This experience helped push my writing and teaching activities heavily in the certification direction. Since then, I've worked on more than 70 certification-related books, and I write about certification topics for numerous Web sites and for *Certification* magazine.

In 1996, while studying for various MCP exams, I became frustrated with the huge, unwieldy study guides that were the only preparation tools available. As an experienced IT professional and former instructor, I wanted "nothing but the facts" necessary to prepare for the exams. From this impetus, Exam Cram emerged in 1997. It quickly became the best-selling computer book series since "...*For Dummies*," and the best-selling certification book series ever. By maintaining an intense focus on subject matter, tracking errata and updates quickly, and following the certification market closely, Exam Cram was able to establish the dominant position in cert prep books.

You will not be disappointed in your decision to purchase this book. If you are, please contact me at etittel@jump.net. All suggestions, ideas, input, or constructive criticism are welcome!

Ed Tittel

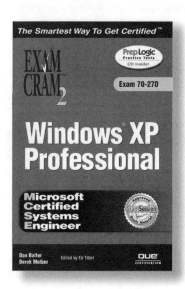

Taking You to the 70-270 Finish Line!

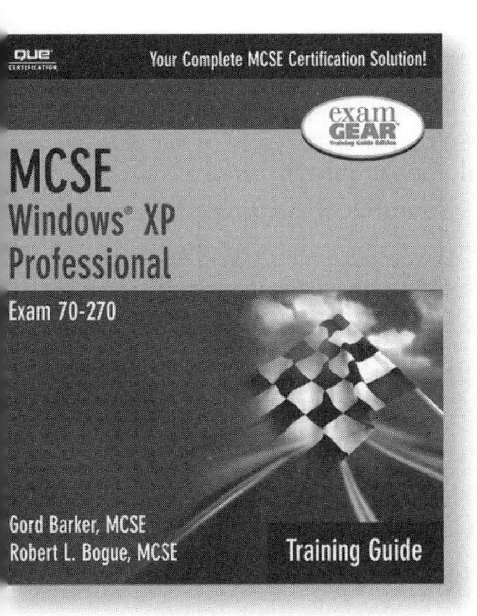

MCSE Training Guide (70-270): Windows XP Professional

Gord Barker and Robert L. Bogue

ISBN 0-7897-2773-0

$49.99 US/$77.99 CAN/£36.50 Net UK

Before you walk into your local testing center, make absolutely sure you're prepared to pass your exam. In addition to the Exam Cram 2 series, consider our Training Guide series. Que Certification's Training Guides have exactly what you need to pass your exam:

- Exam Objectives highlighted in every chapter
- Notes, Tips, Warnings, and Exam Tips advise what to watch out for
- Step-by-Step Exercises for "hands-on" practice
- End-of-chapter Exercises and Exam Questions
- Final Review with Fast Facts, Study and Exam Tips, and another Practice Exam
- A CD that includes PrepLogic Practice Tests for complete evaluation of your knowledge
- Our authors are recognized experts in the field. In most cases, they are current or former instructors, trainers, or consultants – they know exactly what you need to know!

About the Author

Vic Picinich is a computer professional and consultant with more than 25 years experience in the computer field. He presently works as a Microsoft Certified Trainer for Heald College in Stockton, California, with more than 10 years teaching both day and evening classes. Vic has also narrated more than 60 full-length audio training products for AudioWhiz, a Web-based corporation. These include audio self-study training products that help individuals earn certifications from organizations such as Microsoft, CompTIA, Novell, Oracle, and Cisco.

Vic graduated *magna cum laude* from Saint Peter's College in his hometown of Jersey City, New Jersey, with an MBA in Management Information Systems in 1991. He went on to receive further college instruction at New York University in New York City and Heald College, School of Technology, in San Francisco. He holds the following certifications: MCT, MCSE, MCSA, MOS, CTT+, Server+, Network+, and A+.

He enjoys spending time with his family and serving his community by volunteering at his local American Red Cross and the Stockton Police Department. He can be contacted by email at Vic@Picinich.com.

About eITprep

eITprep

eITprep offers a variety of tools that help you prepare for IT certification exams, including books, tests, software, online courses, and IT games. For more information, please visit www.eitgames.com.

Contents at a Glance

Table of Contents

We Want to Hear from You!

As the reader of this book, *you* are our most important critic and commentator. We value your opinion and want to know what we're doing right, what we could do better, what areas you'd like to see us publish in, and any other words of wisdom you're willing to pass our way.

As an executive editor for Que Publishing, I welcome your comments. You can email or write me directly to let me know what you did or didn't like about this book—as well as what we can do to make our books better.

Please note that I cannot help you with technical problems related to the topic of this book. We do have a User Services group, however, where I will forward specific technical questions related to the book.

When you write, please be sure to include this book's title and author as well as your name, email address, and phone number. I will carefully review your comments and share them with the author and editors who worked on the book.

Email: `feedback@quepublishing.com`

Mail: Jeff Riley
Executive Editor
Que Publishing
800 East 96th Street
Indianapolis, IN 46240 USA

For more information about this book or another Que Publishing title, visit our Web site at `www.examcram2.com`. Type the ISBN (excluding hyphens) or the title of a book in the Search field to find the page you're looking for.

Introduction

What Is This Book About?

Welcome to *MCSE Windows XP Professional Practice Questions Exam Cram 2 (Exam 70-270)*! The sole aim of this book is to provide you with practice questions complete with answers and explanations that will help you learn, drill, and review for the Windows XP Professional certification exam.

Who Is This Book For?

If you've studied the 70-270 exam's content and feel you're ready to put your knowledge to the test, but you're not sure that you want to take the real exam yet, this book is for you! Maybe you've answered other practice questions or unsuccessfully taken the real exam, reviewed, and want to do more practice questions before going to take the real exam; this book is for you, too!

What Will You Find in This Book?

As mentioned before, this book is all about practice questions! This book is separated according to the topics you'll find in the 70-270 exam. Each chapter represents an exam topic and in every chapter you'll find three elements:

- *Practice Questions*—These are the numerous questions that will help you learn, drill, and review.
- *Quick-Check Answer Key*—After you've finished answering the questions, you can quickly grade your exam from this section. Only correct answers are given here. No explanations are offered yet!

- *Answers and Explanations*—This section offers you the correct answers as well as further explanation about the content posed in that question. Use this information to learn why an answer is correct and to reinforce the content in your mind for exam day.

You also will find a *Cram Sheet* at the beginning of this book specifically written for this exam. This is a very popular element that is also found in the corresponding *MCSE 70-270 Exam Cram 2* study guide (ISBN 0-7897-2874-5). This item condenses all the necessary facts found in this exam into an easy-to-handle tear card. The CramSheet is something you can carry with you to the exam location and use as a last-second study aid. Be aware that you can't take it into the exam room, though!

Hints for Using This Book

Because this book is a paper practice product, you might want to complete your exams on a separate piece of paper so that you can reuse the exams over and over without having previous answers in your way. Also, a general rule of thumb across all practice question products is to make sure that you're scoring well into the high 80% to 90% range in all topics before attempting the real exam. The higher percentages you score on practice question products, the better your chances for passing the real exam. Of course, we can't guarantee a passing score on the real exam, but we can offer you plenty of opportunities to practice and assess your knowledge levels before you enter the real exam.

Need Further Study?

Are you having a hard time correctly answering these questions? If so, you probably need further review. Be sure to see the sister product to this book, Que Publishing's *MCSE 70-270 Exam Cram 2* (ISBN 0-7897-2874-5) for further review. If you need even further study, check out Que's *MCSE 70-270 Training Guide* (ISBN-0-7897-2773-0).

Installing, Configuring, and Administering Microsoft Windows XP Professional

Quick Check

1. Which of the following commands is needed to perform a clean installation of Microsoft Windows XP from CD-ROM?

   - ☑ A. Winnt.exe
   - ☐ B. Winnt32.exe
   - ☐ C. Setup.exe
   - ☐ D. Setup32.exe

Quick Answer: **18**
Detailed Answer: **19**

2. Which of the following commands is needed to perform an upgrade installation of Microsoft Windows XP from CD-ROM?

   - ☐ A. Setup.exe
   - ☐ B. Winnt.exe
   - ☑ C. Winnt32.exe
   - ☐ D. Setup32.exe
   - ☐ E. Upgrade.exe

Quick Answer: **18**
Detailed Answer: **19**

3. Which of the following commands is needed to perform a clean installation of Microsoft Windows XP over a network?

   - ☐ A. Winnt32.exe
   - ☑ B. Winnt.exe
   - ☐ C. Setup.exe
   - ☐ D. Setup32.exe

Quick Answer: **18**
Detailed Answer: **19**

4. Which of the following commands is needed to perform an upgrade installation of Microsoft Windows XP over a network?

   - ☐ A. Winnt.exe
   - ☑ B. Winnt32.exe
   - ☐ C. Setup.exe
   - ☐ D. Setup32.exe
   - ☐ E. Upgrade.exe

Quick Answer: **18**
Detailed Answer: **19**

Quick Check

5. Which of the following pre-existing hard disk partition types must you have on the client system to hold setup files when installing Microsoft Windows XP over a network? (Select all that apply.)

   - ❑ A. FAT12
   - ❑ B. FAT16
   - ❑ C. FAT32
   - ❑ D. FAT64

Quick Answer: **18**
Detailed Answer: **19**

6. What is the minimum CPU speed required to install Microsoft Windows XP Home Edition?

   - ❑ A. 333MHz
   - ❑ B. 133MHz
   - ❑ C. 300MHz
   - ❑ D. 233MHz

Quick Answer: **18**
Detailed Answer: **19**

7. What is the minimum RAM required to install Microsoft Windows XP Home Edition?

   - ❑ A. 26MB
   - ❑ B. 128MB
   - ❑ C. 64MB
   - ❑ D. 512MB
   - ❑ E. 32MB

Quick Answer: **18**
Detailed Answer: **19**

8. What is the minimum CPU speed required to install Microsoft Windows XP Professional?

   - ❑ A. 333MHz
   - ❑ B. 133MHz
   - ❑ C. 300MHz
   - ❑ D. 233MHz

Quick Answer: **18**
Detailed Answer: **19**

9. What is the minimum RAM required to install Microsoft Windows XP Professional?

   - ❑ A. 64MB
   - ❑ B. 128MB
   - ❑ C. 256MB
   - ❑ D. 512MB
   - ❑ E. 32MB

Quick Answer: **18**
Detailed Answer: **19**

Quick Check

10. What is the maximum RAM allowed to successfully install Microsoft Windows XP Professional?
    - ❑ A. 4GB
    - ❑ B. 8GB
    - ❑ C. 16GB
    - ❑ D. 1TB
    - ❑ E. 2GB

Quick Answer: 18
Detailed Answer: 19

11. What is the maximum RAM allowed to successfully install Microsoft Windows XP Home Edition?
    - ❑ A. 1GB
    - ❑ B. 8GB
    - ❑ C. 16GB
    - ❑ D. 4GB
    - ❑ E. 2GB

Quick Answer: 18
Detailed Answer: 19

12. What is the minimum free hard disk space required to successfully install Microsoft Windows XP Professional?
    - ❑ A. 4.5GB
    - ❑ B. 2.5GB
    - ❑ C. 1.5GB
    - ❑ D. 1GB
    - ❑ E. .5GB

Quick Answer: 18
Detailed Answer: 19

13. What is the minimum free hard disk space required to successfully install Microsoft Windows XP Home Edition?
    - ❑ A. 2GB
    - ❑ B. 1.5GB
    - ❑ C. 4GB
    - ❑ D. 1GB
    - ❑ E. .5GB

Quick Answer: 18
Detailed Answer: 20

14. What is the maximum number of processors allowed in a client system when installing Microsoft Windows XP Home Edition?
    - ❑ A. 2
    - ❑ B. 8
    - ❑ C. 1
    - ❑ D. 4

Quick Answer: 18
Detailed Answer: 20

Quick Check

15. What is the maximum number of processors allowed in a client system when installing Microsoft Windows XP Professional?

Quick Answer: 18
Detailed Answer: 20

- ❑ A. 1
- ❑ B. 2
- ❑ C. 4
- ❑ D. 8

16. Which of the following winnt.exe command-line switches enables accessibility options during the installation of Microsoft Windows XP?

Quick Answer: 18
Detailed Answer: 20

- ❑ A. /a
- ❑ B. /s
- ❑ C. /t
- ❑ D. /u
- ❑ E. /udf:*id*

17. Which of the following winnt.exe command-line switches specifies the source location during the installation of the original Microsoft Windows XP files?

Quick Answer: 18
Detailed Answer: 20

- ❑ A. /u
- ❑ B. /a
- ❑ C. /t
- ❑ D. /s
- ❑ E. /udf:*id*

18. Which of the following winnt.exe command-line switches specifies the drive to hold temporary setup files during the installation of Microsoft Windows XP?

Quick Answer: 18
Detailed Answer: 20

- ❑ A. /u
- ❑ B. /a
- ❑ C. /s
- ❑ D. /t
- ❑ E. /udf:*id*

19. Which of the following winnt.exe command-line switches specifies to perform an unattended setup of Microsoft Windows XP?

Quick Answer: 18
Detailed Answer: 20

- ❑ A. /udf:*id*
- ❑ B. /a
- ❑ C. /s
- ❑ D. /t
- ❑ E. /u

Quick Check

20. Which of the following winnt.exe command-line switches establishes an ID that setup uses to specify how a .UDF file modifies an answer file during an unattended setup of Microsoft Windows XP?

Quick Answer: **18**
Detailed Answer: **20**

- ❑ A. /s
- ❑ B. /a
- ❑ C. /udf
- ❑ D. /t
- ❑ E. /u

21. Which of the following winnt32.exe command-line switches only checks a system for compatibility with Microsoft Windows XP?

Quick Answer: **18**
Detailed Answer: **20**

- ❑ A. /udf:*id*
- ❑ B. /cmdcons
- ❑ C. /debug
- ❑ D. /noreboot
- ❑ E. /checkupgradeonly

22. Which of the following winnt32.exe command-line switches modifies the setup of Microsoft Windows XP by adding a Recovery Console option to the operating system selection screen?

Quick Answer: **18**
Detailed Answer: **20**

- ❑ A. /checkupgradeonly
- ❑ B. /cmdcons
- ❑ C. /debug
- ❑ D. /noreboot
- ❑ E. /udf:*id*

23. Which of the following winnt32.exe command-line switches modifies the setup of Microsoft Windows XP by creating a debug log during installation?

Quick Answer: **18**
Detailed Answer: **20**

- ❑ A. /checkupgradeonly
- ❑ B. /cmdcons
- ❑ C. /debug
- ❑ D. /noreboot
- ❑ E. /udf:*id*

Quick Check

24. Which of the following winnt32.exe command-line switches modifies the setup of Microsoft Windows XP by specifying the system not to reboot after the first stage of installation?

Quick Answer: **18**
Detailed Answer: **20**

- ❑ A. /checkupgradeonly
- ❑ B. /cmdcons
- ❑ C. /debug
- ❑ D. /noreboot
- ❑ E. /udf:*id*

25. Which of the following winnt32.exe command-line switches modifies the setup of Microsoft Windows XP by establishing the *id* (identification) that setup uses to specify how a .UDF (uniqueness database file) modifies an answer file?

Quick Answer: **18**
Detailed Answer: **20**

- ❑ A. /checkupgradeonly
- ❑ B. /cmdcons
- ❑ C. /debug
- ❑ D. /noreboot
- ❑ E. /udf:*id*

26. Which of the following winnt32.exe command-line switches modifies the setup of Microsoft Windows XP by specifying the answer file for an unattended installation?

Quick Answer: **18**
Detailed Answer: **21**

- ❑ A. /checkupgradeonly
- ❑ B. /cmdcons
- ❑ C. /unattend
- ❑ D. /s
- ❑ E. /udf:*id*

27. Which of the following winnt32.exe command-line switches modifies the setup of Microsoft Windows XP by specifying the source location of the original Microsoft Windows XP files?

Quick Answer: **18**
Detailed Answer: **21**

- ❑ A. /checkupgradeonly
- ❑ B. /s
- ❑ C. /debug
- ❑ D. /unattend
- ❑ E. /udf:*id*

28. How can a user obtain an answer file for use in an unattended installation of Microsoft Windows XP? (Select all that apply.)

Quick Answer: **18**
Detailed Answer: **21**

- ❑ A. Create an answer file manually using a text editor.
- ❑ B. Use the Setup Manager Wizard to create an answer file.
- ❑ C. Download an answer file from www.microsoft.com.
- ❑ D. Copy an answer file from a network server.

29. Which of the following levels of user interaction is when the user has no interaction during a fully automated unattended installation of Microsoft Windows XP?

Quick Answer: 18
Detailed Answer: 21

- ❑ A. Fully Automated
- ❑ B. GUI Attended
- ❑ C. Hide Pages
- ❑ D. Provide Defaults
- ❑ E. Read Only

30. Which of the following levels of user interaction is when the user has some interaction during some setup screens during an unattended installation of Microsoft Windows XP?

Quick Answer: 18
Detailed Answer: 21

- ❑ A. Fully Automated
- ❑ B. GUI Attended
- ❑ C. Hide Pages
- ❑ D. Provide Defaults
- ❑ E. Read Only

31. Which of the following levels of user interaction is when the user has some interaction with a Hide Pages unattended installation of Microsoft Windows XP, but only during some setup screens where an administrator did not provide default information?

Quick Answer: 18
Detailed Answer: 21

- ❑ A. Fully Automated
- ❑ B. GUI Attended
- ❑ C. Hide Pages
- ❑ D. Provide Defaults
- ❑ E. Read Only

32. Which of the following levels of user interaction is when the user has some interaction with an unattended installation of Microsoft Windows XP, but only to accept defaults supplied by the administrator or to make changes when necessary?

Quick Answer: 18
Detailed Answer: 21

- ❑ A. Fully Automated
- ❑ B. GUI Attended
- ❑ C. Hide Pages
- ❑ D. Provide Defaults
- ❑ E. Read Only

Quick Check

33. Which of the following levels of user interaction is when the user can only observe an unattended installation of Microsoft Windows XP?
    - ❑ A. Fully Automated
    - ❑ B. GUI Attended
    - ❑ C. Hide Pages
    - ❑ D. Provide Defaults
    - ❑ E. Read Only

Quick Answer: **18**
Detailed Answer: **21**

34. What does RIS stand for in regard to Microsoft Windows XP?
    - ❑ A. Remote Installation Services
    - ❑ B. Remote Installation System
    - ❑ C. Resource Installation Service
    - ❑ D. Remote Input Service

Quick Answer: **18**
Detailed Answer: **21**

35. Which items are required on a single RIS Server when deploying Microsoft Windows XP to clients? (Select all that apply.)
    - ❑ A. Active Directory
    - ❑ B. DHCP
    - ❑ C. DNS
    - ❑ D. RRAS

Quick Answer: **18**
Detailed Answer: **21**

36. What primary function does DHCP provide during a RIS server's deployment of Microsoft Windows XP?
    - ❑ A. Assigns an IP address
    - ❑ B. Locates domain resources
    - ❑ C. Provides IP address resolution
    - ❑ D. Provides MAC address resolution

Quick Answer: **18**
Detailed Answer: **22**

37. What primary function does DNS provide during a RIS server's deployment of Microsoft Windows XP?
    - ❑ A. Assigns an IP address
    - ❑ B. Locates domain resources
    - ❑ C. Provides IP address resolution
    - ❑ D. Provides MAC address resolution

Quick Answer: **18**
Detailed Answer: **22**

38. What primary function does Active Directory provide during a RIS server's deployment of Microsoft Windows XP?
    - ❑ A. Assigns an IP address
    - ❑ B. Locates domain resources
    - ❑ C. Provides IP address resolution
    - ❑ D. Provides MAC address resolution

Quick Answer: **18**
Detailed Answer: **22**

Quick Check

39. Which of the following items are required for the hard disk drive of a RIS server that will be deploying Microsoft Windows XP? (Select all that apply.)

Quick Answer: 18
Detailed Answer: 22

- ❑ A. 2GB or larger
- ☑ B. Two or more partitions
- ☑ C. Formatted with NTFS
- ❑ D. Requires EFS
- ❑ E. Requires DFS

40. What command starts the RIS Setup Wizard?

Quick Answer: 18
Detailed Answer: 22

- ☑ A. Risetup.exe
- ❑ B. Riprep.exe
- ❑ C. Dcpromo.exe
- ❑ D. Riswiz.exe
- ❑ E. Sysprep.exe

41. What command starts the RIPrep Wizard?

Quick Answer: 18
Detailed Answer: 22

- ❑ A. Risetup.exe
- ☑ B. Riprep.exe
- ❑ C. Dcpromo.exe
- ❑ D. Risprep.exe
- ❑ E. Sysprep.exe

42. What command starts the Active Directory Installation Wizard?

Quick Answer: 18
Detailed Answer: 22

- ❑ A. Risetup.exe
- ❑ B. Riprep.exe
- ☑ C. Dcpromo.exe
- ❑ D. Adsetup.exe
- ❑ E. Sysprep.exe

43. Which of the following are true of a RIPrep image that is used in a RIS procedure with Microsoft Windows XP? (Select all that apply.)

Quick Answer: 18
Detailed Answer: 23

- ☑ A. Can be deployed only to client computers with the same HAL (hardware abstraction layer) as the original source computer
- ☑ B. Contains the Microsoft Windows XP operating system and other software applications
- ☑ C. Copies only necessary files and Registry keys to the client system
- ☑ D. Can be deployed to any client computers with a HAL (hardware abstraction layer) supported by Microsoft Windows XP

Quick Check

44. Which of the following are true of a CD-based image that is used in a RIS procedure with Microsoft Windows XP? (Select all that apply.)

Quick Answer: **18**
Detailed Answer: **23**

- ❑ A. Can be deployed only to client computers with the same HAL (hardware abstraction layer) as the original source computer
- ❑ B. Contains only the Microsoft Windows XP operating system
- ❑ C. Are created automatically during the installation of the RIS server
- ❑ D. Copies only necessary files and Registry keys to the client system

45. What command creates the remote boot disk used in a RIS procedure for Microsoft Windows XP?

Quick Answer: **18**
Detailed Answer: **23**

- ❑ A. Risetup.exe
- ❑ B. Riprep.exe
- ❑ C. Dcpromo.exe
- ❑ D. Risdisk.exe
- ❑ E. Rbfg.exe

46. What command removes the unique elements of a fully installed client machine so that it can be duplicated using imaging software such as PowerQuest's DeployCenter (formerly Drive Image Pro) or Symantec's Norton Ghost?

Quick Answer: **18**
Detailed Answer: **23**

- ❑ A. Sysprep.exe
- ❑ B. Riprep.exe
- ❑ C. Dcpromo.exe
- ❑ D. Image.exe
- ❑ E. Rbfg.exe

47. What steps does Microsoft recommend before upgrading a computer system to Microsoft Windows XP? (Select all that apply.)

Quick Answer: **18**
Detailed Answer: **23**

- ❑ A. Ensure that all hardware meets the HCL.
- ❑ B. Ensure that all hardware meets Microsoft Windows XP's minimum system requirements.
- ❑ C. Back up all files.
- ❑ D. Compress any uncompressed drives.

48. What are the choices available during an upgrade installation of Microsoft Windows XP? (Select all that apply.)

Quick Answer: **18**
Detailed Answer: **24**

- ❑ A. Express Upgrade
- ❑ B. Custom Upgrade
- ❑ C. Integrated Upgrade
- ❑ D. Streaming Upgrade

49. What GUI tool is most useful for users upgrading their system to migrate their files and settings over to Microsoft Windows XP?

Quick Answer: 18
Detailed Answer: 24

- ☑ A. FAST
- ❑ B. USMT
- ❑ C. RBFG
- ❑ D. IPCONFIG

50. What command-line tool is most useful for network administrators migrating settings from older systems running Windows 95, Windows 98, or even Windows Me up to Microsoft Windows XP?

Quick Answer: 18
Detailed Answer: 24

- ❑ A. FAST
- ☑ B. USMT
- ❑ C. RBFG
- ❑ D. IPCONFIG

51. What command-line tool is used to create a remote boot disk used in the RIS (remote installation services) process?

Quick Answer: 18
Detailed Answer: 24

- ❑ A. FAST
- ❑ B. USMT
- ☑ C. RBFG
- ❑ D. IPCONFIG

52. What statements are true of Microsoft Windows XP product activation?

Quick Answer: 18
Detailed Answer: 24

- ☑ A. Must occur within 30 days
- ❑ B. Corporate Edition does not require activation
- ❑ C. Can be activated by choosing Start, Activate Windows
- ❑ D. Can be performed only by an administrator

53. What should you do when a network installation of Microsoft Windows XP gives you a message that the system cannot contact a domain controller?

Quick Answer: 18
Detailed Answer: 24

- ☑ A. You should verify that the network cable is properly connected.
- ❑ B. You should verify that you have sufficient hard disk space.
- ❑ C. Check the installation CD.
- ❑ D. Swap out the CD drive.

Quick Check

54. What should you do when the installation process of Microsoft Windows XP gives you a message that there is insufficient disk space? (Select all that apply.)

Quick Answer: 18
Detailed Answer: 25

- ❑ A. You should verify that the network cable is properly connected.
- ❑ B. You should verify that you have sufficient hard disk space.
- ❑ C. Check the installation CD.
- ❑ D. Swap out the CD drive.

55. What should you do when the installation process of Microsoft Windows XP gives you media errors?

Quick Answer: 18
Detailed Answer: 25

- ❑ A. You should verify that the network cable is properly connected.
- ❑ B. You should verify that you have sufficient hard disk space.
- ❑ C. Check the installation CD.
- ❑ D. Swap out the CD drive.

56. What should you do when the installation process of Microsoft Windows XP gives you the error message Non-supported CD Drive?

Quick Answer: 18
Detailed Answer: 25

- ❑ A. You should verify that the network cable is properly connected.
- ❑ B. You should verify that you have sufficient hard disk space.
- ❑ C. Check the installation CD.
- ❑ D. Swap out the CD drive.

57. Which of the following installation logs records setup actions in chronological order?

Quick Answer: 18
Detailed Answer: 25

- ❑ A. Setupact.log
- ❑ B. Setuperr.log
- ❑ C. Netsetup.log
- ❑ D. Setupchron.log

58. Which of the following installation logs records only setup errors?

Quick Answer: 18
Detailed Answer: 25

- ❑ A. Setupact.log
- ❑ B. Setuperr.log
- ❑ C. Netsetup.log
- ❑ D. Error.log

Quick Check

59. Which of the following installation logs records only activity related to joining a network domain or a workgroup?

Quick Answer: **18**
Detailed Answer: **25**

- ❑ A. Setupact.log
- ❑ B. Setuperr.log
- ❑ C. Netsetup.log
- ❑ D. Netset.log

60. You're the desktop administrator for Troy Research. You need to build a RIPrep image of a Windows XP Professional computer. You install Windows XP Professional on a test computer in your lab. You log on to the computer using the local administrator account. You install an antivirus program and four other standard applications. Next, you run RIPrep.exe to create a RIS image of the computer. Then you deploy this image to 60 computers by using RIS. Users complain that when they log on to their computers, the shortcuts for the standard applications are all unavailable.

Quick Answer: **18**
Detailed Answer: **25**

You need to be sure that the RIPrep image includes the shortcuts for the domain user accounts. What should you do?

- ❑ A. Run RIPrep.exe before installing the standard applications, and then open Control Panel. In System Properties, copy the local administrator account profile to the default user profile.
- ❑ B. Open Control Panel. In System Properties, change the local user profile to a roaming profile. Then run RIPrep.exe.
- ❑ C. Open Control Panel. In System Properties, change the local user profile to a mandatory profile. Then run RIPrep.exe.
- ❑ D. Open Control Panel. In System Properties, copy the local administrator account profile to the Default user profile. Grant the Everyone group Allow-Full Control permission on the copied profile. Then run RIPrep.exe.

Quick Check

61. You're a help desk technician for your company. The company is in the process of deploying Windows XP Professional to all client PCs. You upgrade Peter's Windows 98 laptop to Windows XP Professional. After upgrading, Peter states that several older applications no longer work properly. Additionally, a hardware device on his laptop is not yet supported by Windows XP Professional. Peter asks you to reinstall Windows 98 and all applications so that he can use his laptop again.

    You need to restore Peter's laptop to its pre-upgraded state while keeping the applications, documents, and personal data intact. You need to accomplish this in the shortest time. What should you do?

    - ❑ A. On Peter's laptop, run Setup.exe from an original Windows 98 installation CD.
    - ❑ B. Copy Peter's documents and personal data to a shared folder on the network. Reinstall Windows 98 and his applications. Copy the documents and personal data to the My Documents folder on Peter's laptop.
    - ❑ C. On Peter's laptop, use the Add or Remove Programs Wizard to remove the Windows XP Professional installation.
    - ❑ D. On Peter's laptop, use a third-party disk-imaging software utility to apply a disk image that contains Windows 98 and Peter's applications.

Quick Answer: **18**
Detailed Answer: **25**

62. You're the desktop administrator for your company. You plan to install Windows XP Professional on a client computer. The computer contains a PCI video adapter, a PCI network adapter, and an ISA SCSI adapter that hosts the single hard disk and a CD-ROM drive. After starting the installation, you get an error message that states setup cannot find the hard disk. You confirm that the SCSI hard disk is connected and functional. However, the error message reappears when you restart setup. The installation will not resume.

What should you do to complete the installation?

- ❑ A. Restart Setup and install the driver for the SCSI adapter while initially copying the files.
- ❑ B. Disable the APM features in the system BIOS.
- ❑ C. Replace each of the SCSI devices with an equivalent EIDE device.
- ❑ D. Reserve an IRQ for the ISA SCSI adapter in the system BIOS.

Quick Answer: **18**
Detailed Answer: **25**

63. You're the desktop administrator for your organization. You're responsible for automating the deployment of Windows XP Professional to new PCs. You're preparing a Windows XP Professional test PC to be used in disk imaging. You install Windows XP Professional on the test PC and run the SysPrep utility. You use a third-party software package to create a disk image to a new PC and then restart the PC. Instead of completing the Windows XP Professional installation, the PC starts the Windows Welcome program, and prompts you to enter additional setup information.

    Because you're deploying a large number of PCs, you want to be sure the disk image can be used without any additional user interaction. What should you do?

    - ❑ A. Use a network-based RIS server to apply the disk image to new PCs.
    - ❑ B. Use Setup Manager to create a SysPrep Answer File. Copy the Answer File to a floppy disk, and insert that floppy into new PCs when the disk image is applied.
    - ❑ C. On the test computer, run the SysPrep -OEM command. Re-create the disk image by using the third-party software.
    - ❑ D. Create an Unattend.txt Answer File. Run the SysPrep utility and re-create the disk image by using the third-party software.

Quick Answer: **18**
Detailed Answer: **25**

64. You're the desktop administrator for Amusement Software. You do a clean installation of Windows XP Professional on 20 computers. All of these computers are part of a workgroup named Pgm. All the computers in Pgm are configured to require a username and password for logging on. Thirty days after the installation, all users in the Pgm workgroup report that they cannot log on to their computers.

    How should you correct this problem?

    - ❑ A. Restart each computer in Safe mode. Use System Restore, specifying the restore point that was created after the clean installation of Windows XP Professional.
    - ❑ B. On each computer, log on as a local administrator and reset the user password at the next logon.
    - ❑ C. Restart each computer in Safe mode, and change the local account policy expiration from 30 days to zero. Product activation is required.
    - ❑ D. Use the Windows Product Activation Wizard on all computers to activate Windows XP Professional via the Microsoft Clearing House.

Quick Answer: **18**
Detailed Answer: **25**

Quick Check

65. You're the desktop administrator for your company. You are using RIS to install Windows XP Professional on a brand-new computer. You start the computer, but instead of connecting to your network RIS server, the computer displays the error message, Operating system not found. You ensure that the computer has a PXE-compliant NIC that is connecting to your company's network.

You need to start the computer and properly connect to your company's RIS server. What should you do?

- ❑ A. Have a network administrator modify the RIS server permissions to grant your domain user account Allow-Read permission on the RIS images.
- ❑ B. Have a network administrator modify the network DHCP server to include a DHCP reservation for the brand-new computer.
- ❑ C. Modify the computer's BIOS settings, and ensure that the computer is configured to boot from the network.
- ❑ D. Modify the computer's BIOS settings. Be sure the brand-new computer's boot password is the same as the RIS server's Administrator password.

Quick Answer: 18
Detailed Answer: 26

66. You're the desktop administrator for your company's sales department. You need to perform a clean installation of Windows XP Professional on a computer that currently has Windows 98. You start the install, and the text-based portion of Setup finishes successfully. Before the GUI-based portion of Setup begins, the computer stops responding. You research further and find a problem with a device driver.

You want to know which device is causing the problem. What should you do?

- ❑ A. Restart Setup by using the /dushare switch.
- ❑ B. Modify the Boot.ini file to include the /fastdetect switch.
- ❑ C. Restart Setup by using the /dudisable switch.
- ❑ D. Modify the Boot.ini file to include the /sos switch.

Quick Answer: 18
Detailed Answer: 26

Quick Check

67. You're the desktop administrator for your company's advertising department. Phil is a user in the advertising department. Phil's computer currently uses Microsoft Windows NT Workstation 4.0. You need to install Windows XP Professional on Phil's computer. Phil uses an old legacy application that is only compatible with Windows NT Workstation. Phil's computer has two hard disks. The first disk is partitioned as drive C and has 4GB of available space. The second disk is unpartitioned and also has 4GB of available space. Windows NT Workstation 4.0 is currently installed on drive C.

    You want to install Windows XP Professional on the second hard disk, which you will format as drive D. You want to ensure that after Windows XP Professional is installed, Phil can access all files that are on drive C and drive D. What should you do?

    - ❑ A. Before installing Windows XP Professional, install the Active Directory client extensions for Windows NT Workstation 4.0, and then install Windows XP Professional on drive D.
    - ❑ B. Install Windows XP Professional on drive D. Copy Atdisk.sys from drive D back to drive C.
    - ❑ C. Install Windows XP Professional on drive D. Copy Ntfs.sys from drive D back to drive C.
    - ❑ D. Before installing Windows XP Professional, install the most recent Windows NT 4.0 service pack. Then install Windows XP Professional on drive D.

Quick Answer: **18**
Detailed Answer: **26**

Quick Check Answer Key

1. A

2. C

3. B

4. B

5. B and C

6. D

7. C

8. D

9. A

10. A

11. D

12. C

13. B

14. C

15. B

16. A

17. D

18. D

19. E

20. C

21. E

22. B

23. C

24. D

25. E

26. C

27. B

28. A and B

29. A

30. B

31. C

32. D

33. E

34. A

35. A, B, and C

36. A

37. C

38. B

39. A, B, and C

40. A

41. B

42. C

43. A, B, C, and D

44. B and C

45. E

46. A

47. A, B, and C

48. A and B

49. A

50. B

51. C

52. A, B, and C

53. A

54. B

55. C

56. D

57. A

58. B

59. C

60. D

61. C

62. A

63. B

64. D

65. C

66. D

67. D

Answers and Explanations

1. **Answer: A.** The Winnt.exe executable file is located in the \i386 folder on the CD-ROM.

2. **Answer: C.** The Winnt32.exe executable file is located in the \i386 folder on the CD-ROM.

3. **Answer: B.** The Winnt.exe executable file is located in the \i386 folder on the original CD-ROM. You need to create a distribution server that has a file share containing the contents of the entire \i386 folder from the original CD-ROM.

4. **Answer: B.** The Winnt32.exe executable file is located in the \i386 folder on the original CD-ROM. You need to create a distribution server that has a file share containing the contents of the entire \i386 folder from the original CD-ROM.

5. **Answers: B and C.**

   Explanation B. This answer is partially correct. FAT16 (File Allocation Table 16-bit) is commonly used on MS-DOS (Microsoft Disk Operating System) or early (pre-OSR2) Microsoft Windows 95 system hard disks. FAT16 is an acceptable hard disk partition type to hold setup files during a network installation of Microsoft Windows XP.

   Explanation C. This answer is partially correct. FAT32 (File Allocation Table 32-bit) is commonly used on Microsoft Windows 95 OSR2 and Windows 98 system hard disks. FAT32 is an acceptable hard disk partition type to hold setup files during a network installation of Microsoft Windows XP.

6. **Answer: D.** A speed of 233MHz is the minimum speed required to install Microsoft Windows XP Home Edition.

7. **Answer: C.** A total of 64MB is the minimum amount of RAM required to install Microsoft Windows XP Home Edition.

8. **Answer: D.** A speed of 233MHz is the minimum speed required to install Microsoft Windows XP Professional.

9. **Answer: A.** A total of 64MB is the minimum amount of RAM required to install Microsoft Windows XP Professional.

10. **Answer: A.** A total of 4GB is the maximum amount of RAM allowed to successfully install Microsoft Windows XP Professional.

11. **Answer: D.** A total of 4GB is the maximum amount of RAM allowed to successfully install Microsoft Windows XP Home Edition.

12. **Answer: C.** A total of 1.5GB is the minimum amount of free hard disk space required to successfully install Microsoft Windows XP Professional.

13. **Answer: B.** A total of 1.5GB is the minimum amount of free hard disk space required to successfully install Microsoft Windows XP Home Edition.

14. **Answer: C.** A total of one processor is the maximum amount allowed in a client system when installing Microsoft Windows XP Home Edition.

15. **Answer: B.** A total of two processors is the maximum amount allowed in a client system when installing Microsoft Windows XP Professional.

16. **Answer: A.** The /a switch of the winnt.exe command modifies the setup of Microsoft Windows XP by enabling accessibility options.

17. **Answer: D.** The /s switch of the winnt.exe command modifies the setup of Microsoft Windows XP by specifying the source location of the original Microsoft Windows XP files.

18. **Answer: D.** The /t switch of the winnt.exe command modifies the setup of Microsoft Windows XP by specifying the drive to hold temporary setup files.

19. **Answer: E.** The /u switch of the winnt.exe command modifies the setup of Microsoft Windows XP by specifying an unattended setup. Note that the /s switch is then also required, which specifies the source location of the original Microsoft Windows XP files.

20. **Answer: C.** The /udf:id switch of the winnt.exe command modifies the setup of Microsoft Windows XP by establishing the id (identification) that setup uses to specify how a .UDF (uniqueness database file) modifies an answer file.

21. **Answer: E.** The /checkupgradeonly switch of the winnt32.exe command only checks a system for compatibility with—but does not install—Microsoft Windows XP. This switch creates a report that can be printed.

22. **Answer: B.** The /cmdcons switch of the winnt32.exe command modifies the setup of Microsoft Windows XP by adding a Recovery Console option to the operating system selection screen.

23. **Answer: C.** The /debug switch of the winnt32.exe command modifies the setup of Microsoft Windows XP by creating a debug log during installation.

24. **Answer: D.** The /noreboot switch of the winnt32.exe command modifies the setup of Microsoft Windows XP by specifying the system not to reboot after the first stage of installation.

25. **Answer: E.** The /udf:id switch of the winnt23.exe command modifies the setup of Microsoft Windows XP by establishing the id (identification) that setup uses to specify how a .UDF (uniqueness database file) modifies an answer file.

26. **Answer: C.** The /unattend switch of the winnt32.exe command modifies the setup of Microsoft Windows XP by specifying the answer file for an unattended installation.

27. **Answer: B.** The /s switch of the winnt32.exe command modifies the setup of Microsoft Windows XP by specifying the source location of the original Microsoft Windows XP files.

28. **Answers: A and B.**

    Explanation A. This answer is partially correct. A user can create an answer file manually using a text editor such as Microsoft Word, Notepad, or WordPad.

    Explanation B. This answer is partially correct. A user can use the Setup Manager Wizard. The Setup Manager Wizard can be found on the Microsoft Windows XP Professional CD in the \Support\Tools\ folder in a file called Deploy.CAB.

29. **Answer: A.** The user has no interaction during a Fully Automated unattended installation of Microsoft Windows XP.

30. **Answer: B.** The user has some interaction during a GUI (graphical user interface) Attended installation of Microsoft Windows XP, but only during some setup screens. (All text mode installation is done automatically.)

31. **Answer: C.** The user has some interaction with a Hide Pages unattended installation of Microsoft Windows XP, but only during some setup screens where an administrator did not provide default information.

32. **Answer: D.** The user has some interaction with a Provide Defaults unattended installation of Microsoft Windows XP, but only to accept defaults supplied by the Administrator or to make changes when necessary.

33. **Answer: E.** The user can only observe a Read Only unattended installation of Microsoft Windows XP.

34. **Answer: A.** RIS stands for Remote Installation Services. RIS is used to remotely install Microsoft Windows XP over a network.

35. **Answers: A, B, and C.**

    Explanation A. This answer is partially correct. RIS (Remote Installation Services) requires Active Directory when deploying Microsoft Windows XP from a single RIS server.

    Explanation B. This answer is partially correct. RIS requires the DHCP (Dynamic Host Configuration Protocol) Server service when deploying Microsoft Windows XP from a single RIS Server.

Explanation C. This answer is partially correct. RIS requires the DNS (Domain Naming Server) Server service when deploying Microsoft Windows XP from a single RIS Server.

36. **Answer: A.** DHCP stands for Dynamic Host Configuration Protocol. The DHCP Server service running on a server during a RIS server's deployment of Microsoft Windows XP assigns an IP address to client machines.

37. **Answer: C.** IP (Internet Protocol) addresses are resolved with the help of DNS (Domain Naming System). The DNS Server service is required during a RIS (Remote Installation Services) server's deployment of Microsoft Windows XP.

38. **Answer: B.** Domain resources are located with the help of Active Directory. Active Directory is the directory service that acts as a central repository of all domain resources, including users, computers, groups, files, and folders. Domain Controllers hold a copy of the Active Directory.

39. **Answers: A, B, and C.**

    Explanation A. This answer is partially correct. The hard disk drive of a RIS server that will be deploying Microsoft Windows XP must be 2GB or larger.

    Explanation B. This answer is partially correct. The hard disk drive of a RIS server that will be deploying Microsoft Windows XP must have two or more partitions: one for the operating system, and one for the CD image.

    Explanation C. This answer is partially correct. The hard disk drive of a RIS server that will be deploying Microsoft Windows XP must be formatted with NTFS (New Technology File System). Version 5 of NTFS ships with Windows 2000 and above.

40. **Answer: A.** The Risetup.exe command will start the RIS (Remote Installation Services) Setup Wizard. This command should be performed on a server machine on a network that also has Active Directory, DNS (Domain Naming System), and DHCP (Dynamic Host Configuration Protocol) elements in place.

41. **Answer: B.** The Riprep.exe command begins the RIPrep Wizard. RIPrep images are used in RIS (Remote Installation Services) to deploy both the Microsoft Windows XP operating system and other applications.

42. **Answer: C.** The Dcpromo.exe command begins the Active Directory Installation Wizard. Active Directory is required on a network when deploying Microsoft Windows XP with a RIS (Remote Installation Services) server. Dcpromo.exe will promote a member server on a network to a domain controller. It could also demote an existing domain controller on a network back down to a member server. Dcpromo.exe is not used with the Microsoft Windows XP operating system.

43. **Answers: A, B, C, and D.**

    Explanation A. A RIPrep image can be deployed only to client computers with the same HAL (hardware abstraction layer) as the original source computer.

    Explanation B. A RIPrep image contains the Microsoft Windows XP operating system and other software applications.

    Explanation C. A RIPrep image must be created manually.

    Explanation D. A RIPrep image copies only necessary files and Registry keys to the client system. This makes RIPrep faster than CD images, which copies all files to the client machine's hard drive before the setup is started.

44. **Answers: B and C.**

    Explanation B. A CD-based image that is used in a RIS procedure contains only the Microsoft Windows XP operating system.

    Explanation C. A CD-based image that is used in a RIS procedure is created automatically during the installation of the RIS server.

45. **Answer: E.** The Rbfg.exe command creates the remote boot disk used in a RIS procedure for Microsoft Windows XP. Remember the letters of this utility with the mnemonic Remote Boot Floppy Generator.

46. **Answer: A.** The Sysprep.exe command removes the unique elements (such as computer names and SIDs [security identifiers]) of a fully installed client machine so that it can be duplicated. The duplication can then be done using imaging software such as PowerQuest's DeployCenter (formerly Drive Image Pro) or Symantec's Norton Ghost.

47. **Answers: A, B, and C.**

    Explanation A. This answer is partially correct. Before upgrading a computer system to Microsoft Windows XP, Microsoft recommends you ensure all hardware meets the HCL (hardware compatibility list).

    Explanation B. This answer is partially correct. Before upgrading a computer system to Microsoft Windows XP, Microsoft recommends you ensure all hardware meets Microsoft Windows XP's minimum system requirements.

    Explanation C. This answer is partially correct. Before upgrading a computer system to Microsoft Windows XP, Microsoft recommends you uncompress any compressed files.

48. **Answers: A and B.**

    Explanation A. This answer is partially correct. Microsoft actually recommends using the Express Upgrade. The Express Upgrade choice maintains all current system settings and continues to use the current system folder (normally C:\Winnt). There are only two valid upgrade choices available.

    Explanation B. This answer is partially correct. Although a Custom Upgrade is one of only two valid upgrade choices available, Microsoft actually recommends using the Express Upgrade. The Custom Upgrade choice enables you to modify the system folder (normally C:\Winnt), adjust language options, and change the hard disk's formatting type from FAT16 or FAT32 (File Allocation Table, either 16-bit or 32-bit) to NTFS (New Technology File System, version 5).

49. **Answer: A.** FAST stands for the File And Settings Transfer. The FAST Wizard is a GUI tool that is most useful for users upgrading their system to migrate their files and settings over to Microsoft Windows XP. The FAST Wizard is best used by a single computer user upgrading his own single computer.

50. **Answer: B.** USMT stands for the User State Migration Tool. It is not a GUI tool, but rather a command-line tool. The USMT is most useful for network administrators migrating settings from older systems running Windows 95, Windows 98, or even Windows Me up to Microsoft Windows XP.

51. **Answer: C.** RBFG stands for Remote Boot Floppy Generator. It is not a GUI tool, but rather a command-line tool. The RBFG.exe command is used to create a remote boot diskette used in the RIS (Remote Installation Services) process.

52. **Answers: A, B, and C.**

    Explanation A. This answer is partially correct. Microsoft allows up to 30 days to activate Microsoft Windows XP.

    Explanation B. This answer is partially correct. Microsoft has a Corporate Edition of Microsoft Windows XP that does not require activation. It does require a valid product key, as in earlier versions of Windows.

    Explanation C. This answer is partially correct. You can activate Microsoft Windows XP by choosing Start, Activate Windows.

53. **Answer: A.** You should verify that the network cable is properly connected. Also make sure that a domain controller and DNS (Domain Naming System) server are operational on the network. Finally, ensure that the IP (Internet Protocol) address, subnet mask, and default gateway, as well as the administrator's credentials being used, are correct.

54. **Answer: B.** If you receive the message Insufficient Disk Space, you should free up more disk drive space. You could delete a partition, create a new larger partition, or reformat an existing partition in order to free up more disk drive space.

55. **Answer: C.** If you receive any media errors, you should check the installation CD. You should check for a dirty or damaged CD, and then obtain a replacement installation CD.

56. **Answer: D.** If you receive the message Non-supported CD Drive, you should swap out the CD drive for a supported CD drive. You might also consider performing a network installation instead.

57. **Answer: A.** The Setupact.log installation log records all setup actions in chronological order. The Setupact.log is sometimes called the action log. The Setupact.log includes entries made to the Setuperr.log installation error log file as well.

58. **Answer: B.** The Setuperr.log installation log records only setup errors. The Setuperr.log is sometimes called the error log. The Setuperr.log includes severity levels of each error as well.

59. **Answer: C.** The Netsetup.log installation log records only activity related to joining a network domain or a workgroup.

60. **Answer: D.** You should open Control Panel. In System Properties, copy the local administrator account profile to the Default user profile. Grant the Everyone group Allow-Full Control permission on the copied profile. Then run RIPrep.exe.

61. **Answer: C.** On Peter's laptop, you should use the Add or Remove Programs Wizard to remove the Windows XP Professional installation.

62. **Answer: A.** You should restart Setup and install the driver for the SCSI adapter while initially copying the files. SCSI stands for small computer system interface, and ISA stands for industry standard architecture.

63. **Answer: B.** You should use Setup Manager to create a SysPrep Answer File. Copy the Answer File to a floppy disk, and insert the floppy into new PCs when the disk image is applied. Answer Files are perfect to help in this situation.

64. **Answer: D.** You should use the Windows Product Activation Wizard on all computers to activate Windows XP Professional via the Microsoft Clearing House. To reactivate their operating system, users will have to send details of the installation to the Microsoft-run clearing house. They will then receive a product activation code.

65. **Answer: C.** You should modify the computer's BIOS settings, and ensure that the computer is configured to boot from the network.

66. **Answer: D.** You should modify the Boot.ini file to include the /sos switch. The /sos switch in the Boot.ini startup file will display the names of drivers as they are loaded to aid in troubleshooting.

67. **Answer: D.** You should install the most recent Windows NT 4.0 service pack on Phil's computer, and then install Windows XP Professional on drive D.

Establishing, Configuring, and Managing Resources

Quick Check

1. Which of the following file systems offers the best features for use in Microsoft Windows XP?

   - ❑ A. FAT32
   - ❑ B. NTFSv4
   - ❑ C. NTFSv5
   - ❑ D. FAT16

Quick Answer: **38**
Detailed Answer: **39**

2. What command is used to convert a disk partition formatted with FAT to NTFS?

   - ❑ A. Convert.exe
   - ❑ B. Change.exe
   - ❑ C. Fattontfs.exe
   - ❑ D. Fat2ntfs.exe

Quick Answer: **38**
Detailed Answer: **39**

3. What command is used to convert a disk partition formatted with FAT32 to NTFS?

   - ❑ A. Fat2ntfs.exe
   - ❑ B. Change.exe
   - ❑ C. Ntfsv5.exe
   - ❑ D. Convert.exe

Quick Answer: **38**
Detailed Answer: **39**

4. What hard disk partition types can Microsoft Windows XP defragment? (Select all that apply.)

   - ❑ A. NTFS
   - ❑ B. FAT32
   - ❑ C. FAT16
   - ❑ D. FAT12
   - ❑ E. CDFS

Quick Answer: **38**
Detailed Answer: **39**

Quick Check

5. Where is the Microsoft Windows XP defragmenter located?

Quick Answer: 38
Detailed Answer: 39

- ❑ A. Start, Programs, Accessories, Disk Management, Disk Defragmenter
- ❑ B. Start, Programs, System Tools, Disk Defragmenter
- ❑ C. Start, Programs, Accessories, Disk Defragmenter
- ❑ D. Start, Programs, Accessories, System Tools, Disk Defragmenter
- ❑ E. Start, Programs, Disk Management, Disk Defragmenter

6. You're the desktop administrator for your company's network. You're preparing a Microsoft Windows XP Professional computer for Chip, a new user in the promotions department. This computer used to belong to an employee named Alice. Chip needs access to all of Alice's files, but he does not yet have the appropriate permissions. You log on as the local administrator and attempt to reassign permissions so Chip can access Alice's files. Unfortunately, you receive an Access Denied error message.

Quick Answer: 38
Detailed Answer: 39

You need to ensure that Chip can access Alice's file. What should you do?

- ❑ A. Copy Alice's account, and then name the new account Chip.
- ❑ B. Take ownership of the files and folders and give Chip the permission to take ownership.
- ❑ C. Give Chip ownership of the files and folders on the computer.
- ❑ D. Grant Chip the Allow-Change Permissions permission on the files and folders on the computer.

Quick Check

7. You're the desktop administrator for your company. A field sales representative named Linda uses a laptop running Microsoft Windows XP. Linda travels to different locations each day, as well as doing work from home. She does not have a docking station at home, and never uses a docking station. Each time Linda boots her computer, she is prompted to choose either a docked or undocked hardware profile from the Hardware Profile Menu.

   You need to make sure that Linda is not prompted to choose a hardware profile each time she starts her computer. You also need to allow her computer to automatically start with the undocked profile very quickly. How should you adjust Linda's laptop?

   - ❑ A. Modify the Device Manager settings to disable all devices used by the docking station.
   - ❑ B. Modify the BIOS settings and disable support for the docking station.
   - ❑ C. Modify the hardware profiles and remove the docked hardware profile.
   - ❑ D. Configure the hardware profiles so that the undocked hardware profile is the default hardware profile for startup.

Quick Answer: **38**
Detailed Answer: **39**

8. You're a help desk technician for your company. All employees use Windows XP Professional computers. A salesperson named Phil receives a removable disk drive cartridge from his supervisor. Phil states he cannot edit files on the cartridge, and is receiving an Access Denied error message. Phil's supervisor is not in the office. You put the cartridge in the removable drive on your own computer. You receive the very same Access Denied error message when you try to access any files and folders. You decide to call Phil's supervisor.

   The supervisor asks you to grant permission to access the cartridge's contents to Phil only. The supervisor also wants to prevent Phil from changing any permissions on the contents of the cartridge. Which actions should you take? (Select all that apply.)

   - ❑ A. As administrator, take ownership of the files and folders.
   - ❑ B. Grant Phil Allow-Modify permission on the files and folders.
   - ❑ C. As administrator, grant your help desk user account Allow-Full Control permission on the files and folders.
   - ❑ D. Grant Phil Allow-Full Control permission on the files and folders.
   - ❑ E. Grant Phil Allow-Take Ownership permission on the files and folders

Quick Answer: **38**
Detailed Answer: **39**

Quick Check

9. You're a help desk technician for your company. An employee named Annette is using her Microsoft Windows XP Professional laptop to work with a file named Advertising.doc, which is located in a folder named \\Advfiles03\Planning. Annette must make that particular file available on her laptop when she is not in the office. You verify that she has permission to make the file available offline. However, when Annette right-clicks the file, the menu option labeled Make Available Offline is not visible.

   You need to ensure that Annette can make the file available offline. What should you do?

   - ❑ A. Have a network administrator open the properties of the Planning shared folder and be sure the Allow Caching of Files in This Shared Folder check box is selected.
   - ❑ B. Instruct Annette to map a network drive to the \\Advfiles03\Planning folder.
   - ❑ C. Instruct Annette to move the Advertising.doc file from the \\Advfiles03\Planning folder to a shared folder that is formatted as NTFS.
   - ❑ D. Have a network administrator modify the permissions on the Advertising.doc file to grant Annette Allow-Read & Execute permission.

Quick Answer: **38**
Detailed Answer: **39**

10. You're working as a help desk operator in a large corporate environment. Sally calls to complain that she is not able to access any of the data on the \\NT4_CORP\SALES share. You check the share permissions on the share and determine that Sally has Full Control shared folder permissions assigned to her user account. Sally is also able to ping the \\NT4_CORP server. What is your next course of action to help Sally?

    - ❑ A. Verify Sally's membership in other groups to determine whether she is denied access to the share.
    - ❑ B. Verify Sally's NTFS permissions to the file system.
    - ❑ C. Verify that Sally can connect to the \\NT4_CORP server over the network.
    - ❑ D. Verify Sally's shared folder permissions and NTFS permissions.

Quick Answer: **38**
Detailed Answer: **40**

Quick Check

11. You're conducting a security audit on your company's servers to ensure that all confidential data is secure. A consultant has conducted a preliminary review and determined that many of your critical data partitions are unsecured and at risk of being accessed by unauthorized personnel. The consultant has based this conclusion on your shared folder strategy. Your servers are all configured with NTFS, and NTFS permissions have been assigned to groups to control access to the data. Shared folders have been created at the root of each partition and the Domain Users group has been assigned Full Control. Is the poor review from your consultant cause for concern? (Select the two best answers.)

Quick Answer: **38**
Detailed Answer: **40**

- ❑ A. No; NTFS permissions are being used to control access to data.
- ❑ B. Yes; where NTFS and share permissions combine, the least restrictive permission is granted and therefore security will be breached.
- ❑ C. Yes; assigning the Domain Users group Full Control to the share is a security breach.
- ❑ D. No; the consultant you hired is incompetent and should be fired because he does not understand Windows XP share security.

12. As the manager of a high-volume order-processing center, you need to optimize the print environment for your users. A large number of order-entry staff is inputting a high volume of orders. A copy of each order must be printed when the order is entered. All orders are collected in a central location to be filled. Problems arise when printers go offline because the entire staff cannot print. You need a solution that can handle the high volume of print jobs and will allow users to continue printing even if a printer is offline. What should you suggest?

Quick Answer: **38**
Detailed Answer: **40**

- ❑ A. Configure a number of printers to use printer redirection to print to a very fast and reliable printer.
- ❑ B. Buy a faster and more reliable printer.
- ❑ C. Set up a large number of network printers and configure the users' workstations to point to a number of the printers.
- ❑ D. Use printer pooling to create one printer with multiple physical devices.

Quick Check

13. You've configured your server with FAT partitions (the D: drive) and want to convert them to FAT32. You issue the following command, but find the system will not convert the drive:

```
Convert d: /fs:fat32
```

What is the cause of the problem? (Select the two best answers.)

- ❑ A. The syntax for the command is Convert d: /fs:ntfs.
- ❑ B. You need to back up the FAT file system and reformat the drive as FAT32 and then restore from backup.
- ❑ C. You should use the Format command to convert the drive.
- ❑ D. You cannot convert from FAT to FAT32 in Windows XP.

Quick Answer: **38**
Detailed Answer: **40**

14. As the support technician for a large company, you're called in to fix the president's PC. The president read in a magazine that Windows XP computers are secure only if they are configured with NTFS-formatted partitions. He then proceeded to convert his hard drive from FAT to NTFS using the format utility. He is now very concerned that his PC will not boot. What should you tell him?

- ❑ A. The president should stop reading computer magazines.
- ❑ B. You will have to reinstall Windows to access the newly formatted drive to recover the data.
- ❑ C. The data is lost because the drive was formatted rather than converted.
- ❑ D. The president should have used the correct command switches with the format utility.

Quick Answer: **38**
Detailed Answer: **40**

15. As the network administrator of your company, you want to create a large number of user accounts with secure home directories. What is the most efficient way to secure these directories?

- ❑ A. Create a shared folder named Users on a FAT or FAT32 partition and create subfolders for each user. Then share out the Users folders so all users can access it.
- ❑ B. Create a shared folder named Users on an NTFS partition and create subfolders for each user (each user directory is secured so only one user can access it).
- ❑ C. Create a folder named Users on an NTFS partition and create subfolders for each user. Then share each subfolder so that only one user can access it.
- ❑ D. Create a shared folder named Users on a FAT or FAT32 partition and create subfolders for each user. Then share out each subfolder so that only one user can access it.

Quick Answer: **38**
Detailed Answer: **41**

Quick Check

16. You're troubleshooting a resource access issue for a user on your network. Mikayla is not able to access data when accessing the shared data folder over the network. If Mikayla logs on locally at the computer where the shared data is stored, she can access the data directly from the file system. Where should you start troubleshooting her access problems?

Quick Answer: **38**
Detailed Answer: **41**

- ❑ A. Check the NTFS permissions assigned to Mikayla. She has been assigned Deny - Full Control.
- ❑ B. Check the NTFS permissions assigned to Mikayla. They are blocking her from accessing the resource when she attaches from the network.
- ☑ C. Check the shared folder permissions assigned to Mikayla. She has been assigned Deny - Full Control.
- ❑ D. Mikayla needs to be a member of the Authenticated User group to access resources from over the network.

17. As the network administrator for a large accounting firm, you're developing a strategy to secure a shared data folder for the executives in your company. You created a folder called EXECDATA on a partition formatted with NTFS. Security is of prime concern, so you deny the Everyone group Full Control permissions to the folder. You then grant the Executives group Full Control permissions to the folder. To allow access to the resource over the network, you share the folder and grant Full Control access to the Executives group. Executives are not able to access the resource. What is the problem with your strategy?

Quick Answer: **38**
Detailed Answer: **41**

- ❑ A. The Administrators group must be granted Full Control so that the resource can be managed properly.
- ☑ B. By denying full control to the Everyone group, all users are blocked from the resource regardless of group membership.
- ❑ C. The executives should be accessing all resources locally, so shared permissions should not be assigned.
- ❑ D. Future investigation is required to determine whether this is an NTFS or a shared folder issue.

Quick Check

18. As the network administrator of a large company, you create a shared folder with the permissions presented in Table 2.1.

Quick Answer: 38
Detailed Answer: 41

Table 2.1 Shared Folder Permissions

User/Group	Shared Folder Permission
Mikayla	Allow Change
Sales	Deny Full Control
Executives	Allow Full Control

Mikayla is a member of the Sales group and the Executives group. What are Mikayla's effective permissions on the shared folder?

- ❑ A. Full Control
- ❑ B. Change
- ❑ C. Read
- ❑ D. No access will be allowed
- ❑ E. Not enough information is presented to calculate permissions

19. As the network administrator of a large company, you create a shared folder with the permissions presented in Table 2.2. The shared resource is located on a partition formatted as NTFS.

Quick Answer: 38
Detailed Answer: 42

Table 2.2 Shared Folder Permissions

User/Group	Shared Folder Permission	NTFS Permissions
Mikayla	Allow Read	Allow Read
Sales	Allow Read	
Executives	Allow Full Control	

Mikayla and John are members of the Sales group and the Executives group. What are Mikayla's and John's effective permissions on the resource?

- ❑ A. Mikayla has Read; John has Read.
- ❑ B. Mikayla has Read; John has no access.
- ❑ C. Mikayla has no access; John has Read.
- ❑ D. Mikayla has Full Control; John has Full Control.
- ❑ E. Mikayla has Full Control; John has no access.
- ❑ F. Mikayla has no access; John has Full Control.
- ❑ G. Not enough information is presented to calculate permissions.

Quick Answer: **38**

Detailed Answer: **42**

20. You're working the help desk late one night when a user calls to complain that when she moves a file from one network share to another, the permissions are getting messed up (the shared folders are on separate partitions). Table 2.3 presents the existing NTFS permissions on the file being moved. Table 2.4 presents the NTFS permissions on the target folder.

Table 2.3 Source File NTFS Permissions

User/Group	NTFS Permission
Executives	Allow Full Control (inherited from the parent folder)
Sales	Deny Full Control

Table 2.4 Target Folder NTFS Permissions

User/Group	NTFS Permission
Sales	Allow Full Control

When the user moves the file to the target folder, what will the effective permissions be on the file?

- ❑ A. Executives has Allow Full Control; Sales has Allow Full Control.
- ❑ B. Executives has Deny Full Control; Sales has Deny Full Control.
- ❑ C. Executives has Allow Full Control; Sales has Deny Full Control.
- ❑ D. Executives has no permissions; Sales has Deny Full Control.
- ❑ E. Executives has no permissions; Sales has Allow Full Control.
- ❑ F. Executives has Deny Full Control; Sales has no permissions.
- ❑ G. Executives has Allow Full Control; Sales has no permissions.
- ❑ H. Not enough information is presented to calculate permissions.

Quick Check

21. You're working the help desk late one night when a user calls to complain that when she moves a file from one folder to another folder (on the same partition), the permissions are getting messed up. Table 2.5 presents the existing NTFS permissions on the file being moved. Table 2.6 presents the NTFS permissions on the target folder.

Quick Answer: 38
Detailed Answer: 42

Table 2.5 Source File NTFS Permissions

User/Group	NTFS Permission
Executives	Allow Full Control (inherited from the parent folder)
Sales	Deny Full Control

Table 2.6 Target Folder NTFS Permissions

User/Group	NTFS Permission
Sales	Allow Full Control

When the user moves the file to the target folder, what will the effective permissions be on the file?

- ❑ A. Executives has Allow Full Control; Sales has Allow Full Control.
- ❑ B. Executives has Deny Full Control; Sales has Deny Full Control.
- ❑ C. Executives has Allow Full Control; Sales has Deny Full Control.
- ❑ D. Executives has no permissions; Sales has Deny Full Control.
- ❑ E. Executives has no permissions; Sales has Allow Full Control.
- ❑ F. Executives has Deny Full Control; Sales has no permissions.
- ❑ G. Executives has Allow Full Control; Sales has no permissions.
- ❑ H. Not enough information is presented to calculate permissions.

22. You're the administrator of a large consulting organization. All the consultants are equipped with notebook computers. There is a set of template files that all consultants should have with them at all times. These templates change frequently. Which feature of Windows XP Professional should you use to keep these templates available to the consultants as they travel away from the network?

   - ❑ A. Use Group Policy Objects to force the templates to a directory on the consultant computers.
   - ❑ B. Have the logon scripts for each user copy the necessary files to each machine.
   - ❑ C. Use the Offline Folders feature to share a folder as Offline Enabled.
   - ❑ D. On each consultant computer, select the share where the templates are and select Make Available Offline.

Quick Answer: **38**
Detailed Answer: **43**

Quick Check Answer Key

1. C

2. A

3. D

4. A, B, and C

5. D

6. B

7. C

8. A

9. A

10. B

11. A, D

12. D

13. B, D

14. C

15. B

16. C

17. B

18. D

19. B

20. E

21. D

22. D

Answers and Explanations

1. **Answer: C.** NTFSv5 (New Technology File System version 5) offers the best features for use with Microsoft Windows XP. NTFSv5 includes optimum reliability and, more importantly, the best security available in Windows. NTFSv4 does not offer all that NTFSv5 does, including disk quotas, disk compression, and built-in encryption. NTFSv5 cannot be used when dual-booting Microsoft Windows XP with most earlier operating systems.

2. **Answer: A.** The Convert.exe command converts a disk partition formatted with FAT (File Allocation Table, 16-bit) to NTFS (New Technology File System version 5). An example of proper syntax would be convert.exe C: /FS:NTFS.

3. **Answer: D.** The Convert.exe command will convert a disk partition formatted with FAT32 (File Allocation Table, 32-bit) to NTFS (New Technology File System version 5). An example of proper syntax would be convert.exe D: /FS:NTFS.

4. **Answers: A, B, and C.**

   Explanation A. NTFS stands for New Technology File System. Microsoft Windows XP can defragment this type of hard disk format.

   Explanation B. FAT32 stands for File Allocation Table, 32-bit. Microsoft Windows XP can defragment this type of hard disk format.

   Explanation C. FAT16 stands for File Allocation Table, 16-bit. Microsoft Windows XP can defragment this type of hard disk format. Note that FAT16 is also commonly referred to as simply FAT.

5. **Answer: D.** The Microsoft Windows XP defragmenter is located under Start, Programs, Accessories, System Tools, Disk Defragmenter.

6. **Answer: B.** You should take ownership of the files and folders and give Chip the permission to take ownership.

7. **Answer: C.** You should modify the hardware profiles and remove the docked hardware profile.

8. **Answer: A.** As administrator, you should take ownership of the files and folders.

9. **Answer: A.** You should have a network administrator open the properties of the Planning shared folder and be sure the Allow Caching of Files in This Shared Folder check box is selected.

10. **Answer: B.** Sally is able to connect to the share and access some of the data on it. Because of this, you can confirm that the shared folder is accessible. Remember that share permissions are assigned at the folder level and are then applied from that point in the directory structure down. The only reason why Sally would not be able to access all the data in the share has to do with NTFS permissions. When NTFS and share permissions are combined, the most restrictive permission applies. Answer A is incorrect because Sally can access the share. Answer C is incorrect because Sally can ping the server and can access some of the data from the share. Answer D is incorrect because shared folder permissions are not the cause of Sally's difficulties.

11. **Answers: A, D.** Answer A is correct; NTFS is being used to control access to resources. When NTFS and share permissions are combined, the most restrictive permission becomes the user's effective permissions. Answer D is also correct; the consultant you've hired is not qualified to conduct a security audit for your company. Answer B is incorrect because NTFS and share permissions do not combine in the manner described. An argument could be made for answer C, but technically it is not correct if NTFS permissions are being managed properly in your environment.

12. **Answer: D.** Answer D is the best answer for this scenario. Printer pooling allows one printer to point to multiple physical print devices. This allows workstations to be configured so they point to one network printer. If a printer fails, the pooling function will allow jobs to be routed to another printer. Answer A is not correct because redirection forwards jobs from one printer to another printer. Answer B would help, but is not the best solution. Answer C is incorrect because the users would need to change their printer configuration to print to a new printer if their current printer failed.

13. **Answers: B, D.** The convert command only enables you to convert FAT or FAT32 to NTFS. If you would like to change a FAT partition to FAT32, you need to back up your data, reformat the drive, and then restore the data. Answer A is incorrect because this command converts the drive to NTFS. Answer C is incorrect because formatting a drive is not the same as converting a drive. During a format all data is lost. Converting a drive allows the data to be retained.

14. **Answer: C.** Although answer A is tempting, it is not in your best interest to get the president upset. Technically, answer C is correct and the data is lost. Answers B and D are incorrect because the format utility cannot be used to convert a drive under any circumstances.

15. **Answer: B.** The key to this question is understanding the limitations of FAT and FAT32 partitions. Remember that FAT and FAT32 do not support folder- and file-level security. For this reason, they are not very efficient for creating user home directories (because these directories are typically secure). Answer A is incorrect because the user folders would not be secure. Answer C is incorrect because this requires a large effort (creating all the individual user shares). This effort is not required on NTFS partitions, where we can use file and folder security to secure the resource. To simplify the creating process, you can use the %Username% environment variable to create user home directories and assign NTFS permissions automatically when configuring the user home directory property of a user account. Answer D is incorrect because this requires a large effort (creating all the individual user shares). Answer B represents the most efficient answer.

16. **Answer: C.** You must remember how shared folder and NTFS permissions are applied when a user accesses a resource over the network. In this case, Mikayla can access a resource if she accesses the resource while logged on locally (she is accessing the resource directly from the file system), but cannot access the same resource from over the network. This situation points to a shared folder permission issue. When Mikayla is accessing the resource locally, shared folder permissions are not processed. You also know that Mikayla has NTFS permissions to the resource because she can access it locally. For these reasons, C is correct. Answer A is incorrect because Mikayla can access the resource if logged on locally. Answer B is incorrect because NTFS permissions cannot be applied for network access versus local access. Answer D is incorrect because membership in Authenticated Users cannot be changed (it is a built-in group).

17. **Answer: B.** Expect a number of questions regarding troubleshooting permissions. The correct answer for this question revolves around the calculation of effective NTFS permissions. Remember that if a user is denied permission, it overrides all other permissions granted to the user. In this case, denying Full Control to the Everyone group effectively denies access to all users on the network. Answer A is incorrect because no such requirement exists in Windows XP (or any other version of Windows). Answer C is incorrect because users need to be able to access resources from across the network. Answer D is incorrect because the problem is an NTFS permission issue.

18. **Answer: D.** Remember that shared folder permissions combine unless a deny permission has been assigned. In this case, the Deny Full Control permission assigned to the Executives group will block Mikayla from this resource. Answers A, B, and C are incorrect because the effective permissions are Deny Full Control. Answer E is incorrect because the permission table and group member is provided. This is all the information you need to calculate effective permissions.

19. **Answer: B.** When calculating effective permissions, you need to remember how both shared folder permissions and NTFS permissions work with each other. You also must remember that not being in the access control list of a resource is the same as not having permissions to a resource. In this question, Mikayla and John both have the same effective shared folder permissions (Full Control). This is true because shared folder permissions add up to give you the effective permissions (unless the deny permission is assigned). The question, however, asks for Mikayla and John's effective permissions on the resource. To calculate the overall effective permissions, you also need to look at the NTFS permissions assigned to the users. Mikayla has Read permissions explicitly assigned to her user account. John does not have any NTFS permissions at all. The overall effective permissions are the most restrictive of the shared folder and NTFS permissions combined. For this reason, Mikayla receives Full Control shared folder permissions plus Read NTFS permissions for a total effective permission of Read. John receives Full Control shared folder permission plus no NTFS permissions for a total effective permission of no access (or no permissions assigned).

20. **Answer: E.** Again, recall the rules when you move files on NTFS partitions:

- When you move a folder or file within a single NTFS partition, the folder or file retains its original permissions.
- When you move a folder or file between NTFS partitions, the folder or file inherits the permissions of the destination folder. When you move a folder or file between partitions, you're creating a new version of the resource and therefore inherit permissions.
- When you move a folder or file to a non-NTFS partition, all permissions are lost (this is because non-NTFS partitions do not support NTFS permissions).

In this question, we're moving a file between two different partitions, so the effective permissions on the target file are Sales Full Control.

21. **Answer: D.** Again, remember the rules when you move files on NTFS partitions:

- When you move a folder or file within a single NTFS partition, the folder or file retains its original permissions.
- When you move a folder or file between NTFS partitions, the folder or file inherits the permissions of the destination folder. When you move a folder or file between partitions, you're creating a new version of the resource and therefore inherit permissions.

- When you move a folder or file to a non-NTFS partition, all permissions are lost (this is because non-NTFS partitions do not support NTFS permissions).

  In this question, you're moving a file on the same partition, so the effective permissions on the target file are Sales Deny Full Control. In this case, you must also be aware of the fact that only explicitly assigned permissions carry over.

22. **Answer: D.** Although you could use Group Policy Objects to force the templates to be copied to the local machine, the fact that they change frequently means that this will be resource-intensive (and not the best option) for the administrator. Logon scripts can be used to copy the templates each time the user logs in; however, this will significantly delay the user's logon if the templates are very large. The question didn't specify the size of the templates. You can't share a folder as Offline Enabled. The client must request, or set, offline status for a share, or a folder underneath a remote share.

Setting Up, Managing, and Troubleshooting Security Accounts and Policies

Quick Check

1. You're a help desk technician for your company. Sarah is an executive at your company. Because Sarah travels frequently, she uses a Windows XP Professional portable computer that has a smart card reader. Sarah asks you to configure her computer so that she can dial in to the company network when she is out of the office. The company security policy states that dial-in users must use smart cards when they connect to the network, and that the users must use the strongest form of encryption possible. The company security policy further states that client computers must disconnect if the routing and remote access server does not support both smart card authentication and the strongest possible authentication.

   You need to configure the dial-up connection properties on Sarah's computer to dial in to the company network. Your solution must ensure that company security policies are enforced.

   Which of the following should you do? (Select all that apply.)

   - ❑ A. Select the Advanced (Custom Settings) security option.
   - ❑ B. Select the Maximum Strength Encryption item from the data encryption list.
   - ❑ C. Select the Extensible Authentication Protocol (EAP) option, and select Smart Card or other Certificate from the EAP list.
   - ❑ D. Select the Require Data Encryption check box.

Quick Answer: **64**
Detailed Answer: **65**

Quick Check

2. You're a help desk technician for your company. Mary is a member of your company's sales department. Mary asks you to configure her XP portable computer so that she can dial in to the company network when she is out of the office. The company uses two servers for Routing and Remote Access: One is a Microsoft Windows 2000 Server, and the other is a Windows NT 4.0 Server. Each server contains four modems. Each modem connects to a dial-up telephone line, and a single telephone number distributes incoming calls across the eight telephone lines.

   Company security policy requires that dial-up logon credentials be encrypted and use the maximum possible security when they are transmitted. You need to ensure that Mary can dial in and log on by using her domain user account. You also need to ensure that company security policy is enforced.

   How should you configure the security settings for the dial-up connection?

   - ❑ A. Select the Typical (Recommended Settings) option. Select the Require Secured Password list item from the validation list.
   - ❑ B. Select the Typical (Recommended Settings) option. Select the Require Data Encryption (Disconnect If None) check box.
   - ❑ C. Select the Advanced (Custom Settings) option. On the Advanced Security Settings tab, clear all check boxes except the MS-CHAP v2 check box.
   - ❑ D. Select the Typical (Recommended Settings) option. Select the Automatically Use My Windows Logon Name and Password (and Domain) check box.

Quick Answer: **64**
Detailed Answer: **65**

3. You're the desktop administrator for your organization. All employees have Windows XP Professional computers. All employees are members of the local Users group on their own computers. A user in the marketing department has a removable disk cartridge drive on his computer. The disk cartridge contains an unsupported, third-party file system. When he tries to save data to the disk cartridge, the user is prompted to reformat the disk cartridge. However, he receives an Access Denied error message when attempting to reformat.

   You need to enable the user to save data to the disk cartridge. What should you do?

   - ❑ A. Grant the user Allow-Full Control permission on the disk cartridge.
   - ❑ B. Instruct the user to format the cartridge as FAT32.
   - ❑ C. Remove the Read-Only attribute from the disk cartridge.
   - ❑ D. Configure the local security settings to enable the user to format and eject removable media.

Quick Answer: **64**
Detailed Answer: **65**

Quick Check

4. You're a help desk technician for Parker Research. All employees use Windows XP Professional computers. A user named Amy reports a problem browsing the Internet. She says that she cannot use a search to browse to www.parkerresearch.com. You use Remote Assistance to examine search engines on Amy's computer. When you try to use the search engine, you receive the following warning message: You cannot send HTML forms. When you try to use other search engines on Amy's computer, you receive the same message. Amy verifies that she is able to use the search engine to browse the company intranet without problems.

Quick Answer: **64**
Detailed Answer: **65**

You need to ensure that Amy can use any search engine to browse the Internet from her computer. What should you do?

- ❑ A. On Amy's computer, open the Security properties for Microsoft Internet Explorer. Add www.parkerresearch.com to the Trusted Sites list. Clear the Require Server Verification for All Sites in This Zone check box.
- ❑ B. Inform Amy to use https:// instead of http:// when typing the URLs for the search engines. Tell Amy to ensure that Internet Explorer displays a lock icon in its status bar, before she submits information in a form on a Web page.
- ❑ C. On Amy's computer, open the Security properties for Internet Explorer. In the security settings for the Internet zone, select the Submit Non-Encrypted Form Data option.
- ❑ D. Tell Amy to click the Search button on the Internet Explorer toolbar and then type her search keywords in the Web form displayed by Internet Explorer.

Quick Check

5. You're a help desk technician for Loftware, Inc. Loftware, Inc. maintains a secure intranet Web site at intranet.loftwareinc.com. All employees use Windows XP Professional computers. A user named Kate reports that she cannot access the secure Web site by using Internet Explorer. When she types http://intranet.loftware.com into the Internet Explorer address bar, an error message reports that a digital certificate is not from a trusted source. You verify that the intranet Web server is using a digital certificate issued by your company's Enterprise CA (certificate authority). The Enterprise CA is located on a server named certificates.loftwareinc.com.

   You need to ensure that Kate can access the secure intranet Web site without receiving an error message. What should you do?

   - ❑ A. On Kate's computer, open the Security properties for Internet Explorer. Add intranet.loftwareinc.com to the Trusted Sites list.
   - ❑ B. Ask a network administrator to modify the properties for IIS (Internet Information Services) on intranet.loftwareinc.com and set the SSL port number to 443.
   - ❑ C. On Kate's computer, open the Security properties for Internet Explorer. Open the Trusted Sites dialog box and select the Require Server Verification for All Sites in This Zone check box.
   - ❑ D. On Kate's computer, open Internet Explorer's list of certificates. Import a copy of the certificate used by the intranet.loftwareinc.com server into Kate's Trusted Publishers Certificates store.

Quick Answer: **64**
Detailed Answer: **65**

Quick Check

6. You're a help desk technician for your company. Your company uses a custom database application to analyze revenue information. The database application saves data to files with a .dcp file extension. The .dcp files are stored in the same shared folder as many shared Microsoft Word 2002 documents. Your supervisor informs you that the application's .dcp files are becoming corrupted. Each time the files get corrupted, they must be restored from a tape backup, which is time- and resource-consuming. Users with portable computers often select the Word 2002 documents in the shared folder to be made available offline. You find that several users also select the .dcp files to be made available offline.

   You need to ensure that users cannot make .dcp files available offline. Your solution must not affect user access to the other files in the folder. What should you do?

   - ❑ A. Ask a network administrator to modify the file permissions on the .dcp files to assign all users the Deny-Change permission.
   - ❑ B. Modify the file share that contains the .dcp files and disable offline file caching.
   - ❑ C. Ask a network administrator to modify the domain security policy by adding the .dcp file type to the File Not Caching domain group policy.
   - ❑ D. Use Remote Assistance to disable offline files on the local computer policy of all portable computers.

Quick Answer: **64**
Detailed Answer: **65**

Quick Check

7. You're the administrator of your company's network. The network includes an Active Directory domain. A new employee named Jane is hired to help deploy Windows XP Professional to 150 new computers. You create a new domain user account for Jane and add the account to the Domain Users group. Jane can install Windows XP Professional on the new computers, but she cannot add the computers to the Active Directory domain.

   You verify that the computers are connected to the network and that they are receiving IP configuration information from the company's DHCP server. You need to ensure that Jane can add the new computers to the Active Directory domain. You also need to be sure Jane does not receive any unnecessary security privileges on the network. What should you do?

   - ❑ A. Add Jane's domain account to the Server Operators domain user group.
   - ❑ B. On a domain controller, use the Local Computer Policy MMC to add Jane's domain user account to the Add Workstations to Domain user right policy.
   - ❑ C. Use the Delegation of Control Wizard to grant Jane's domain user account the right to create new objects in the computers container.
   - ❑ D. Install the Active Directory users and computers MMC on Jane's Windows XP Professional computer. Add Jane's domain user account to the domain Administrators domain user group.

Quick Answer: 64
Detailed Answer: 65

Quick Check

Quick Answer: 64
Detailed Answer: 65

8. You're a help desk technician for your company. All users have Windows XP Professional computers. Eight users run a custom application named Payroll on their computers. Payroll stores user passwords in a file named Secure.ini. By default, the Secure.ini file is stored in a folder named C:\Winnt\PayrollApp. The actual location and name of the file can be changed by an administrator. Each Secure.ini file is unique. Each computer contains a single logical drive C: formatted as NTFS in order to comply with the company's security policy.

   You need to be sure that the Secure.ini files get encrypted. What should you do?

   - ❑ A. Create a folder named C:\Files. Copy the Secure.ini file to the C:\Files folder. In the properties of the C:\Files folder, select the option to encrypt the contents of the folder. Accept the default settings on the Confirm Attributes Changes dialog box. Configure Payroll to use the C:\Files\Secure.ini file.
   - ❑ B. In the Properties of the C:\Winnt\PayrollApp folder, use Windows Explorer to select the option to encrypt the contents of the folder. Accept the default settings on the Confirm Attributes Changes dialog box.
   - ❑ C. Have a network administrator share a new encrypted folder named SecureFiles on a network server. Permit users to read the files contained within the folder. Copy the Secure.ini file from each computer into the SecureFiles folder. On each computer, configure Payroll to use the Passwords.ini file in the SecureFiles folder.
   - ❑ D. Create a folder named C:\Files. Move the Secure.ini file to the C:\Files folder. Instruct the user of each computer to open the properties of the C:\Files folder and select the option to encrypt the contents of the folder. Accept the default settings on the Confirm Attributes Changes dialog box. Configure Payroll to use the C:\Files\Secure.ini files.

Quick Check

9. You're a help desk technician for your company. Mike and Valerie are users in your company's sales department. Mike and Valerie both use Windows XP Professional laptop computers. They also use Internet Explorer to connect to a Web-based Internet email service. Mike reports that he is required to provide a username and password each time he accesses that Web site. Valerie, however, is not required to log on each separate time she accesses the Web site because the site remembers her username and password.

   Quick Answer: 64
   Detailed Answer: 65

   You need to configure Mike's computer so that the Web site can remember his username and password. How should you configure Internet Explorer on Mike's computer?

   - ❑ A. Set the privacy configuration for first-party cookies to Accept.
   - ❑ B. Modify the security configuration on Mike's laptop so that the Internet email Web site is included in the Trusted Sites list.
   - ❑ C. Modify the privacy configuration so that the Always Allow Session Cookies check box is selected.
   - ❑ D. Set the security level for the Internet zone to medium on Mike's computer.

10. You and Steve are the desktop administrators for your company. You install a printer on your Windows XP Professional computer. You share this printer on the company network.

    Quick Answer: 64
    Detailed Answer: 66

    You want to ensure that only members of the ITAdmins local group can use this printer, and that only you and Steve can manage the printer and all print jobs. You also want to ensure that members of the ITAdmins local group can manage only their own print jobs. How should you configure security on this printer?

    - ❑ A. Grant Allow-Print permission to the ITAdmins group. Grant Allow-Manage Documents permission to your user account and Steve's user account.
    - ❑ B. Grant Allow-Print permission to the ITAdmins group. Grant Allow-Manage Documents and Allow-Manage Printers permissions to your user account and Steve's user account.
    - ❑ C. Grant Allow-Manage Documents permission to the ITAdmins group. Grant Allow-Manage printers permission to your user account and Steve's user account.
    - ❑ D. Grant Allow-Print permission to the ITAdmins group. Remove Allow-Manage Documents permission from the Creator Owner group. Grant Allow-Manage Printers permission to your user account and Steve's user account.

Quick Check

11. You're the desktop administrator for Computers, Ltd. A graphics designer named Paul saves all his files in the My Documents folder on his Windows XP Professional computer. Paul now needs to work on several different computers each day to complete his work. He needs to be able to access his files at any time. You implement a roaming user profile and home directory for Paul. However, Paul mentions that when he uses his roaming profile, it takes more than 10 minutes for him to log on to other computers.

Quick Answer: **64**
Detailed Answer: **66**

You need to reduce the amount of time it takes for Paul to log on to other computers when using his roaming profile. What should you do?

- ❑ A. Log on as a local administrator on Paul's computer. Edit the local group policy to exclude directories in roaming profiles.
- ❑ B. Change the UNC path of Paul's roaming profile to his home directory folder.
- ❑ C. Log on as a local administrator on Paul's computer. Change the roaming profile to a local profile.
- ❑ D. Log on as a local administrator on Paul's computer. In the properties of the My Documents folder, change the target folder location to Paul's home directory.

12. You're the desktop administrator for your company's research department. The IT manager for the research department creates a custom policy that will apply to a custom application that is loaded on the department's Windows XP Professional computers. He deploys this policy by using Group Policy. When you inspect the research department's computers, you find out that the application has not been modified by the policy.

Quick Answer: **64**
Detailed Answer: **66**

You want to examine the Windows XP Professional computers to find out whether the custom policy is affecting the correct location in the Registry. Which command should you run?

- ❑ A. MSInfo32.exe
- ❑ B. GPEdit.exe
- ❑ C. GPResult.exe
- ❑ D. RGP.exe

Quick Check

13. You're the desktop administrator for Compco, Ltd. The company's network contains 800 Windows XP Professional computers. All the computers are members of a single Active Directory domain. The computers' hard disks are formatted as NTFSv5. Compco's software developers release a new custom application. The application uses a .dll file named AppLibrary.dll, which is installed in a folder named \Program Files\Compco\CompcoApp. The company's software help desk technicians complain that many users experience problems when they use the application. You notice that the AppLibrary.dll file was deleted on the client computers. Compco's software developers recommend that you modify the file permissions on AppLibrary.dll so that users have only Read permission on the file.

    You need to ensure that all users have only Read permission on the AppLibrary.dll file on all 800 Windows XP Professional computers. What should you do?

    - ❑ A. Write a logon script that moves the AppLibrary.dll file into the Windows\System32 folder. Ensure that Windows file protection is enabled on all 800 Windows XP Professional computers. Apply that logon script to all domain user accounts.
    - ❑ B. Use the Security Configuration and Analysis console to create a new security template that modifies file permissions on AppLibrary.dll. Use the Active Directory group policy to import and then apply the template to all 800 Windows XP Professional computers.
    - ❑ C. Repackage the customer application in a Windows Installer package. Have a domain administrator create a GPO that advertises the package to all domain user accounts.
    - ❑ D. Write a VBScript file named Fix.vbs that modifies the file permissions on AppLibrary.dll.

Quick Answer: **64**
Detailed Answer: **66**

14. What component of the Active Directory Structure used with Microsoft Windows XP is a distinct named set of attributes that represent a network resource, such as a user or computer account?

    - ❑ A. OU
    - ❑ B. Class
    - ❑ C. Object
    - ❑ D. Domain
    - ❑ E. Tree

Quick Answer: **64**
Detailed Answer: **66**

Quick Check

15. What component of the Active Directory structure used with Microsoft Windows XP is a logical grouping of objects, such as computers, accounts, domains, or OUs?

    - ☐ A. Object
    - ☐ B. Class
    - ☐ C. OU
    - ☐ D. Domain
    - ☐ E. Site

Quick Answer: **64**
Detailed Answer: **66**

16. What component of the Active Directory structure used with Microsoft Windows XP is a container used to organize objects of a domain into logical administrative groups?

    - ☐ A. Object
    - ☐ B. Class
    - ☐ C. OU
    - ☐ D. Domain
    - ☐ E. Tree

Quick Answer: **64**
Detailed Answer: **66**

17. What component of the Active Directory structure used with Microsoft Windows XP holds all network objects and information about only all objects it contains, and acts as a security boundary?

    - ☐ A. Object
    - ☐ B. Class
    - ☐ C. OU
    - ☐ D. Domain
    - ☐ E. Tree

Quick Answer: **64**
Detailed Answer: **66**

18. What component of the Active Directory structure used with Microsoft Windows XP is a hierarchical grouping of one or more domains that share a contiguous namespace?

    - ☐ A. Object
    - ☐ B. Class
    - ☐ C. Tree
    - ☐ D. Domain
    - ☐ E. Forest

Quick Answer: **64**
Detailed Answer: **66**

Quick Check

19. What component of the Active Directory structure used with Microsoft Windows XP is a hierarchical grouping of one or more domain trees that have different namespaces?

Quick Answer: 64
Detailed Answer: 66

- ❑ A. Site
- ❑ B. Class
- ❑ C. OU
- ❑ D. Forest
- ❑ E. Domain

20. What component of the Active Directory structure used with Microsoft Windows XP is a geographical grouping of one or more IP subnets connected by high-speed links?

Quick Answer: 64
Detailed Answer: 66

- ❑ A. Site
- ❑ B. Class
- ❑ C. OU
- ❑ D. Tree

21. What item in Active Directory used with Microsoft Windows XP contains a formal definition of contents and structure of Active Directory, such as classes, class properties, and attributes?

Quick Answer: 64
Detailed Answer: 67

- ❑ A. Schema
- ❑ B. Global Catalog
- ❑ C. DN
- ❑ D. RDN
- ❑ E. GUID

22. What item in Active Directory used with Microsoft Windows XP is a central repository of information about all objects in an entire forest?

Quick Answer: 64
Detailed Answer: 67

- ❑ A. Schema
- ❑ B. Global Catalog
- ❑ C. DN
- ❑ D. RDN
- ❑ E. GUID

23. What item in Active Directory used with Microsoft Windows XP uniquely identifies an object within the entire Active Directory forest?

Quick Answer: 64
Detailed Answer: 67

- ❑ A. Schema
- ❑ B. Global Catalog
- ❑ C. DN
- ❑ D. RDN
- ❑ E. UPN

Quick Check

24. What item in Active Directory used with Microsoft Windows XP identifies an object only within a single domain?

Quick Answer: 64
Detailed Answer: 67

- ❑ A. Schema
- ❑ B. Global Catalog
- ❑ C. DN
- ❑ D. RDN
- ❑ E. UPN

25. What item in Active Directory used with Microsoft Windows XP is a unique 128-bit character string assigned to objects when they're created?

Quick Answer: 64
Detailed Answer: 67

- ❑ A. Schema
- ❑ B. Global Catalog
- ❑ C. UPN
- ❑ D. RDN
- ❑ E. GUID

26. What item in Active Directory used with Microsoft Windows XP is the common, friendly name given to a user account?

Quick Answer: 64
Detailed Answer: 67

- ❑ A. Schema
- ❑ B. Global Catalog
- ❑ C. DN
- ❑ D. UPN
- ❑ E. GUID

27. What Microsoft Windows XP built-in local group can perform all administrative tasks on the local system?

Quick Answer: 64
Detailed Answer: 67

- ❑ A. Administrators
- ❑ B. Backup Operators
- ❑ C. Guests
- ❑ D. Power Users
- ❑ E. Remote Desktop Users

28. What Microsoft Windows XP built-in local group can use Backup to back up and restore data on the local computer?

Quick Answer: 64
Detailed Answer: 67

- ❑ A. Administrators
- ❑ B. Backup Operators
- ❑ C. Guests
- ❑ D. Power Users
- ❑ E. Users

Quick Check

29. What Microsoft Windows XP built-in local group can be used for granting temporary access to resources?

    ❑ A. Administrators
    ❑ B. Backup Operators
    ❑ C. Guests
    ❑ D. Power Users
    ❑ E. Remote Desktop Users

Quick Answer: 64
Detailed Answer: 67

30. What Microsoft Windows XP built-in local group can only create and modify local user accounts on the local computer, share resources, install programs, and install device drivers, among other simple tasks?

    ❑ A. Administrators
    ❑ B. Backup Operators
    ❑ C. Guests
    ❑ D. Power Users
    ❑ E. Users

Quick Answer: 64
Detailed Answer: 67

31. What Microsoft Windows XP built-in local group can log on locally through the Remote Desktop Connection?

    ❑ A. Administrators
    ❑ B. Backup Operators
    ❑ C. Guests
    ❑ D. Power Users
    ❑ E. Remote Desktop Users

Quick Answer: 64
Detailed Answer: 67

32. What Microsoft Windows XP built-in local group can perform only everyday tasks for which it has been assigned permissions?

    ❑ A. Administrators
    ❑ B. Backup Operators
    ❑ C. Users
    ❑ D. Power Users
    ❑ E. Remote Desktop Users

Quick Answer: 64
Detailed Answer: 67

33. Which Microsoft Windows XP built-in local group includes all users and computers that have been authenticated?

    ❑ A. Authenticated Users
    ❑ B. Administrators
    ❑ C. Guest
    ❑ D. Power Users

Quick Answer: 64
Detailed Answer: 67

Quick Check

34. Which Microsoft Windows XP built-in system group includes all users that have logged on through Task Scheduler?

Quick Answer: 64
Detailed Answer: 68

- ❑ A. Everyone
- ❑ B. Batch
- ❑ C. Creator
- ❑ D. Dialup

35. What Microsoft Windows XP built-in system group is best described as a placeholder in an inheritable ACE?

Quick Answer: 64
Detailed Answer: 68

- ❑ A. Authenticated Users
- ❑ B. Batch
- ❑ C. Creator Group
- ❑ D. Dialup
- ❑ E. Everyone

36. Which Microsoft Windows XP built-in system group includes all users that have logged in using a standard 56Kbps phone connection?

Quick Answer: 64
Detailed Answer: 68

- ❑ A. Everyone
- ❑ B. Batch
- ❑ C. Creator
- ❑ D. Dialup

37. What Microsoft Windows XP built-in system group is best described as including authenticated users and guests?

Quick Answer: 64
Detailed Answer: 68

- ❑ A. Authenticated Users
- ❑ B. Batch
- ❑ C. Creator Group
- ❑ D. Dialup
- ❑ E. Everyone

38. What Microsoft Windows XP built-in system group is best described as including all users logging on locally or through a remote desktop connection?

Quick Answer: 64
Detailed Answer: 68

- ❑ A. Everyone
- ❑ B. Interactive
- ❑ C. Local System
- ❑ D. Text Service
- ❑ E. Text Terminal Server Users

Quick Check

39. What Microsoft Windows XP built-in system group is best described as a service account that's used by the operating system?

Quick Answer: 64
Detailed Answer: 68

- ❑ A. Everyone
- ❑ B. Interactive
- ❑ C. Local System
- ❑ D. Text Service
- ❑ E. Text Terminal Server Users

40. What Microsoft Windows XP built-in system group is best described as including all security principals that have logged on as a service, with membership in this group controlled by the operating system?

Quick Answer: 64
Detailed Answer: 68

- ❑ A. Everyone
- ❑ B. Interactive
- ❑ C. Local System
- ❑ D. Text Service
- ❑ E. Text Terminal Server Users

41. What Microsoft Windows XP built-in system group is best described as including all users who have logged on to a Terminal Services server that uses Terminal Services version 4.0 application compatibility mode?

Quick Answer: 64
Detailed Answer: 68

- ❑ A. Everyone
- ❑ B. Interactive
- ❑ C. Local System
- ❑ D. Text Service
- ❑ E. Text Terminal Server Users

42. What items are true of group policies in Microsoft Windows XP? (Select all that apply.)

Quick Answer: 64
Detailed Answer: 68

- ❑ A. GPedit.msc is the replacement for the POLEdit.exe used in earlier Windows versions.
- ❑ B. Group policies can be stored locally.
- ❑ C. Group policies are more flexible than system policies.
- ❑ D. System policies are more flexible than group policies.
- ❑ E. Group policies can be stored in Active Directory.

Quick Check

43. Which security template for Microsoft Windows XP is a compatibility template, and is also referred to as the Basic template?

    Quick Answer: 64
    Detailed Answer: 68

    - ❑ A. Compatws.inf
    - ❑ B. Securews.inf
    - ❑ C. Hisecws.inf
    - ❑ D. Rootsec.inf

44. Which security template for Microsoft Windows XP is a more secure template in regard to account policy and auditing?

    Quick Answer: 64
    Detailed Answer: 68

    - ❑ A. Compatws.inf
    - ❑ B. Securews.inf
    - ❑ C. Hisecws.inf
    - ❑ D. Rootsec.inf

45. Which security template for Microsoft Windows XP is a highly secure template provided for Microsoft Windows XP workstations running in native mode only?

    Quick Answer: 64
    Detailed Answer: 68

    - ❑ A. Compatws.inf
    - ❑ B. Securews.inf
    - ❑ C. Hisecws.inf
    - ❑ D. Rootsec.inf

46. Which security template for Microsoft Windows XP applies the default settings to the root of the system drive that Windows XP was originally installed with?

    Quick Answer: 64
    Detailed Answer: 69

    - ❑ A. Compatws.inf
    - ❑ B. Securews.inf
    - ❑ C. Hisecws.inf
    - ❑ D. Rootsec.inf

47. Which of the following are true in Microsoft Windows XP with regard to EFS? (Select all that apply.)

    Quick Answer: 64
    Detailed Answer: 69

    - ❑ A. EFS is available only on NTFSv5 partitions.
    - ❑ B. EFS is transparent to the end user.
    - ❑ C. EFS uses public key encryption.
    - ❑ D. EFS uses shared key encryption.
    - ❑ E. An appointed recovery system agent can open the files as well.

Quick Check

48. When working with a file encrypted with EFS in Microsoft Windows XP from one NTFS partition to another computer's FAT partition, which of the following are true? (Select all that apply.)

Quick Answer: 64
Detailed Answer: 69

- ❑ A. Copy the file as normal and it will remain encrypted.
- ❑ B. Copy the file as normal and it will become unencrypted.
- ❑ C. Move the file as normal and it will become unencrypted.
- ❑ D. Move the file as normal and it will remain encrypted.

49. When working with a file encrypted with EFS in Microsoft Windows XP from an NTFS partition to a FAT partition, including floppy disks, which of the following are true? (Select all that apply.)

Quick Answer: 64
Detailed Answer: 69

- ❑ A. Move the file as normal and it will remain encrypted.
- ❑ B. Copy the file as normal and it will remain encrypted.
- ❑ C. Move the file as normal and it will become unencrypted.
- ❑ D. Copy the file as normal and it will become unencrypted.

50. When working with a file encrypted with EFS in Microsoft Windows XP from one NTFS partition to another computer's NTFS partition, which of the following are true? (Select all that apply.)

Quick Answer: 64
Detailed Answer: 69

- ❑ A. Copy the file as normal and it will remain encrypted.
- ❑ B. Copy the file as normal and it will become unencrypted.
- ❑ C. Move the file as normal and it will remain encrypted.
- ❑ D. Move the file as normal and it will become unencrypted.

51. When working with a file encrypted with EFS in Microsoft Windows XP from one NTFS partition to another NTFS partition on the same computer, which of the following are true? (Select all that apply.)

Quick Answer: 64
Detailed Answer: 69

- ❑ A. Move the file as normal and it will remain encrypted.
- ❑ B. Copy the file as normal and it will become unencrypted.
- ❑ C. Copy the file as normal and it will remain encrypted.
- ❑ D. Move the file as normal and it will become unencrypted.

52. When working with a Microsoft Windows XP computer in a workgroup, which of the following are true regarding user password hints? (Select all that apply.)

Quick Answer: 64
Detailed Answer: 69

- ❑ A. They dramatically lower security.
- ❑ B. They dramatically increase security.
- ❑ C. They are visible to the administrator only.
- ❑ D. They are visible to all users.

Quick Answer: **64**

Detailed Answer: **70**

53. You're the desktop administrator for your company. The company's network consists of 20 Microsoft Windows XP computers. All hardware and installed applications are the same on each computer. A user named Steve in the marketing department forgets his password on a regular basis, causing you much concern and administrative effort regarding security.

    What should you do?

    - ☑ A. Create a password reset disk for Steve, and instruct him in its use.
    - ❑ B. Assign Steve the password of *password*, and click the setting for User Cannot Change Password.
    - ❑ C. Assign Steve the password of *noexpire*, and click the setting for Password Never Expires.
    - ❑ D. Assign Steve the password of logon, and click the setting for User Must Change Password at Next Logon.

Quick Check Answer Key

1. A, B, and C
2. C
3. D
4. A
5. D
6. C
7. B
8. D
9. A
10. B
11. D
12. C
13. B
14. C
15. B
16. C
17. D
18. C
19. D
20. A
21. A
22. B
23. C
24. D
25. E
26. D
27. A
28. B
29. C
30. D
31. E
32. C
33. A
34. B
35. C
36. D
37. E
38. B
39. C
40. D
41. E
42. A, B, and E
43. A
44. B
45. C
46. D
47. A, B, C, and E
48. B and C
49. C and D
50. A and C
51. A and C
52. A and D
53. A

Answers and Explanations

1. **Answers: A, B, and C.**

   Explanation A. You need to select the Advanced (Custom Settings) security option to get things started.

   Explanation B. Select the Maximum Strength Encryption item from the data encryption list. This is required in this situation.

   Explanation C. Smart Cards require you to select the Extensible Authentication Protocol (EAP) option, and select Smart Card or other Certificate from the EAP list. Remember Smart Cards means EAP.

2. **Answer: C.** Select the Advanced (Custom Settings) option. On the Advanced Security Settings tab, clear all check boxes except the MS-CHAP v2 (Microsoft Challenge Handshake Authentication Protocol Version 2) check box.

3. **Answer: D.** You should configure the local security settings to enable the user to format and eject removable media.

4. **Answer: A.** You must open the security properties for Microsoft Internet Explorer on Amy's computer. Add www.parkerresearch.com to the Trusted Sites list. Finally, clear the Require Server Verification for All Sites in This Zone check box.

5. **Answer: D.** On Kate's computer, you need to add a trusted certificate. Open Internet Explorer's list of certificates. Import a copy of the certificate used by the intranet.loftwareinc.com server into Kate's Trusted Publishers certificates store.

6. **Answer: C.** A configuration adjustment by a network admin is needed. Ask a network administrator to modify the Domain Security Policy by adding the .dcp file type to the File Not Caching domain group policy.

7. **Answer: B.** On a domain controller, you must use the Local Computer Policy Microsoft Management Console (MMC) to add Jane's domain user account to the Add Workstations to Domain user right policy.

8. **Answer: D.** You should create a folder named C:\Files. Move the Secure.ini file to the C:\Files folder. Instruct the user of each computer to open the properties of the C:\Files folder and select the option to encrypt the contents of the folder. Accept the default settings on the Confirm Attributes Changes dialog box. Configure Payroll to use the C:\Files\Secure.ini files.

9. **Answer: A.** You need to set the privacy configuration for first-party cookies to Accept.

10. **Answer: B.** You should grant Allow-Print permission to the ITAdmins group. Also, grant the Allow-Manage Documents and Allow-Manage Printers permissions to your and Steve's user accounts.

11. **Answer: D.** You should log on as a local administrator on Paul's computer. In the properties of the My Documents folder, change the Target folder location to Paul's home directory.

12. **Answer: C.** To examine a Windows XP Professional PC to find out whether a custom policy is affecting the correct location in the Registry, run the GPResult.exe command.

13. **Answer: B.** Use the Security Configuration and Analysis console to create a new security template that modifies file permissions on AppLibrary.dll. Use the Active Directory group policy to import and then apply the template to all 800 Windows XP Professional computers.

14. **Answer: C.** An object is a distinct named set of attributes that represent a network resource, such as a user or computer account. An example would be JSmith or Printer05.

15. **Answer: B.** A class is a logical grouping of objects, such as computers, accounts, domains, or OUs (organizational units).

16. **Answer: C.** OU stands for organizational unit, which is a container used to organize objects of a domain into logical administrative groups. An example would be the SalesOU, which would be functionally equivalent to a sales department, having users, computers, and printers.

17. **Answer: D.** A domain holds all network objects and information only about all objects it contains. A domain is considered a security boundary. In Microsoft Windows XP, security settings do not cross from one domain to another.

18. **Answer: C.** A tree is a hierarchical grouping, like a pyramid structure, of one or more Microsoft Windows XP domains that share a contiguous (similar, touching) namespace. An example would be eITprep.com, sales.eITprep.com, and products.eITprep.com.

19. **Answer: D.** A forest is a hierarchical grouping, like a pyramid structure, of one or more Microsoft Windows XP domain trees that have different namespaces. An example would be eITprep.com and sales.eITprep.com, connected over to AudioWhiz.com and products.AudioWhiz.com.

20. **Answer: A.** A site is a geographical grouping of one or more IP (Internet Protocol) subnets connected by high-speed links. An example would be a Microsoft Windows XP single domain with sites in Sacramento, San Francisco, and Los Angeles, California.

21. **Answer: A.** The schema contains a formal definition of contents and structure of Active Directory, such as classes, class properties, and attributes. Examples of each of these items would be User, Firstname, and John.

22. **Answer: B.** The Global Catalog is a central repository of information about all objects in an entire forest. The Global Catalog maintains a subset of attributes for each and every single object in the entire forest to help with searches.

23. **Answer: C.** DN stands for distinguished name. The distinguished name of an object uniquely identifies it within the entire Active Directory forest.

24. **Answer: D.** RDN stands for relative distinguished name. The relative distinguished name is a portion of the full distinguished name. The RDN identifies an object only within a single domain.

25. **Answer: E.** GUID stands for globally unique identifier. The globally unique identifier is a unique 128-bit character string assigned to objects when they are created in Active Directory. The GUID of an object never changes, even if the object is renamed or moved.

26. **Answer: D.** UPN stands for user principal name. The user principal name is the common, friendly name given to a user account that looks like an email address. An example would be AnneJohnson@ABCompany.com.

27. **Answer: A.** The Administrators built-in local group can perform all administrative tasks on the local system. The built-in Administrator account is a member of this group by default.

28. **Answer: B.** The Backup Operators built-in local group can use Microsoft Windows XP Backup to back up and restore data on the local computer.

29. **Answer: C.** The Guests built-in local group can be used for granting temporary access to resources. This is a very limited account.

30. **Answer: D.** The Power Users built-in local group can create and modify local user accounts on the local computer, share resources, install programs, and install device drivers.

31. **Answer: E.** The Remote Desktop Users built-in local group can log on locally through the Remote Desktop Connection.

32. **Answer: C.** The Users built-in local group can perform everyday tasks for which they have been assigned permissions. All new accounts added to a Microsoft Windows XP computer are added to this account.

33. **Answer: A.** The Authenticated Users Microsoft Windows XP built-in system group includes all users and computers whose identities have been authenticated. Authenticated Users does not include the Guest account.

34. **Answer: B.** The Batch Microsoft Windows XP built-in system group includes all users who have logged on through a batch facility such as Task Scheduler.

35. **Answer: C.** The Creator Group Microsoft Windows XP built-in system group is a placeholder in an inheritable ACE (access control entry).

36. **Answer: D.** The Dialup Microsoft Windows XP built-in system group includes all users who are logged in through a dial-up connection.

37. **Answer: E.** The Everyone Microsoft Windows XP built-in system group includes authenticated users and guests.

38. **Answer: B.** The Interactive Microsoft Windows XP built-in system group includes all users logging on locally or through a remote desktop connection.

39. **Answer: C.** The Local System Microsoft Windows XP built-in system group is a service account that is used by the operating system.

40. **Answer: D.** The Service Microsoft Windows XP built-in system group includes all security principals that have logged on as a service. Membership in the Service group is controlled by the operating system.

41. **Answer: E.** The Terminal Server Users Microsoft Windows XP built-in system group includes all users who have logged on to a Terminal Services server that uses Terminal Services version 4.0 application compatibility mode.

42. **Answers: A, B, and E.**

    Explanation A. GPedit.msc is the replacement for the POLEdit.exe used in earlier Windows versions. GPedit.msc is the snap-in for the Microsoft console.

    Explanation B. Group policies can be stored locally.

    Explanation E. Group policies can be stored in Active Directory.

43. **Answer: A.** Compatws.inf is a compatibility template, also referred to as the Basic template. It sets up permissions for local users group so that legacy programs are more likely to run. Compatws.inf is not considered secure.

44. **Answer: B.** Securews.inf is a more secure template in regards to account policy and auditing. It removes all members from the Power Users group, but ACLs (access control lists) are not modified. Securews.inf is considered somewhat secure.

45. **Answer: C.** Hisecws.inf is a highly secure template provided for Microsoft Windows XP workstations running in native mode only. It requires all network communications to be digitally signed and encrypted. Hisecws.inf changes the ACLs (access control lists) to give Power Users the ability to create shares and change the system time.

46. **Answer: D.** Rootsec.inf applies the default settings to the root of the system drive that Microsoft Windows XP was originally installed with. Rootsec.inf does not override settings that have been changed, and is therefore considered not secure.

47. **Answers: A, B, C, and E.**

    Explanation A. EFS (Encrypting File System) is only available on NTFSv5 (New Technology File System version 5) partitions.

    Explanation B. EFS is transparent to the end user.

    Explanation C. EFS uses public key encryption.

    Explanation E. EFS has an appointed recovery system agent who can open the files as well.

48. **Answers: B and C.**

    Explanation B. EFS stands for Encrypting File System. Copy the file as normal and it will become unencrypted.

    Explanation C. Move the file as normal and it will become unencrypted.

49. **Answers: C and D.**

    Explanation C. Move the file as normal and it will become unencrypted.

    Explanation D. EFS stands for Encrypting File System. Copy the file as normal and it will become unencrypted.

50. **Answers: A and C.**

    Explanation A. EFS stands for Encrypting File System. Copy the file as normal and it will remain encrypted.

    Explanation C. Move the file as normal and it will remain encrypted.

51. **Answers: A and C.**

    Explanation A. Move the file as normal and it will remain encrypted.

    Explanation C. EFS stands for Encrypting File System. Copy the file as normal and it will remain encrypted.

52. **Answers: A and D.**

    Explanation A. When working with a Microsoft Windows XP computer in a workgroup, user password hints dramatically lower security.

    Explanation D. When working with a Microsoft Windows XP computer in a workgroup, user password hints are visible to all users.

53. **Answer: A.** You should create a password reset disk for Steve. Click Start, Settings, Control Panel, User Accounts, Related Tasks, Prevent a Forgotten Password. This will start the Forgotten Password Wizard. Any newly created password reset disk will invalidate older disks.

Implementing and Managing User and Desktop Settings

Quick Check

1. What is another name for a collection of data and folders that store a user's desktop environment and application settings along with personal data in Microsoft Windows XP?

Quick Answer: **97**
Detailed Answer: **99**

- ❑ A. Control Panel
- ❑ B. Desktop settings
- ❑ C. User profiles
- ❑ D. Hardware profiles

2. What settings are contained in a user profile in Microsoft Windows XP? (Select all that apply.)

Quick Answer: **97**
Detailed Answer: **99**

- ❑ A. Accessories
- ❑ B. Application settings
- ❑ C. Control Panel
- ❑ D. Printer settings
- ❑ E. Taskbar settings

3. What Microsoft Windows XP user profile settings contain the settings for Calculator, Notepad, and Paint?

Quick Answer: **97**
Detailed Answer: **99**

- ❑ A. Accessories
- ❑ B. Application settings
- ❑ C. Control Panel
- ❑ D. Printer settings
- ❑ E. Windows Explorer settings

4. What Microsoft Windows XP user profile settings contain user profile[nd]aware applications, such as Microsoft Word and Excel?

Quick Answer: **97**
Detailed Answer: **99**

- ❑ A. Accessories
- ❑ B. Application settings
- ❑ C. Control Panel
- ❑ D. Printer settings
- ❑ E. Taskbar settings

Quick Check

5. What Microsoft Windows XP user profile settings contain specific information on network printers (but not local printers)?
   - ❑ A. Accessories
   - ❑ B. Application settings
   - ❑ C. Windows Explorer settings
   - ❑ D. Printer settings
   - ❑ E. Taskbar settings

Quick Answer: **97**
Detailed Answer: **99**

6. What Microsoft Windows XP user profile settings contain the display and mouse settings?
   - ❑ A. Windows Explorer settings
   - ❑ B. Application settings
   - ❑ C. Control Panel
   - ❑ D. Printer settings
   - ❑ E. Taskbar settings

Quick Answer: **97**
Detailed Answer: **99**

7. What Microsoft Windows XP user profile settings contain taskbar settings for each user in his own user profile?
   - ❑ A. Accessories
   - ❑ B. Application settings
   - ❑ C. Control Panel
   - ❑ D. Printer settings
   - ❑ E. Taskbar settings

Quick Answer: **97**
Detailed Answer: **99**

8. What Microsoft Windows XP user profile settings contain all Microsoft Explorer settings and mapped drive information?
   - ❑ A. Accessories
   - ❑ B. Windows Explorer settings
   - ❑ C. Control Panel
   - ❑ D. Printer settings
   - ❑ E. Taskbar settings

Quick Answer: **97**
Detailed Answer: **99**

9. What user profile folders are there in Microsoft Windows XP? (Select all that apply.)
   - ❑ A. Desktop
   - ❑ B. NetHood
   - ❑ C. PrintHood
   - ❑ D. SendTo
   - ❑ E. Start Menu

Quick Answer: **97**
Detailed Answer: **100**

Quick Check

10. What user profile folder in Microsoft Windows XP contains all profile-aware applications information?
    - ❑ A. Application Data
    - ❑ B. Cookies
    - ❑ C. Desktop
    - ❑ D. Favorites
    - ❑ E. NetHood

Quick Answer: **97**
Detailed Answer: **100**

11. What user profile folder in Microsoft Windows XP contains all Microsoft Internet Explorer cookies?
    - ❑ A. Application Data
    - ❑ B. Cookies
    - ❑ C. NetHood
    - ❑ D. PrintHood
    - ❑ E. Start Menu

Quick Answer: **97**
Detailed Answer: **100**

12. What user profile folder in Microsoft Windows XP contains all desktop items, including files and shortcuts?
    - ❑ A. Application Data
    - ❑ B. Cookies
    - ❑ C. Desktop
    - ❑ D. Favorites
    - ❑ E. NetHood

Quick Answer: **97**
Detailed Answer: **100**

13. What user profile folder in Microsoft Windows XP contains all of a user's favorite Microsoft Internet Explorer bookmarks?
    - ❑ A. Application Data
    - ❑ B. Cookies
    - ❑ C. Desktop
    - ❑ D. Favorites
    - ❑ E. NetHood

Quick Answer: **97**
Detailed Answer: **100**

14. What user profile folder in Microsoft Windows XP contains shortcuts of where Network Neighborhood items are located?
    - ❑ A. Application Data
    - ❑ B. Cookies
    - ❑ C. Desktop
    - ❑ D. Favorites
    - ❑ E. NetHood

Quick Answer: **97**
Detailed Answer: **100**

Quick Check

15. What user profile folder in Microsoft Windows XP contains shortcuts of where print folder items are located?

Quick Answer: 97
Detailed Answer: 100

- ❑ A. Application Data
- ❑ B. Cookies
- ❑ C. Desktop
- ❑ D. NetHood
- ❑ E. PrintHood

16. What user profile folder in Microsoft Windows XP contains simple shortcuts to applications?

Quick Answer: 97
Detailed Answer: 100

- ❑ A. Application Data
- ❑ B. Cookies
- ❑ C. Desktop
- ❑ D. Favorites
- ❑ E. SendTo

17. What user profile folder in Microsoft Windows XP contains shortcuts to recently used documents?

Quick Answer: 97
Detailed Answer: 100

- ❑ A. Application Data
- ❑ B. Cookies
- ❑ C. Recent
- ❑ D. SendTo
- ❑ E. Start Menu

18. What user profile folder in Microsoft Windows XP contains shortcuts to executable programs from the user's Start menu?

Quick Answer: 97
Detailed Answer: 100

- ❑ A. Application Data
- ❑ B. Cookies
- ❑ C. Desktop
- ❑ D. Favorites
- ❑ E. Start Menu

19. What are valid types of user profiles in Microsoft Windows XP? (Select all that apply.)

Quick Answer: 97
Detailed Answer: 100

- ❑ A. Remote user profile
- ❑ B. Local user profile
- ❑ C. Mandatory user profile
- ❑ D. Roaming user profile

Quick Check

20. What type of user profile in Microsoft Windows XP is created the very first time a user logs on to the computer?

Quick Answer: **97**
Detailed Answer: **101**

- ❑ A. Hardware user profile
- ❑ B. Local user profile
- ❑ C. Mandatory user profile
- ❑ D. Roaming user profile

21. What type of user profile in Microsoft Windows XP is created by an administrator and cannot be permanently modified by a user?

Quick Answer: **97**
Detailed Answer: **101**

- ❑ A. Forced user profile
- ❑ B. Local user profile
- ❑ C. Mandatory user profile
- ❑ D. Roaming user profile

22. What type of user profile in Microsoft Windows XP allows a user to log on to different computers and receive the same user profile settings?

Quick Answer: **97**
Detailed Answer: **101**

- ❑ A. Identical user profile
- ❑ B. Local user profile
- ❑ C. Mandatory user profile
- ❑ D. Roaming user profile

23. What types of deployment options are there in Microsoft Windows XP? (Select all that apply.)

Quick Answer: **97**
Detailed Answer: **101**

- ❑ A. Assign
- ❑ B. Direct
- ❑ C. Distribute
- ❑ D. Publish

24. What is true about publishing software packages in Microsoft Windows XP? (Select all that apply.)

Quick Answer: **97**
Detailed Answer: **101**

- ❑ A. Published applications are advertised.
- ❑ B. Published applications are not advertised.
- ❑ C. Published applications can be installed through Add/Remove Programs.
- ❑ D. Published applications can be installed through invocation.

Quick Check

25. When are software packages assigned to a computer installed in Microsoft Windows XP?
    - ❑ A. The next time the computer is started, and after a user logs on
    - ❑ B. The next time the computer is started, but before a user can log on
    - ❑ C. The next time Active Directory replicates throughout the network
    - ❑ D. Immediately

Quick Answer: **97**
Detailed Answer: **101**

26. What types of files are non–Microsoft Installer (.MSI) software packages published as in Microsoft Windows XP?
    - ❑ A. .MSI
    - ❑ B. .ZAP
    - ❑ C. .EPS
    - ❑ D. .PPT

Quick Answer: **97**
Detailed Answer: **102**

27. What types of files are Microsoft Installer software packages published as in Microsoft Windows XP?
    - ❑ A. .ZAP
    - ❑ B. .MSI
    - ❑ C. .EPS
    - ❑ D. .XLS

Quick Answer: **97**
Detailed Answer: **102**

28. What types of files are patches to Microsoft Installer software packages published as in Microsoft Windows XP?
    - ❑ A. .ZAP
    - ❑ B. .MSI
    - ❑ C. .MSP
    - ❑ D. .MST

Quick Answer: **97**
Detailed Answer: **102**

29. What types of files are modifications to Microsoft Installer software packages assigned as in Microsoft Windows XP?
    - ❑ A. .ZAP
    - ❑ B. .MSI
    - ❑ C. .MSP
    - ❑ D. .MST

Quick Answer: **97**
Detailed Answer: **102**

30. How can a required CD key be entered with an installer package in Microsoft Windows XP?
    - ❑ A. .ZAP
    - ❑ B. .MSI
    - ❑ C. .MSP
    - ❑ D. msiexec

Quick Answer: **97**
Detailed Answer: **102**

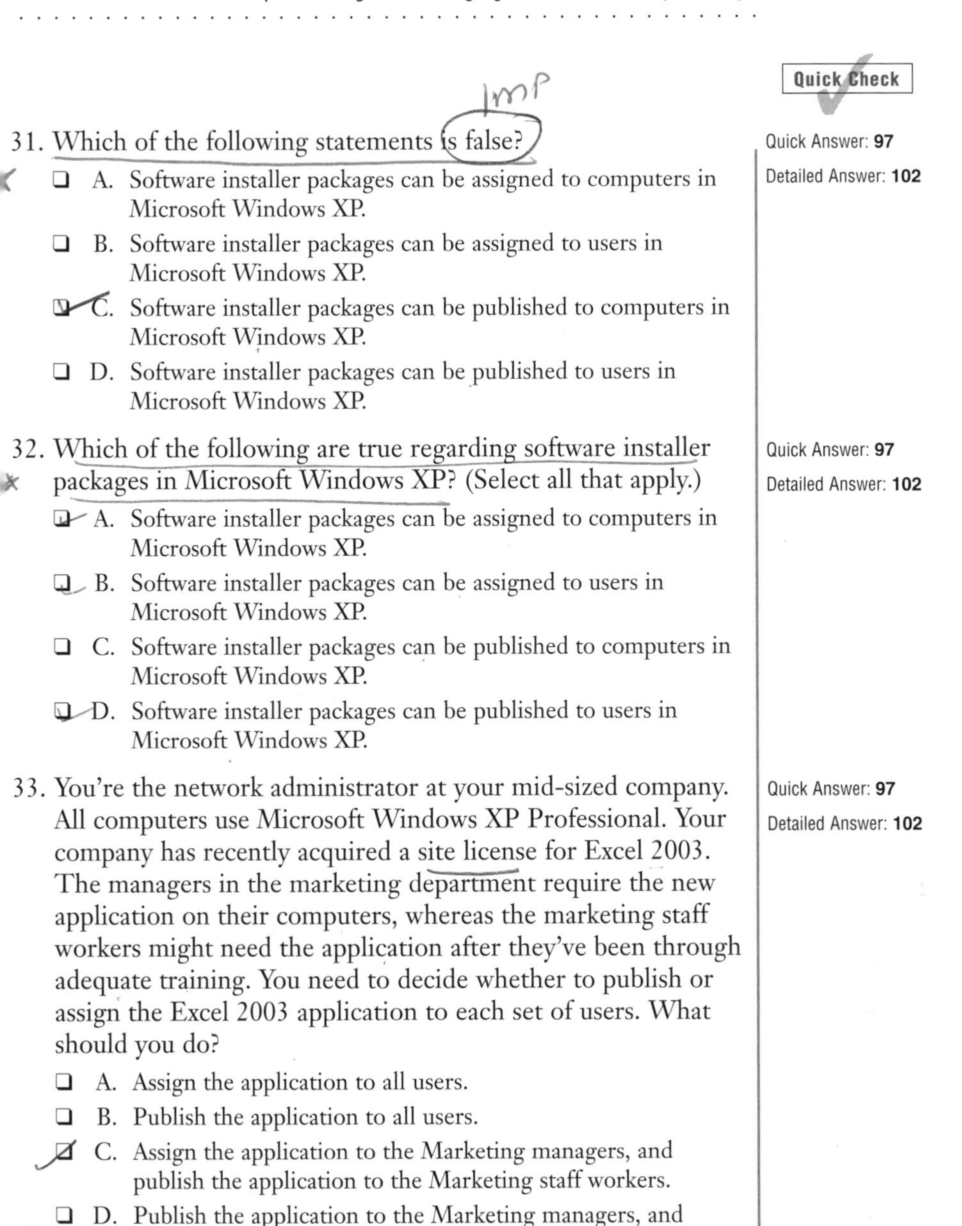

Quick Check

31. Which of the following statements is false?

    ❑ A. Software installer packages can be assigned to computers in Microsoft Windows XP.

    ❑ B. Software installer packages can be assigned to users in Microsoft Windows XP.

    ❑ C. Software installer packages can be published to computers in Microsoft Windows XP.

    ❑ D. Software installer packages can be published to users in Microsoft Windows XP.

Quick Answer: **97**
Detailed Answer: **102**

32. Which of the following are true regarding software installer packages in Microsoft Windows XP? (Select all that apply.)

    ❑ A. Software installer packages can be assigned to computers in Microsoft Windows XP.

    ❑ B. Software installer packages can be assigned to users in Microsoft Windows XP.

    ❑ C. Software installer packages can be published to computers in Microsoft Windows XP.

    ❑ D. Software installer packages can be published to users in Microsoft Windows XP.

Quick Answer: **97**
Detailed Answer: **102**

33. You're the network administrator at your mid-sized company. All computers use Microsoft Windows XP Professional. Your company has recently acquired a site license for Excel 2003. The managers in the marketing department require the new application on their computers, whereas the marketing staff workers might need the application after they've been through adequate training. You need to decide whether to publish or assign the Excel 2003 application to each set of users. What should you do?

    ❑ A. Assign the application to all users.

    ❑ B. Publish the application to all users.

    ❑ C. Assign the application to the Marketing managers, and publish the application to the Marketing staff workers.

    ❑ D. Publish the application to the Marketing managers, and assign the application to the Marketing staff workers.

Quick Answer: **97**
Detailed Answer: **102**

Quick Check

34. Which of the following are not true of Microsoft Installer software packages that are published in Microsoft Windows XP? (Select all that apply.)

- ❑ A. Published software applications self-repair (or reinstall) if they are deleted by the user.
- ❑ B. Published software applications do not self-repair (or reinstall) if they are deleted by the user.
- ❑ C. Published software applications can be published only to users and not to computers.
- ❑ D. Published software applications can be published only to computers and not to users.

Quick Answer: **97**
Detailed Answer: **102**

35. Which of the following words best describes what occurs when Microsoft Installer software packages are auto-installed after a user double-clicks on an unknown file type in Microsoft Windows XP?

- ❑ A. Invocation
- ❑ B. Replication
- ❑ C. Self-production
- ❑ D. Auto-production

Quick Answer: **97**
Detailed Answer: **103**

36. Which of the following words describe ways that you can configure deployment of software installation packages in Microsoft Windows XP? (Select all that apply.)

- ❑ A. Replicate
- ❑ B. Force
- ❑ C. Assign
- ❑ D. Publish

Quick Answer: **97**
Detailed Answer: **103**

37. How do you add more input locales to a computer in Microsoft Windows XP?

- ❑ A. Start, Control Panel, Regional Options, Input Locale tab
- ❑ B. Start, Settings, Control Panel, Regional Options, Add, Input Locale tab
- ❑ C. Start, Settings, Control Panel, Regional Options, Input Locale tab
- ❑ D. Start, Settings, Control Panel, Input Locale tab

Quick Answer: **97**
Detailed Answer: **103**

38. How do you see what languages are available to a computer in Microsoft Windows XP?

- ❑ A. Start, Control Panel, Regional Options, General tab
- ❑ B. Start, Settings, Control Panel, Regional Options, Input Locale tab
- ❑ C. Start, Settings, Control Panel, Regional Options, General tab
- ❑ D. Start, Settings, Control Panel, General tab

Quick Answer: **97**
Detailed Answer: **103**

39. How do you see what the exact default language is on a computer in Microsoft Windows XP?

Quick Answer: 97
Detailed Answer: 103

- ❑ A. Start, Control Panel, Regional Options, General tab
- ❑ B. Start, Settings, Control Panel, Regional Options, General tab
- ❑ C. Start, Settings, Control Panel, Regional Options, Default Languages tab
- ❑ D. Start, Settings, Control Panel, General tab, Default Languages button

40. Where are changes made by an administrator to a user's roaming profile copied to in Microsoft Windows XP?

Quick Answer: 97
Detailed Answer: 103

- ❑ A. DRIVERS subdirectory
- ❑ B. Network server
- ❑ C. Workstation
- ❑ D. WINXP subdirectory

41. Where are changes made by a locally logged-on Microsoft Windows XP computer user copied to?

Quick Answer: 97
Detailed Answer: 103

- ❑ A. Domain controller
- ❑ B. Local hard drive
- ❑ C. File and print server
- ❑ D. Proxy server

42. Where are changes made to a local user profile on a Microsoft Windows XP PC copied to?

Quick Answer: 97
Detailed Answer: 103

- ❑ A. DNS server
- ❑ B. File and print server
- ❑ C. Local hard drive
- ❑ D. DHCP server

43. Where does a shortcut appear when a user has a software installation package assigned on a Microsoft Windows XP computer?

Quick Answer: 97
Detailed Answer: 103

- ❑ A. On the user's Start, Settings, Programs menu
- ❑ B. On the user's Start, Search menu
- ❑ C. On the user's Start, Programs menu
- ❑ D. On the user's Start, Settings, Add/Remove Programs menu

44. What are the four phases of the software life cycle, in order, according to Microsoft?

Quick Answer: 97
Detailed Answer: 103

- ❑ A. Preparation, deployment, maintenance, and removal
- ❑ B. Preparation, maintenance, deployment, and removal
- ❑ C. Preparation, removal, deployment, and maintenance
- ❑ D. Preparation, deployment, removal, and maintenance

Quick Check

45. Which item is not one of the four phases of the software life cycle, according to Microsoft?
    - ❑ A. Preparation
    - ❑ B. Deployment
    - ❑ C. Testing
    - ❑ D. Maintenance
    - ❑ E. Removal

Quick Answer: **97**
Detailed Answer: **103**

46. What does *GPO* stand for when applying settings in Microsoft Windows XP?
    - ❑ A. Group Policy Object
    - ❑ B. Group Program Object
    - ❑ C. General Protection Object
    - ❑ D. General Procedure Object

Quick Answer: **97**
Detailed Answer: **103**

47. What can Active Directory do with group policies for a Microsoft Windows XP client, when updating deployed software?
    - ❑ A. Either uninstall the old application or upgrade on top of it.
    - ❑ B. Only uninstall the old application.
    - ❑ C. Only upgrade on top of it.
    - ❑ D. Neither uninstall the old application nor upgrade on top of it.

Quick Answer: **97**
Detailed Answer: **104**

48. What type of upgrade cannot be performed in Active Directory with group policies for a Microsoft Windows XP client, when publishing upgrades to deployed software?
    - ❑ A. Mandatory upgrades for computers
    - ❑ B. Optional upgrades for computers
    - ❑ C. Mandatory upgrades for users
    - ❑ D. Optional upgrades for users

Quick Answer: **97**
Detailed Answer: **104**

49. What types of upgrades can Active Directory do with group policies for a Microsoft Windows XP client, when publishing upgrades to deployed software? (Select all that apply.)
    - ❑ A. Mandatory upgrades for computers
    - ❑ B. Optional upgrades for computers
    - ❑ C. Mandatory upgrades for users
    - ❑ D. Optional upgrades for users

Quick Answer: **97**
Detailed Answer: **104**

Quick Check

50. What feature of Microsoft Windows XP regularly goes online to check the Microsoft site called Windows Update?
   - ❑ A. Automatic Windows
   - ❑ B. Automatic Updates
   - ❑ C. Active Directory Updates
   - ❑ D. Active Directory Replication

Quick Answer: **97**
Detailed Answer: **104**

51. How do you adjust the Automatic Updates feature settings of Microsoft Windows XP, which regularly goes online to check the Microsoft site called Windows Update?
   - ❑ A. Right-click My Computer, choose Automatic Updates
   - ❑ B. Right-click My Computer, choose Properties, Automatic Updates tab
   - ❑ C. Right-click My Computer, choose Properties, Windows Updates tab
   - ❑ D. Double-click My Computer, choose Properties, Automatic Updates tab

Quick Answer: **97**
Detailed Answer: **104**

52. What are the available settings on the Automatic Updates tab of System Properties on a Microsoft Windows XP computer? (Select all that apply.)
   - ❑ A. Download the Updates Automatically and Notify Me When They Are Ready to Be Installed.
   - ❑ B. Notify Me Before Downloading Any Updates and Notify Me Again Before Installing Them on My Computer.
   - ❑ C. Turn Off Automatic Updating. I Want to Update My Computer Manually.
   - ❑ D. Turn On Automatic Updating. I Want to Update My Computer Automatically.

Quick Answer: **97**
Detailed Answer: **104**

53. How many monitors can Microsoft Windows XP Professional support?
   - ❑ A. 1
   - ❑ B. 10
   - ❑ C. 2
   - ❑ D. 8

Quick Answer: **97**
Detailed Answer: **104**

54. What is the name of the feature in Microsoft Windows XP that allows portable computer users to spread their desktop across both their laptop computer as well as one additional external monitor?
   - ❑ A. Double View
   - ❑ B. Dual View
   - ❑ C. Double Play
   - ❑ D. Double See

Quick Answer: **97**
Detailed Answer: **104**

Quick Check

55. Where are monitor settings configured in Microsoft Windows XP?

Quick Answer: 97
Detailed Answer: 104

- ❑ A. Start, Settings, Control Panel, Display Panel
- ❑ B. Start, Settings, Display
- ❑ C. Start, Settings, Display Panel
- ❑ D. Start, Settings, Control Panel, Display

56. What is the name of the default theme that Microsoft Windows XP uses when originally installed?

Quick Answer: 97
Detailed Answer: 105

- ❑ A. Windows Classic
- ❑ B. Luna
- ❑ C. Windows Classic (large)
- ❑ D. Windows Regular

57. What does the Windows taskbar now allow when you have several similar open window items hidden on the taskbar?

Quick Answer: 97
Detailed Answer: 105

- ❑ A. Copying
- ❑ B. Replicating
- ❑ C. Pasting
- ❑ D. Grouping

58. What is the new default functionality of the Start menu in Microsoft Windows XP?

Quick Answer: 97
Detailed Answer: 105

- ❑ A. Allow speed of program access.
- ❑ B. Allow speed of replication.
- ❑ C. Keep icons visible to the end user.
- ❑ D. Keep icons hidden from the end user.

59. How do you revert to the old-style functionality of the Start menu in Microsoft Windows XP?

Quick Answer: 97
Detailed Answer: 105

- ❑ A. Double-click the taskbar, Properties, Start Menu tab, Classic Start Menu
- ❑ B. Start, Classic Start Menu
- ❑ C. Start, Menu tab, Classic Start Menu
- ❑ D. Right-click the taskbar, Properties, Start Menu tab, Classic Start Menu

60. What is the new name of the System Tray in Microsoft Windows XP?

Quick Answer: 97
Detailed Answer: 105

- ❑ A. System Area
- ❑ B. Classic Start Menu
- ❑ C. Menu tab
- ❑ D. Notification Area

Quick Check

61. How do you launch the Program Compatibility Wizard in Microsoft Windows XP?

- ❑ A. Start, Programs, Accessories, Program Compatibility Wizard
- ❑ B. Start, Programs, Program Compatibility Wizard
- ❑ C. Start, Accessories, Program Compatibility Wizard
- ❑ D. Start, Programs, Accessibility, Program Compatibility Wizard

Quick Answer: **97**
Detailed Answer: **105**

62. What are the choices listed by the Program Compatibility Wizard when selecting a compatibility mode for a program in Microsoft Windows XP? (Select all that apply.)

- ❑ A. Microsoft Windows 3.11
- ❑ B. Microsoft Windows 95
- ❑ C. Microsoft Windows NT 4.0 (Service Pack 5)
- ❑ D. Microsoft Windows 98/Windows Me
- ❑ E. Microsoft Windows 2000

Quick Answer: **97**
Detailed Answer: **105**

63. Where does the Fax applet appear in Microsoft Windows XP?

- ❑ A. In Control Panel when not installed
- ❑ B. In Control Panel when installed
- ❑ C. In Settings when installed
- ❑ D. On the desktop when installed

Quick Answer: **97**
Detailed Answer: **105**

64. What appears in Control Panel when you install a fax/modem hardware device in Microsoft Windows XP?

- ❑ A. Modem applet
- ❑ B. In User Profiles
- ❑ C. In Hardware Profiles
- ❑ D. Fax applet

Quick Answer: **97**
Detailed Answer: **105**

65. What items can be configured under the Fax applet in Control Panel when you have a fax/modem hardware device in Microsoft Windows XP? (Select all that apply.)

- ❑ A. Where your received faxes will be stored
- ❑ B. The number of retries when faxing
- ❑ C. User security permissions
- ❑ D. Where your sent faxes will be stored
- ❑ E. How many copies of faxes your boss will receive

Quick Answer: **97**
Detailed Answer: **106**

66. What is true about the fax printer in your printer folder in Microsoft Windows XP?

- ❑ A. It cannot be deleted.
- ❑ B. It cannot be shared.
- ❑ C. It cannot be copied.
- ❑ D. It cannot be renamed.

Quick Answer: **97**
Detailed Answer: **106**

Quick Check

67. Which of these settings is not available on the Automatic Updates tab of System Properties on a Microsoft Windows XP computer?

   - ❑ A. Download the Updates Automatically and Notify Me When They Are Ready to Be Installed.
   - ❑ B. Notify Me Before Downloading Any Updates and Notify Me Again Before Installing Them on My Computer.
   - ❑ C. Turn Off Automatic Updating. I Want to Update My Computer Manually.
   - ❑ D. Turn On Automatic Updating. I Want to Update My Computer Automatically.

Quick Answer: **97**
Detailed Answer: **106**

68. How many additional external monitors can a laptop using Microsoft Windows XP Professional support?

   - ❑ A. 10
   - ❑ B. 1
   - ❑ C. 2
   - ❑ D. 8

Quick Answer: **97**
Detailed Answer: **106**

69. What is the new name of the wizard in Microsoft Windows XP that provides a compatibility mechanism for older programs?

   - ❑ A. Program Compatibility Wizard
   - ❑ B. Program Companion Wizard
   - ❑ C. Program Composer Wizard
   - ❑ D. Program Completeness Wizard

Quick Answer: **97**
Detailed Answer: **106**

70. What choices are not listed by the Program Compatibility Wizard when selecting a compatibility mode for a program in Microsoft Windows XP? (Select all that apply.)

   - ❑ A. Microsoft Windows 3.11
   - ❑ B. Microsoft Windows 95
   - ❑ C. Microsoft Windows NT 4.0 (Service Pack 5)
   - ❑ D. Microsoft Windows 2000
   - ❑ E. Microsoft Windows .NET Server 2003

Quick Answer: **97**
Detailed Answer: **106**

71. What does the Program Compatibility Wizard do in Microsoft Windows XP?

    - ❑ A. It allows Microsoft Windows XP to trick a program into running a PC program that would normally be incompatible.
    - ❑ B. It allows Microsoft Windows XP to trick a program into running a mainframe program that would normally be incompatible.
    - ❑ C. It allows Microsoft Windows XP to trick a program into running a Novell program that would normally be incompatible.
    - ❑ D. It allows Microsoft Windows XP to trick a program into running a Unix program that would normally be incompatible.

Quick Answer: **97**
Detailed Answer: **106**

72. You're using a brand-new computer running Microsoft Windows XP. You don't have any third-party image-editing application software installed. You would like to view a faxed document. What Microsoft Windows XP feature is included on your computer to accomplish this task?

    - ❑ A. Modem/Fax applet in Control Panel
    - ❑ B. Notepad
    - ❑ C. WordPad
    - ❑ D. Windows Picture and Fax Viewer

Quick Answer: **97**
Detailed Answer: **106**

73. Tommy is trying to configure a fax/modem that he just installed on a Microsoft Windows XP computer. He cannot see the Advanced Options tab described in the hardware documentation.

    What must Tommy do to see the Advanced Options tab?

    - ❑ A. Log off, and then log back on as himself.
    - ❑ B. Log off, and then log back on as Print Server Operator.
    - ❑ C. Log off, and then log back on as Server Operator.
    - ❑ D. Log off, and then log back on as Administrator.
    - ❑ E. Log off, and then log back on as Guest.

Quick Answer: **97**
Detailed Answer: **107**

74. What services in Microsoft Windows XP include StickyKeys, FilterKeys, SoundSentry, ShowSounds, MouseKeys, Magnifier, and Narrator?

    - ❑ A. Accessory services
    - ❑ B. Mouse Option services
    - ❑ C. Physically Challenged services
    - ❑ D. Accessibility services

Quick Answer: **97**
Detailed Answer: **107**

Quick Check

75. What items are included in Microsoft Windows XP Accessibility services? (Select all that apply.)

Quick Answer: 97
Detailed Answer: 107

- ❑ A. StickyKeys
- ❑ B. FilterKeys
- ❑ C. SoundSentry
- ❑ D. ShowSounds
- ❑ E. MouseKeys

76. What item under Microsoft Windows XP Accessibility services enables you to press multiple keystroke combinations, one key at a time?

Quick Answer: 97
Detailed Answer: 107

- ❑ A. StickyKeys
- ❑ B. FilterKeys
- ❑ C. SoundSentry
- ❑ D. ShowSounds
- ❑ E. MouseKeys

77. What item under Microsoft Windows XP Accessibility services informs the keyboard to ignore repeated keystrokes or mistaken brief keystrokes?

Quick Answer: 97
Detailed Answer: 107

- ❑ A. StickyKeys
- ❑ B. FilterKeys
- ❑ C. SoundSentry
- ❑ D. Magnifier
- ❑ E. Narrator

78. What item under Microsoft Windows XP Accessibility services flashes visual warnings for the hearing impaired whenever your computer makes a sound?

Quick Answer: 97
Detailed Answer: 107

- ❑ A. StickyKeys
- ❑ B. FilterKeys
- ❑ C. SoundSentry
- ❑ D. ShowSounds
- ❑ E. MouseKeys

79. What item under Microsoft Windows XP Accessibility services has programs show captions whenever the program makes a sound or speaks?

Quick Answer: 97
Detailed Answer: 107

- ❑ A. StickyKeys
- ❑ B. FilterKeys
- ❑ C. SoundSentry
- ❑ D. ShowSounds
- ❑ E. Narrator

80. What item under Microsoft Windows XP Accessibility services enables you tocontrol the mouse with the numeric keypad included on most keyboards?

Quick Answer: **97**
Detailed Answer: **107**

- ❑ A. StickyKeys
- ❑ B. FilterKeys
- ❑ C. SoundSentry
- ❑ D. ShowSounds
- ❑ E. MouseKeys

81. What item under Microsoft Windows XP Accessibility services increases the size of a portion of the screen for the visually impaired?

Quick Answer: **97**
Detailed Answer: **107**

- ❑ A. StickyKeys
- ❑ B. FilterKeys
- ❑ C. SoundSentry
- ❑ D. Magnifier
- ❑ E. Narrator

82. What item under Microsoft Windows XP Accessibility services reads aloud any menu options and title bar expressions using speech synthesis?

Quick Answer: **98**
Detailed Answer: **107**

- ❑ A. StickyKeys
- ❑ B. FilterKeys
- ❑ C. SoundSentry
- ❑ D. ShowSounds
- ❑ E. Narrator

83. What items are included in Microsoft Windows XP Accessibility services? (Select all that apply.)

Quick Answer: **98**
Detailed Answer: **108**

- ❑ A. Keyboard
- ❑ B. FilterKeys
- ❑ C. SoundSentry
- ❑ D. ShowSounds
- ❑ E. MouseKeys

84. What feature in Microsoft Windows XP enables a user to request remote help from an expert?

Quick Answer: **98**
Detailed Answer: **108**

- ❑ A. StickyKeys
- ❑ B. FilterKeys
- ❑ C. SoundSentry
- ❑ D. Remote Assistance

Quick Check

85. What feature in Microsoft Windows XP enables a user to request remote help from an expert, who can then see the user's desktop?

- ❑ A. MouseKeys
- ❑ B. FilterKeys
- ❑ C. Remote Assistance
- ❑ D. SoundSentry

Quick Answer: **98**
Detailed Answer: **108**

86. What feature in Microsoft Windows XP enables a user to request remote help from an expert, who can then control the user's desktop?

- ❑ A. Remote Assistance
- ❑ B. StickyKeys
- ❑ C. SoundForge
- ❑ D. MouseKeys

Quick Answer: **98**
Detailed Answer: **108**

87. What feature in Microsoft Windows XP enables a user to request remote help from an expert, who can then chat with the user using text?

- ❑ A. MouseKeys
- ❑ B. Remote Assistance
- ❑ C. FilterKeys
- ❑ D. StickyKeys

Quick Answer: **98**
Detailed Answer: **108**

88. What feature in Microsoft Windows XP allows a user to request remote help from an expert, who can then actually chat with the user using voice?

- ❑ A. Remote Assistance
- ❑ B. SoundSentry
- ❑ C. SoundBlaster
- ❑ D. ShowSounds

Quick Answer: **98**
Detailed Answer: **108**

89. What feature in Microsoft Windows XP enables a user to request remote help from an expert, who can then actually chat with the user using voice?

- ❑ A. ShowSounds
- ❑ B. SoundSentry
- ❑ C. Remote Assistance
- ❑ D. SoundBlaster

Quick Answer: **98**
Detailed Answer: **108**

Quick Check

90. What feature in Microsoft Windows XP enables a user to request remote help from an expert, who can then send files from the user's system?
    - ❑ A. NTFS
    - ❑ B. Remote Assistance
    - ❑ C. DSL
    - ❑ D. Fax applet

Quick Answer: 98
Detailed Answer: 108

91. What feature in Microsoft Windows XP enables a user to request remote help from an expert, who can then receive files from the user's system?
    - ❑ A. Cable
    - ❑ B. Fax applet
    - ❑ C. DSL
    - ❑ D. Remote Assistance

Quick Answer: 98
Detailed Answer: 108

92. What are the three ways to request assistance from an expert using Remote Assistance in Microsoft Windows XP? (Select all that apply.)
    - ❑ A. Using Windows Messenger
    - ❑ B. Fax applet
    - ❑ C. Using a MAPI-enabled email client
    - ❑ D. Using a file

Quick Answer: 98
Detailed Answer: 109

93. What is the status of the Remote Assistance feature in Microsoft Windows XP by default?
    - ❑ A. Disabled by default
    - ❑ B. Enabled by Add/Remove Programs
    - ❑ C. Enabled by Add/Remove Hardware
    - ❑ D. Enabled by default

Quick Answer: 98
Detailed Answer: 109

94. Remote Assistance is the feature in Microsoft Windows XP that enables a user to request remote help from an expert or other knowledgeable person. It is enabled by default.

    What items appear on the expert's (or helper's) Remote Assistance Console in Microsoft Windows XP? (Select all that apply.)
    - ❑ A. Take Control
    - ❑ B. Send a File
    - ❑ C. Start Talking
    - ❑ D. Settings
    - ❑ E. Remove Control

Quick Answer: 98
Detailed Answer: 109

Quick Check

95. Remote Assistance is the feature in Microsoft Windows XP that enables a user to request remote help from an expert or other knowledgeable person. It is enabled by default.

    What item appears on the expert's (or helper's) Remote Assistance Console in Microsoft Windows XP and actually requests taking control of a user's system?

    - ☑ A. Take Control
    - ❑ B. Send a File
    - ❑ C. Start Talking
    - ❑ D. Settings
    - ❑ E. Help

Quick Answer: **98**
Detailed Answer: **109**

96. Remote Assistance is the feature in Microsoft Windows XP that enables a user to request remote help from an expert or other knowledgeable person. It is enabled by default.

    What item appears on the expert's (or helper's) Remote Assistance Console in Microsoft Windows XP and sends the user a file that is needed; for example, a hardware driver file?

    - ❑ A. Take Control
    - ☑ B. Send a File
    - ❑ C. Start Talking
    - ❑ D. Disconnect
    - ❑ E. Help

Quick Answer: **98**
Detailed Answer: **109**

97. Remote Assistance is the feature in Microsoft Windows XP that enables a user to request remote help from an expert or other knowledgeable person. It is enabled by default.

    What item appears on the expert's (or helper's) Remote Assistance Console in Microsoft Windows XP and starts a VOIP session?

    - ❑ A. Take Control
    - ❑ B. Send a File
    - ☑ C. Start Talking
    - ❑ D. Settings
    - ❑ E. Disconnect

Quick Answer: **98**
Detailed Answer: **109**

Quick Check

98. Remote Assistance is the feature in Microsoft Windows XP that enables a user to request remote help from an expert or other knowledgeable person. It is enabled by default.

    What item appears on the expert's (or helper's) Remote Assistance Console in Microsoft Windows XP and enables the expert to adjust the console size and speaker settings?

    - ❑ A. Take Control
    - ❑ B. Send a File
    - ❑ C. Start Talking
    - ❑ D. Settings
    - ❑ E. Disconnect

Quick Answer: **98**
Detailed Answer: **109**

99. Remote Assistance is the feature in Microsoft Windows XP that enables a user to request remote help from an expert or other knowledgeable person. It is enabled by default.

    What item appears on the expert's (or helper's) Remote Assistance Console in Microsoft Windows XP and ends the expert's Remote Assistance session?

    - ❑ A. Take Control
    - ❑ B. Send a File
    - ❑ C. Start Talking
    - ❑ D. Settings
    - ❑ E. Disconnect

Quick Answer: **98**
Detailed Answer: **109**

100. Remote Assistance is the feature in Microsoft Windows XP that enables a user to request remote help from an expert or other knowledgeable person. It is enabled by default.

    What item appears on the expert's (or helper's) Remote Assistance Console in Microsoft Windows XP and provides help information for the expert's Remote Assistance session?

    - ❑ A. Take Control
    - ❑ B. Help
    - ❑ C. Start Talking
    - ❑ D. Settings
    - ❑ E. Disconnect

Quick Answer: **98**
Detailed Answer: **109**

101. What are the names of the built-in accounts used with Remote Assistance in Microsoft Windows XP? (Select all that apply.)

    - ❑ A. ControlAssistant
    - ❑ B. XPRAssistant
    - ❑ C. HelpAssistant
    - ❑ D. Support_*hex*

Quick Answer: **98**
Detailed Answer: **110**

Quick Check

102. What account used with Remote Assistance in Microsoft Windows XP is enabled only when you have an open request to another user for Remote Assistance?

- ❑ A. RCAssistant
- ❑ B. XPAssistant
- ❑ C. HelpAssistant
- ❑ D. Support_*hex*

Quick Answer: **98**
Detailed Answer: **110**

103. What account used with Remote Assistance in Microsoft Windows XP is enabled only when you request Remote Assistance directly from Microsoft?

- ❑ A. RemoteAssistant
- ❑ B. XPAssist
- ❑ C. HelpAssistant
- ❑ D. Support_*hex*

Quick Answer: **98**
Detailed Answer: **110**

104. You are the desktop administrator for your company. You upgrade all the client computers from Microsoft Windows NT Workstation 4.0 to Windows XP Professional. After upgrading, a user named Veronica complains that her computer now uses display settings of 640×480 resolution with only 16 colors. Veronica is unable to change these settings, and she also wants to be able to select Windows XP themes.

You need to allow Veronica to use these Windows XP interface options. What should you do?

- ❑ A. On the Color Management tab of the Advanced Display settings, add the color profile for Veronica's monitor.
- ❑ B. Update the driver for the video adapter to support increased screen resolution and color depth.
- ❑ C. In the Advanced Properties for the video adapter, clear the Enable Write Combining check box.
- ❑ D. Roll back the current video adapter driver to the previous Windows NT Workstation 4.0 video adapter driver.

Quick Answer: **98**
Detailed Answer: **110**

105. You're a help desk technician for your organization. When you first arrive at the organization, all client computers run Microsoft NT Workstation 4.0. You upgrade those computers. The computers now run either Microsoft Windows XP Professional or Windows 2000 Professional. Users now complain of display problems. When they run an application named Focus, their displays become garbled or their computers do not display the Focus application window correctly. Users do not experience this problem when running any other applications.

Quick Answer: **98**
Detailed Answer: **110**

How should you reconfigure each user's computer?

- ❑ A. In the Monitor properties, adjust the screen refresh rate to a lower value.
- ❑ B. In the Display settings, adjust the screen resolution to a lower value.
- ❑ C. In the Compatibility settings for the Focus application, select the Run in 256 Colors check box.
- ❑ D. In the Advanced Display settings, configure the display DPI settings to 120 dots per inch.

106. You're a desktop administrator for the Museum of Fine Arts in Boston. You're configuring a Windows XP Professional desktop computer for an employee named Melody, who will be using the Magnifier utility. You need to configure her computer so that Melody can more easily distinguish between interface fonts and colors. You also need to configure Melody's screen to display fonts and colors designed to be read easily.

Quick Answer: **98**
Detailed Answer: **110**

What should you do?

- ❑ A. Enable the Invert Colors setting for the Magnifier utility's configuration screen.
- ❑ B. Enable the Use High Contrast Display setting in Accessibility options.
- ❑ C. In the Display Properties, change the Appearance settings to use the Windows Classic theme instead of the Windows XP theme.
- ❑ D. Change the system display settings to enable large fonts in the display properties.

Quick Check

107. You're a desktop administrator for your company. All employees use Microsoft Windows XP Professional computers. All employees have been made members of the local Power Users group on their computers. There are three standard daily work shifts, and employees share their computers with other employees who work the different shifts. Each client computer has a predefined set of desktop icons and shortcuts, in addition to the standard system icons.

Quick Answer: **98**
Detailed Answer: **110**

All users must be able to access these icons and shortcuts. Users can place their own icons and shortcuts on the desktop, but these icons and shortcuts should not be visible to other users of their computer. You want to prevent users from adding or removing any icons and shortcuts to their default desktop. However, you also want to allow users to customize their own personal desktops. What should you do?

- ❑ A. For the Power Users group, remove Allow-Modify permission from the Documents and Settings\All Users folder.
- ❑ B. For each individual user, remove Allow-Full Control and Allow-Modify permissions from the Document and Settings\%username% folder.
- ❑ C. For the Power Users group, assign the Deny-Full Control permission on the Documents and Settings folder.
- ❑ D. For the Power Users group, assign the Deny-Full Control permission on the Documents and Settings/Default User folder.

108. You're the desktop administrator for Acme World Imports. The company has a main office in Seattle and a branch office in Berlin, Germany. An employee named Ursula travels to and from the branch office. During Ursula's last trip, the desktop administrator at the Berlin office configured Ursula's Microsoft Windows XP Professional laptop to display the German date and time settings. When Ursula returns to the main office in Seattle, all of her email messages display the German date and time settings.

Quick Answer: **98**
Detailed Answer: **110**

You need to change Ursula's date and time settings back to the English format. What should you do?

- ❑ A. In the Date and Time options, select the English language.
- ❑ B. In the Regional and Language options, apply the English user interface.
- ❑ C. In the Regional and Language options, apply the English input language keyboard.
- ❑ D. In the Regional and Language options, apply the English (United States) Standards and Formats.

109. You're a help desk technician for your company. You create a Windows installer package and a transform file with custom changes for a third-party application. You install the Windows installer package on your Microsoft Windows XP Professional computer. However, when the installation is complete, you find none of the custom changes were applied.

You need to install the Windows installer package as well as the custom changes on your computer only. What should you do?

- ❑ A. Create a .zap file for the package, and redeploy the package.
- ❑ B. Start the Windows Installer service, and install the package.
- ❑ C. Install the Windows installer package by using an .mst file.
- ❑ D. From the command prompt on your computer, use the Msiexec.exe utility to repair the package.

Quick Answer: **98**
Detailed Answer: **110**

110. You're the desktop administrator for RetroFun Toys. The management of RetroFun Toys requires a standard user profile be created for all domain user accounts. This standard profile must be protected so that domain users cannot make any permanent changes to it.

You create a company standard user profile. You require all domain user accounts to use this profile. A little while later, however, users claim that changes they make to their desktop actually are overwriting the standard profile settings you created.

What should you do to be sure that permanent changes cannot be made to the standard user profile?

- ❑ A. Open the local default user profile. Rename ntuser.dat to ntuser.man.
- ❑ B. Enable the local group policy to exclude directories in roaming profile for all users in the RetroFun Toys domain.
- ❑ C. Open Control Panel, System Properties, and copy the standard user profile to the profile server. Grant the Everyone group Allow-Full Control permission on the copied profile. Change the profile type from Local to Roaming.
- ❑ D. Open Control Panel, System Properties, and copy the standard user profile folder to the profile server. Grant the Everyone group Allow-Full Control permission on the newly copied profile. Name the directory that contains the standard user profile to standard.man.

Quick Answer: **98**
Detailed Answer: **110**

Quick Check

111. You're a desktop administrator for TransWorld Imports. You've installed Microsoft Windows XP Professional on a laptop for a user named Bryan. Bryan travels between the main office in Chicago and the branch office in Tokyo. Bryan needs to create documents in both the English and Japanese languages.

You need to provide an easy method for Bryan to switch between languages. You also need to enable Bryan to create documents in the selected language immediately. How should you configure the regional and language options on Bryan's laptop?

- ❑ A. In the Advanced options, select Japanese as the language for non-Unicode programs. In the Language options, add the Japanese keyboard layout.
- ❑ B. In the Languages options, configure the Language bar to show additional Language bar icons.
- ❑ C. In the Languages options, select the Install Files for Complex Script and Right-to-Left Languages (Including Thai) check box.
- ❑ D. In the Languages options, select the Install Files for East Asian Languages check box. Add Japanese as an input language.

Quick Answer: **98**
Detailed Answer: **110**

112. You're a desktop administrator for America West Airlines. You just finished upgrading a client computer to Microsoft Windows XP Professional. Before the upgrade, the computer had the Multilanguage edition of Windows 2000 Professional installed. Users now complain, however, that the Regional and Language options no longer provides the option to switch between the English and Japanese user interfaces. Now only the English user interface can be used.

You need to configure the computer to use both the Japanese and English user interfaces. What should you do?

- ❑ A. Use the Regional and Language options to install files for East Asian languages, and to switch between the English to the Japanese user interfaces.
- ❑ B. Use the Regional and Language options to add the Japanese Input Language.
- ❑ C. Run Muisetup.exe from the original Multilanguage CD-ROM to install the Japanese user interface. Restart the computer.
- ❑ D. Use the Regional and Language options to install files for complex script and right-to-left languages, and to switch between the English to the Japanese user interfaces.

Quick Answer: **98**
Detailed Answer: **110**

Quick Check Answer Key

1. C
2. A, B, C, D, and E
3. A
4. B
5. D
6. C
7. E
8. B
9. A, B, C, D, and E
10. A
11. B
12. C
13. D
14. E
15. E
16. E
17. C
18. E
19. B, C, and D
20. B
21. C
22. D
23. A and D
24. B, C, and D
25. B
26. B
27. B
28. C
29. D
30. D
31. C
32. A, B, and D
33. C
34. A and D
35. A
36. C and D
37. C
38. C
39. B
40. B
41. B
42. C
43. C
44. A
45. C
46. A
47. A
48. B
49. A, C, and D
50. B
51. B
52. A, B, and C
53. B
54. B
55. D
56. B
57. D
58. D
59. D
60. D
61. A
62. B, C, D, and E
63. B
64. D
65. A, B, C, and D
66. B
67. D
68. B
69. A
70. A and E
71. A
72. D
73. D
74. D
75. A, B, C, D, and E
76. A
77. B
78. C
79. D
80. E
81. D

Quick Check Answer Key

82. E
83. B, C, D, and E
84. D
85. C
86. A
87. B
88. A
89. C
90. B
91. D
92. A, C, and D
93. D
94. A, B, C, and D
95. A
96. B
97. C
98. D
99. E
100. B
101. C and D
102. C
103. D
104. B
105. C
106. B
107. A
108. D
109. C
110. A
111. D
112. C

Answers and Explanations

1. **Answer: C.** User profiles are another name for a collection of data and folders that store a user's desktop environment and application settings along with personal data in Microsoft Windows XP. A user profile is automatically created the first time a user logs in to a Microsoft Windows XP system.

2. **Answers: A, B, C, D, and E.**

   Explanation A. Accessories are one item contained in a user profile in Microsoft Windows XP. Specific items include the settings for Calculator, Notepad, and Paint.

   Explanation B. Application settings are one item contained in a user profile in Microsoft Windows XP. Specific items include user profile[nd]aware applications, such as Microsoft Word and Excel.

   Explanation C. Control Panel is one item contained in a user profile in Microsoft Windows XP. Specific items include the display and mouse settings.

   Explanation D. Printer settings are one item contained in a user profile in Microsoft Windows XP. Specific information on network printers (but not local printers) is included.

   Explanation E. Taskbar settings are one item contained in a user profile in Microsoft Windows XP. All taskbar settings are included for each user in her own user profile.

3. **Answer: A.** Accessories contains the settings for Calculator, Notepad, and Paint.

4. **Answer: B.** Application settings contain user profile[nd]aware applications, such as Microsoft Word and Excel.

5. **Answer: D.** Printer settings contain specific information on network printers (but not local printers).

6. **Answer: C.** Control Panel contains the display and mouse settings.

7. **Answer: E.** Taskbar settings contain taskbar settings for each user in his own user profile.

8. **Answer: B.** Windows Explorer settings contain all Microsoft Explorer settings and mapped drive information.

9. **Answers: A, B, C, D, and E.**

   Explanation A. The Desktop folder contains all desktop items, including files and shortcuts.

   Explanation B. The NetHood folder contains shortcuts of where Network Neighborhood items are located.

   Explanation C. The PrintHood folder contains shortcuts of where print folder items are located.

   Explanation D. The SendTo folder contains simple shortcuts to applications.

   Explanation E. The Start Menu folder contains shortcuts to executable programs from the user's Start menu.

10. **Answer: A.** The Application Data folder contains all profile-aware applications information.

11. **Answer: B.** The Cookies folder contains all Microsoft Internet Explorer cookies.

12. **Answer: C.** The Desktop folder contains all desktop items, including files and shortcuts.

13. **Answer: D.** The Favorites folder contains all of a user's favorite Microsoft Internet Explorer bookmarks.

14. **Answer: E.** The NetHood folder contains shortcuts of where Network Neighborhood items are located.

15. **Answer: E.** The PrintHood folder contains shortcuts of where print folder items are located.

16. **Answer: E.** The SendTo folder contains simple shortcuts to applications.

17. **Answer: C.** The Recent folder contains shortcuts to recently used documents.

18. **Answer: E.** The Start Menu folder contains shortcuts to executable programs from the user's Start menu.

19. **Answers: B, C, and D.**

    Explanation B. Local user profiles are created the very first time a user logs on to the computer. Local user profiles are stored on the local hard drive, as are all future changes.

    Explanation C. Mandatory user profiles are created by administrators. A user cannot permanently modify changes to this type of profile. Mandatory user profiles are most commonly used in Microsoft Windows NT 4 and earlier domains. Mandatory user profiles are stored on the network server, as are all future changes.

Explanation D. Roaming user profiles enable users to log on to different computers and receive the same user profile settings. Roaming user profiles also enable users to have access to all their documents stored on a central network server, instead of just one local machine. Roaming user profiles are stored on the network server, as are all future changes.

20. **Answer: B.** Local user profiles are created the very first time a user logs on to the computer. Local user profiles are stored on the local hard drive, as are all future changes.

21. **Answer: C.** Mandatory user profiles are created by administrators. A user cannot permanently modify changes to this type of profile. Mandatory user profiles are most commonly used in Microsoft Windows NT 4 and earlier domains. Mandatory user profiles are stored on the network server, as are all future changes.

22. **Answer: D.** Roaming user profiles enable users to log on to different computers and receive the same user profile settings. Roaming user profiles also enable users to have access to all their documents stored on a central network server, instead of just one local machine. Roaming user profiles are stored on the network server, as are all future changes.

23. **Answers: A and D.**

    Explanation A. You can assign software packages, such as .MSI (Microsoft Installer) files, in Microsoft Windows XP. There is another method of deploying software packages.

    Explanation D. You can publish software packages, such as .MSI (Microsoft Installer) files, in Microsoft Windows XP. There is another method of deploying software packages.

24. **Answers: B, C, and D.**

    Explanation B. Published applications are not advertised.

    Explanation C. Published applications can be installed through Add/Remove Programs in Control Panel.

    Explanation D. Published applications can be installed through invocation. By simply clicking on a data file with the new filename extension association (such as .DOC for Microsoft Word or .XLS for Microsoft Excel), the new software is installed.

25. **Answer: B.** Software packages assigned to a computer are installed the next time the computer is started, but before a user can log on in Microsoft Windows XP.

26. **Answer: B.** Non-Microsoft Installer (.MSI) software packages are published in Microsoft Windows XP as the .ZAP file type.
27. **Answer: B.** Microsoft Installer software packages are published in Microsoft Windows XP as the .MSI file type.
28. **Answer: C.** The .MSP (patch files) file types are deployed separately as .MSP files.
29. **Answer: D.** The .MST (modification files) file type must be assigned to .MSI (Microsoft Installer) packages at the time of deployment.
30. **Answer: D.** The msiexec command can enter a required CD key with an installer package in Microsoft Windows XP with the following syntax: msiexec /a <path_to_MSI_file> PIDKEY="[CD-Key]". You'll need to enter in the appropriate path and CD key in this command.
31. **Answer: C.** This response is a false statement. Software installer packages cannot be published to computers in Microsoft Windows XP. This is the only exception to software installer capabilities.
32. **Answers: A, B, and D.**

    Explanation A. Software installer packages can be assigned to computers in Microsoft Windows XP.

    Explanation B. Software installer packages can be assigned to users in Microsoft Windows XP.

    Explanation D. Software installer packages can be published to users in Microsoft Windows XP.
33. **Answer: C.** Assigning applications to the Marketing managers (users) is correct, since they require the application right away. The Marketing staff workers (also users) might eventually need the application, so merely publishing the application to them is the best response for now. Answer A is incorrect, since all users do not need the application right away. Answer B is incorrect, since the Marketing managers need the application right away. Answer D is incorrect and actually is reverse of the best solution.
34. **Answers: A and D.**

    Explanation A. This response is a false statement. Published software applications do not self-repair (or reinstall) if they are deleted by the user.

    Explanation D. This response is a false statement. Published software applications can only be published to users and not to computers. Also note that software applications can be assigned to either computers or users.

35. **Answer: A.** Invocation is the word that best describes what occurs when Microsoft Installer software packages are auto-installed after a user double-clicks on an unknown file type in Microsoft Windows XP.

36. **Answers: C and D.**

    Explanation C. You can assign software installation packages in Microsoft Windows XP. There is another deployment method as well.

    Explanation D. You can publish software installation packages in Microsoft Windows XP. There is another deployment method as well.

37. **Answer: C.** You add more locales by selecting Start, Settings, Control Panel, Regional Options, Input Locale tab.

38. **Answer: C.** You can see what languages are available to a computer in Microsoft Windows XP by selecting Start, Settings, Control Panel, Regional Options, General tab.

39. **Answer: B.** You can see what the exact default language is on a computer in Microsoft Windows XP by selecting Start, Settings, Control Panel, Regional Options, General tab. Scroll through the box labeled Your System Is Configured to Read and Write Documents in Multiple Languages to find the default.

40. **Answer: B.** Changes made by an administrator to a user's roaming profile are copied to a network server.

41. **Answer: B.** Changes made by a Microsoft Windows XP computer user are copied to the local hard drive.

42. **Answer: C.** Changes made to a local user profile on a Microsoft Windows XP PC are copied to the local hard drive.

43. **Answer: C.** A shortcut appears on the user's Start, Programs menu when a software installation package is assigned.

44. **Answer: A.** According to Microsoft, the four phases of the software life cycle, in order, are preparation, deployment, maintenance, and removal. Note that testing is not listed, but should be performed throughout the entire software life cycle.

45. **Answer: C.** According to Microsoft, the four phases of the software life cycle, in order, are preparation, deployment, maintenance, and removal. Note that testing is not listed by Microsoft as a distinct software life cycle phase, but should be performed throughout the entire process.

46. **Answer: A.** GPO stands for Group Policy Object when applying settings in Microsoft Windows XP.

47. **Answer: A.** Active Directory can either uninstall old applications or upgrade on top of them with group policies for Microsoft Windows XP clients, when updating deployed software.

48. **Answer: B.** Active Directory cannot use group policies for a Microsoft Windows XP client to do optional upgrades for computers of deployed software.

49. **Answers: A, C, and D.**

    Explanation A. Active Directory can use group policies for a Microsoft Windows XP client to do mandatory upgrades for computers of deployed software.

    Explanation C. Active Directory can use group policies for a Microsoft Windows XP client to do mandatory upgrades for users of deployed software.

    Explanation D. Active Directory can use group policies for a Microsoft Windows XP client to do optional upgrades for users of deployed software.

50. **Answer: B.** The Automatic Updates feature of Microsoft Windows XP regularly goes online to check the Microsoft site called Windows Update.

51. **Answer: B.** The Automatic Updates feature of Microsoft Windows XP regularly goes online to check the Microsoft site called Windows Update. You can adjust these settings by right-clicking My Computer and choosing Properties, Automatic Updates tab.

52. **Answers: A, B, and C.**

    Explanation A. There are two other valid responses on the Automatic Updates tab of System Properties on a Microsoft Windows XP computer.

    Explanation B. There are two other valid responses on the Automatic Updates tab of System Properties on a Microsoft Windows XP computer.

    Explanation C. There are two other valid responses on the Automatic Updates tab of System Properties on a Microsoft Windows XP computer.

53. **Answer: B.** Microsoft Windows XP can support 10 monitors.

54. **Answer: B.** The feature in Microsoft Windows XP that allows portable computer users to spread their desktop across both their laptop computer as well as one additional external monitor is called Dual View.

55. **Answer: D.** Monitor settings are configured in Microsoft Windows XP through the Start, Settings, Control Panel, Display.

56. **Answer: B.** The default theme that Microsoft Windows XP uses when originally installed is bright and colorful and is called Luna.

57. **Answer: D.** The taskbar now allows grouping of similar items when you have several similar open window items hidden on it.

58. **Answer: D.** The new default Start menu in Microsoft Windows XP tries to keep icons hidden from the end user, providing a neater appearance. This is a noticeable change in the philosophy of the Windows operating system.

59. **Answer: D.** The new default Start menu in Microsoft Windows XP tries to keep icons hidden from the end user, providing a neater appearance. To change it back to the old-style functionality, right-click the taskbar, choose Properties, choose Start Menu tab, and select the Classic Start Menu option.

60. **Answer: D.** The new name of the System Tray in Microsoft Windows XP is the Notification Area.

61. **Answer: A.** The new name of the new wizard in Microsoft Windows XP that provides a compatibility mechanism for older programs is the Program Compatibility Wizard. Launch it by Start, Programs, Accessories, Program Compatibility Wizard.

62. **Answers: B, C, D, and E.**

    Explanation B. This is one of the available choices when selecting a compatibility mode for a program in the Program Compatibility Wizard in Microsoft Windows XP.

    Explanation C. This is one of the available choices when selecting a compatibility mode for a program in the Program Compatibility Wizard in Microsoft Windows XP.

    Explanation D. This is one of the available choices when selecting a compatibility mode for a program in the Program Compatibility Wizard in Microsoft Windows XP.

    Explanation E. This is one of the available choices when selecting a compatibility mode for a program in the Program Compatibility Wizard in Microsoft Windows XP.

63. **Answer: B.** The Fax applet appears in Control Panel when installed in Microsoft Windows XP. It does not appear otherwise.

64. **Answer: D.** The Fax applet appears in Control Panel when installed in Microsoft Windows XP. It does not appear elsewhere otherwise.

65. **Answers: A, B, C, and D.**

    Explanation A. The Fax applet appears in Control Panel only when installed in Microsoft Windows XP, and has many settings.

    Explanation B. The Fax applet appears in Control Panel only when installed in Microsoft Windows XP, and has many settings.

    Explanation C. The Fax applet appears in Control Panel only when installed in Microsoft Windows XP, and has many settings.

    Explanation D. The Fax applet appears in Control Panel only when installed in Microsoft Windows XP, and has many settings.

66. **Answer: B.** The fax printer in your printer folder in Microsoft Windows XP cannot be shared.

67. **Answer: D.** This is not one of the three valid responses found on the Automatic Updates tab of System Properties on a Microsoft Windows XP computer. The other three responses actually appear on the Automatic Updates tab.

68. **Answer: B.** Microsoft Windows XP can support only one additional external monitor from a laptop. This feature is called Dual View and it works similar to the multiple monitors feature.

69. **Answer: A.** The new name of the new wizard in Microsoft Windows XP that provides a compatibility mechanism for older programs is the Program Compatibility Wizard.

70. **Answers: A and E.**

    Explanation A. This is not one of the available choices when selecting a compatibility mode for a program in the Program Compatibility Wizard in Microsoft Windows XP.

    Explanation E. This is not one of the available choices when selecting a compatibility mode for a program in the Program Compatibility Wizard in Microsoft Windows XP.

71. **Answer: A.** The Program Compatibility Wizard in Microsoft Windows XP tricks a program into running a PC program that would normally be incompatible.

72. **Answer: D.** The ability to view faxes is done through the Windows Picture and Fax Viewer, which is installed as part of Microsoft Windows XP. Answer A is incorrect because it would be used to control device settings. Answers B and C are incorrect because both Notepad and WordPad are better designed to work with view text files, not faxes.

73. **Answer: D.** The Fax applet appears in Control Panel when installed in Microsoft Windows XP. It does not appear elsewhere otherwise.

74. **Answer: D.** Accessibility services include StickyKeys, FilterKeys, SoundSentry, ShowSounds, MouseKeys, Magnifier, and Narrator in Microsoft Windows XP.

75. **Answers: A, B, C, D, and E.**

    Explanation A. There are several other items included in Microsoft Windows XP Accessibility services.

    Explanation B. There are several other items included in Microsoft Windows XP Accessibility services.

    Explanation C. There are several other items included in Microsoft Windows XP Accessibility services.

    Explanation D. Accessibility services include StickyKeys, FilterKeys, SoundSentry, ShowSounds, MouseKeys, Magnifier, and Narrator in Microsoft Windows XP.

    Explanation E. There are several other items included in Microsoft Windows XP Accessibility services.

76. **Answer: A.** StickyKeys enables you to press multiple keystroke combinations, one key at a time.

77. **Answer: B.** FilterKeys informs the keyboard to ignore repeated keystrokes or mistaken brief keystrokes.

78. **Answer: C.** SoundSentry flashes visual warnings for the hearing impaired whenever your computer makes a sound.

79. **Answer: D.** ShowSounds has programs show captions whenever the program makes a sound or speaks.

80. **Answer: E.** MouseKeys enables you to control the mouse with the numeric keypad included on most keyboards.

81. **Answer: D.** Magnifier increases the size of a portion of your screen for the visually impaired.

82. **Answer: E.** Narrator reads aloud any menu options and title bar expressions using speech synthesis.

83. **Answers: B, C, D, and E.**

    Explanation B. There are several other items included in Microsoft Windows XP Accessibility services.

    Explanation C. There are several other items included in Microsoft Windows XP Accessibility services.

    Explanation D. Accessibility services include StickyKeys, FilterKeys, SoundSentry, ShowSounds, MouseKeys, Magnifier, and Narrator in Microsoft Windows XP.

    Explanation E. There are several other items included in Microsoft Windows XP Accessibility services.

84. **Answer: D.** Remote Assistance is the feature in Microsoft Windows XP that enables a user to request remote help from an expert or other knowledgeable person.

85. **Answer: C.** Remote Assistance is the feature in Microsoft Windows XP that enables a user to request remote help from an expert or other knowledgeable person. An expert can then see the user's desktop.

86. **Answer: A.** Remote Assistance is the feature in Microsoft Windows XP that enables a user to request remote help from an expert or other knowledgeable person. An expert can then control the user's desktop.

87. **Answer: B.** Remote Assistance is the feature in Microsoft Windows XP that enables a user to request remote help from an expert or other knowledgeable person. An expert can then chat with the user using text.

88. **Answer: A.** Remote Assistance is the feature in Microsoft Windows XP that enables a user to request remote help from an expert or other knowledgeable person. An expert can then actually chat with the user using voice.

89. **Answer: C.** Remote Assistance is the feature in Microsoft Windows XP that enables a user to request remote help from an expert or other knowledgeable person. An expert can then actually chat with the user using voice.

90. **Answer: B.** Remote Assistance is the feature in Microsoft Windows XP that enables a user to request remote help from an expert or other knowledgeable person. An expert can then send files from the user's system.

91. **Answer: D.** Remote Assistance is the feature in Microsoft Windows XP that enables a user to request remote help from an expert or other knowledgeable person. An expert can then receive files from the user's system.

92. **Answers: A, C, and D.**

    Explanation A. There are two other ways besides Windows Messenger to request assistance from an expert using Remote Assistance in Microsoft Windows XP.

    Explanation C. There are two other ways besides email to request assistance from an expert using Remote Assistance in Microsoft Windows XP. MAPI stands for Messaging Application Programming Interface, a system in Microsoft Windows that allows email programs to work together.

    Explanation D. There are two other ways besides using a file to request assistance from an expert using Remote Assistance in Microsoft Windows XP.

93. **Answer: D.** Remote Assistance is the feature in Microsoft Windows XP that enables a user to request remote help from an expert or other knowledgeable person. It is enabled by default.

94. **Answers: A, B, C, and D.**

    Explanation A. The Remote Assistance Console contains a Take Control function.

    Explanation B. The Remote Assistance Console contains a Send a File function.

    Explanation C. The Remote Assistance Console contains a Start Talking function.

    Explanation D. The Remote Assistance Console contains a Settings function.

95. **Answer: A.** Take Control will actually request taking control of a user's system.

96. **Answer: B.** Send a File will send the user a file that is needed; for example, a hardware driver file.

97. **Answer: C.** Start Talking will start a VOIP (Voice Over Internet Protocol) session. Both the user and the expert need proper hardware for this to work: sound card, microphone, and speakers or headset.

98. **Answer: D.** Settings will allow the expert to adjust the console size and speaker settings.

99. **Answer: E.** Disconnect will end the expert's Remote Assistance session.

100. **Answer: B.** Help will provide help information as usual for the expert's Remote Assistance session.

101. **Answers: C and D.**

Explanation C. HelpAssistant is one of the two built-in accounts used with Remote Assistance in Microsoft Windows XP. HelpAssistant is enabled only when you have an open request to another user for Remote Assistance.

Explanation D. Support_hex (a random hexadecimal number) is one of the built-in accounts used with Remote Assistance in Microsoft Windows XP. Support_hex is used when you request Remote Assistance directly from Microsoft.

102. **Answer: C.** HelpAssistant is one of the two built-in accounts used with Remote Assistance in Microsoft Windows XP. HelpAssistant is enabled only when you have an open request to another user for Remote Assistance. After invitations have expired, this account is disabled.

103. **Answer: D.** Support_hex (a random hexadecimal number) is one of the two built-in accounts used with Remote Assistance in Microsoft Windows XP. Support_hex is used when you request Remote Assistance directly from Microsoft.

104. **Answer: B.** You should update the driver for the video adapter to support increased screen resolution and color depth.

105. **Answer: C.** You should adjust the Compatibility settings for the Focus application by selecting the Run in 256 Colors check box.

106. **Answer: B.** You should enable the Use High Contrast Display setting in Accessibility options.

107. **Answer: A.** You should adjust the Power Users group by removing the Allow-Modify permission from the Documents and Settings\All Users folder.

108. **Answer: D.** In the Regional and Language options, you should apply the English (United States) Standards and Formats.

109. **Answer: C.** You should install the Windows installer package by using an .mst file. The Msiexec.exe program is a part of Windows Installer that uses a dynamic link library, Msi.dll, to read package files (.msi), apply transforms (.mst), and include any other command-line options.

110. **Answer: A.** You should open the local default user profile. Rename ntuser.dat to ntuser.man, which is a mandatory profile.

111. **Answer: D.** Configure Bryan's laptop by going to Languages options and selecting the Install Files for East Asian Languages check box. Add Japanese as an input language.

112. **Answer: C.** Run Muisetup.exe from the original Multilanguage CD-ROM to install the Japanese user interface. Restart the computer. MUI stands for Multilingual User Interface.

Installing, Configuring, and Troubleshooting Hardware Devices and Drivers

Quick Check

1. What can be done in Microsoft Windows XP in Device Manager under Display Adapters? (Select all that apply.)

   Quick Answer: **143**
   Detailed Answer: **145**

   - ❑ A. Install a new display adapter.
   - ❑ B. Remove a display adapter.
   - ❑ C. Update drivers for a display adapter.
   - ❑ D. Install a new monitor.

2. What can be done in Microsoft Windows XP in Device Manager under Monitors? (Select all that apply.)

   Quick Answer: **143**
   Detailed Answer: **145**

   - ❑ A. Install a new monitor.
   - ❑ B. Remove a monitor.
   - ❑ C. Update drivers for a monitor.
   - ❑ D. Install a new display adapter.

3. What devices are supported in Microsoft Windows XP for laptops? (Select all that apply.)

   Quick Answer: **143**
   Detailed Answer: **145**

   - ❑ A. PCMCIA
   - ❑ B. USB
   - ❑ C. IEEE 1394
   - ❑ D. Infrared

4. What power-saving technologies are supported in Microsoft Windows XP for laptops? (Select all that apply.)

   Quick Answer: **143**
   Detailed Answer: **145**

   - ❑ A. ACPI
   - ❑ B. APM
   - ❑ C. PnP
   - ❑ D. Windows Update

Quick Check

5. You have Microsoft Windows XP installed on a laptop. Normally you either use a power adapter (when using a modem) or a docking station (when using a NIC). You need to configure the laptop to conserve battery life when neither a power adapter nor a docking station is available. What should you do?

   - ❑ A. Create a new hardware profile.
   - ❑ B. Disable the modem and network adapter PCMCIA cards.
   - ❑ C. Configure the Undocked hardware profile as the default.
   - ❑ D. Disable the Server service in Services.

Quick Answer: **143**
Detailed Answer: **146**

6. Which Power Scheme setting will maintain constant power when plugged in or while running on batteries?

   - ❑ A. Always On
   - ❑ B. Home Office/Desk
   - ❑ C. Max Battery
   - ❑ D. Minimal Power Management
   - ❑ E. Portable/Laptop

Quick Answer: **143**
Detailed Answer: **146**

7. Which Power Scheme setting will maintain constant power when plugged in?

   - ❑ A. Always On
   - ❑ B. Home Office/Desk
   - ❑ C. Max Battery
   - ❑ D. Minimal Power Management
   - ❑ E. Presentation

Quick Answer: **143**
Detailed Answer: **146**

8. Which Power Scheme setting will maintain constant power when plugged in, but power down within 1 minute of inactivity if running on batteries?

   - ❑ A. Presentation
   - ❑ B. Home Office/Desk
   - ❑ C. Max Battery
   - ❑ D. Minimal Power Management
   - ❑ E. Portable/Laptop

Quick Answer: **143**
Detailed Answer: **146**

9. Which Power Scheme setting will maintain constant power when plugged in, but will power down within 15 minutes of inactivity if running on batteries?

   - ❑ A. Always On
   - ❑ B. Home Office/Desk
   - ❑ C. Presentation
   - ❑ D. Minimal Power Management
   - ❑ E. Portable/Laptop

Quick Answer: **143**
Detailed Answer: **146**

Quick Check

10. Which Power Scheme setting will shut down everything within 30 minutes of inactivity when plugged in, with everything shutting down faster if running on batteries?

Quick Answer: **143**
Detailed Answer: **146**

- ❑ A. Always On
- ❑ B. Home Office/Desk
- ❑ C. Max Battery
- ❑ D. Minimal Power Management
- ❑ E. Portable/Laptop

11. Which Power Scheme setting will always keep the monitor on, whether plugged in or running on batteries, and keep the rest of the system active while plugged in?

Quick Answer: **143**
Detailed Answer: **146**

- ❑ A. Always On
- ❑ B. Presentation
- ❑ C. Max Battery
- ❑ D. Minimal Power Management
- ❑ E. Portable/Laptop

12. What are the two types of power option alarms that can be set in Microsoft Windows XP? (Select all that apply.)

Quick Answer: **143**
Detailed Answer: **146**

- ❑ A. Low Battery alarm
- ❑ B. Critical Battery alarm
- ❑ C. Yellow Alert
- ❑ D. Orange Alert
- ❑ E. Red Alert

13. What is the power option alarm that can be set in Microsoft Windows XP to indicate that your batteries are starting to get low?

Quick Answer: **143**
Detailed Answer: **146**

- ❑ A. Low Battery alarm
- ❑ B. Critical Battery alarm
- ❑ C. Yellow Alert
- ❑ D. Orange Alert
- ❑ E. Red Alert

14. What is the power option alarm that can be set in Microsoft Windows XP to indicate that your batteries are extremely low?

Quick Answer: **143**
Detailed Answer: **146**

- ❑ A. Low Battery alarm
- ❑ B. Critical Battery alarm
- ❑ C. Yellow Alert
- ❑ D. Orange Alert
- ❑ E. Red Alert

Quick Check

15. What are the two types of Advanced Power Options settings that can be configured in Microsoft Windows XP? (Select all that apply.)

Quick Answer: **143**
Detailed Answer: **146**

- ❑ A. Low Battery alarm
- ❑ B. Critical Battery alarm
- ❑ C. Standby
- ❑ D. Hibernate

16. What is the Advanced Power Options setting in Microsoft Windows XP that is the low power state that runs your computer using minimal power?

Quick Answer: **143**
Detailed Answer: **146**

- ❑ A. Low Battery alarm
- ❑ B. Critical Battery alarm
- ❑ C. Standby
- ❑ D. Hibernate

17. What is the Advanced Power Options setting in Microsoft Windows XP that is the low power state that copies the contents of RAM onto a hard drive for later use?

Quick Answer: **143**
Detailed Answer: **147**

- ❑ A. Low Battery alarm
- ❑ B. Critical Battery alarm
- ❑ C. Standby
- ❑ D. Hibernate

18. Where are keyboards installed in Microsoft Windows XP?

Quick Answer: **143**
Detailed Answer: **147**

- ❑ A. Keyboards
- ❑ B. Mice and Other Pointing Devices
- ❑ C. Keyboards and Mice
- ❑ D. Mouse

19. Where are mice installed in Microsoft Windows XP?

Quick Answer: **143**
Detailed Answer: **147**

- ❑ A. Keyboards
- ❑ B. Mice and Other Pointing Devices
- ❑ C. Keyboards and Mice
- ❑ D. Mouse

20. Where are graphic tablets installed in Microsoft Windows XP?

Quick Answer: **143**
Detailed Answer: **147**

- ❑ A. Keyboards
- ❑ B. Mice and Other Pointing Devices
- ❑ C. Keyboards and Mice
- ❑ D. Mouse

Quick Check

21. What variation of the System File Checker command scans all protected system files immediately in Microsoft Windows XP?
    - ❑ A. Sfc.exe /scannow
    - ❑ B. Sfc.exe /scanonce
    - ❑ C. Sfc.exe /scanboot
    - ❑ D. Sfc.exe /cancel
    - ❑ E. Sfc.exe /quiet

Quick Answer: 143
Detailed Answer: 147

22. What variation of the System File Checker command scans all protected system files at the next reboot in Microsoft Windows XP?
    - ❑ A. Sfc.exe /scannow
    - ❑ B. Sfc.exe /scanonce
    - ❑ C. Scf.exe /enable
    - ❑ D. Sfc.exe /purgecache
    - ❑ E. Sfc.exe /cachesize=x

Quick Answer: 143
Detailed Answer: 147

23. What variation of the System File Checker command scans all protected system files at every reboot in Microsoft Windows XP?
    - ❑ A. Sfc.exe /scannow
    - ❑ B. Sfc.exe /scanonce
    - ❑ C. Sfc.exe /scanboot
    - ❑ D. Sfc.exe /purgecache
    - ❑ E. Sfc.exe /cachesize=x

Quick Answer: 143
Detailed Answer: 147

24. What variation of the System File Checker command cancels all pending scans of protected system files in Microsoft Windows XP?
    - ❑ A. Sfc.exe /scannow
    - ❑ B. Sfc.exe /scanonce
    - ❑ C. Sfc.exe /scanboot
    - ❑ D. Sfc.exe /cancel
    - ❑ E. Sfc.exe /quiet

Quick Answer: 143
Detailed Answer: 147

25. What variation of the System File Checker command replaces incorrect system files without prompting in Microsoft Windows XP?
    - ❑ A. Sfc.exe /scannow
    - ❑ B. Sfc.exe /scanonce
    - ❑ C. Sfc.exe /scanboot
    - ❑ D. Sfc.exe /cancel
    - ❑ E. Sfc.exe /quiet

Quick Answer: 143
Detailed Answer: 147

Quick Check

26. What variation of the System File Checker command sets system file protection back to default in Microsoft Windows XP?

Quick Answer: 143
Detailed Answer: 147

- ☐ A. Scf.exe /enable
- ☐ B. Sfc.exe /scanonce
- ☐ C. Sfc.exe /scanboot
- ☐ D. Sfc.exe /cancel
- ☐ E. Sfc.exe /quiet

27. What variation of the System File Checker command purges the file cache and then immediately rescans protected system files in Microsoft Windows XP?

Quick Answer: 143
Detailed Answer: 147

- ☐ A. Sfc.exe /scannow
- ☐ B. Sfc.exe /scanonce
- ☐ C. Sfc.exe /scanboot
- ☐ D. Sfc.exe /purgecache
- ☐ E. Sfc.exe /quiet

28. What variation of the System File Checker command sets the file cache size for protected system files in Microsoft Windows XP?

Quick Answer: 143
Detailed Answer: 147

- ☐ A. Sfc.exe /scannow
- ☐ B. Sfc.exe /scanonce
- ☐ C. Sfc.exe /cachesize=
- ☐ D. Sfc.exe /cancel
- ☐ E. Sfc.exe /quiet

29. What is the definition of a driver in Microsoft Windows XP?

Quick Answer: 143
Detailed Answer: 147

- ☐ A. A program that controls a device
- ☐ B. A database used by the operating system to store configuration information
- ☐ C. A signal informing a program that an event occurred
- ☐ D. An instruction to a computer or a device to perform a specific task

30. You're the network administrator at your company. Several users have recently caused device driver conflicts on their computers by attaching their personal digital cameras to their Microsoft Windows XP computers at work. You need to stop the installation of devices by end users. What level of driver signing should you configure?

Quick Answer: 143
Detailed Answer: 147

- ☐ A. Ignore
- ☐ B. Warn
- ☐ C. Block
- ☐ D. Screen

Quick Check

31. You're the network administrator at your company. A user named Bob attaches his new color printer to his Microsoft Windows XP computer. Bob follows the prompts during installation of the drivers, and ignores a warning message that the new color printer's drivers are not digitally signed by Microsoft Windows XP. When Bob tries to reboot his computer, it freezes. Soon after you're called to his desk, you realize that there must be a device driver conflict on his computer. What level of driver signing should you have configured on Bob's machine to have prevented this scenario?

    - ❑ A. Ignore
    - ❑ B. Warn
    - ❑ C. Deny
    - ❑ D. Block

Quick Answer: **143**
Detailed Answer: **147**

32. Where are all the original Microsoft Windows XP driver files contained?

    - ❑ A. C:\Drivers
    - ❑ B. Driverguide.com
    - ❑ C. Drivers.com
    - ❑ D. Driver.cab

Quick Answer: **143**
Detailed Answer: **148**

33. What is the name of the command-line utility that will verify all of a computer's digitally signed Microsoft Windows XP driver files?

    - ❑ A. Verify.exe
    - ❑ B. Drivers.exe /verify
    - ❑ C. Drivers.exe /v
    - ❑ D. Verifier.exe

Quick Answer: **143**
Detailed Answer: **148**

34. What is the name of the feature in Microsoft Windows XP that enables you to revert to an older version of a driver that worked before the new driver you just tried to install failed?

    - ❑ A. Driver Verify
    - ❑ B. Driver Signature
    - ❑ C. Driver Scanning
    - ❑ D. Driver Rollback

Quick Answer: **143**
Detailed Answer: **148**

Quick Check

35. Which of the following statements are true about resolving hardware conflicts in Microsoft Windows XP? (Select all that apply.)

Quick Answer: **143**
Detailed Answer: **148**

- ❑ A. Allow Microsoft Windows XP to attempt to resolve any hardware resource conflicts first.
- ❑ B. Hardware made by the same manufacturer will never conflict with each other.
- ❑ C. Microsoft Windows XP is capable of sharing resources (such as IRQs—interrupt requests) among several different hardware devices.
- ❑ D. Avoid using the Registry Editor except as a last resort.

36. Which of the following statements are true about managing and configuring multiple CPUs in Microsoft Windows XP? (Select all that apply.)

Quick Answer: **143**
Detailed Answer: **148**

- ❑ A. Microsoft Windows XP Professional can support up to two CPUs.
- ❑ B. Microsoft Windows XP can support ASMP.
- ❑ C. Adding a CPU to your system is called *scaling*.
- ❑ D. Microsoft Windows XP Professional supports SMP.

37. Which of the following statements are true about installing and managing network adapters in Microsoft Windows XP? (Select all that apply.)

Quick Answer: **143**
Detailed Answer: **148**

- ❑ A. Network adapters are installed using Add/Remove Hardware in Control Panel.
- ❑ B. Each network adapter has its own icon under Network and Dial-up Connection icon.
- ❑ C. Network adapters in the same computer do not have to be identical.
- ❑ D. Network adapters in the same computer have to be identical.

38. Which of the following files are used in the Microsoft Windows XP boot process? (Select all that apply.)

Quick Answer: **143**
Detailed Answer: **148**

- ❑ A. Boot.ini
- ❑ B. Bootsect.dos
- ❑ C. Hal.dll
- ❑ D. Ntdetect.com
- ❑ E. Ntldr
- ❑ F. Ntoskrnl.exe
- ❑ G. System

39. Which of the following Boot.ini switches boots a Microsoft Windows XP computer using a standard VGA driver?

Quick Answer: 143
Detailed Answer: 149

- ❑ A. /basevideo
- ❑ B. /noguiboot
- ❑ C. /sos
- ❑ D. /bootlog
- ❑ E. /safeboot:network

40. Which of the following Boot.ini switches boots a Microsoft Windows XP computer without displaying the graphical start-up screen?

Quick Answer: 143
Detailed Answer: 149

- ❑ A. /basevideo
- ❑ B. /noguiboot
- ❑ C. /sos
- ❑ D. /bootlog
- ❑ E. /safeboot:minimal

41. Which of the following Boot.ini switches displays the device driver names of a Microsoft Windows XP computer as they are loaded?

Quick Answer: 143
Detailed Answer: 149

- ❑ A. /basevideo
- ❑ B. /noguiboot
- ❑ C. /sos
- ❑ D. /bootlog
- ❑ E. /safeboot:network

42. Which of the following Boot.ini switches enables boot logging on a Microsoft Windows XP computer?

Quick Answer: 143
Detailed Answer: 149

- ❑ A. /basevideo
- ❑ B. /noguiboot
- ❑ C. /safeboot:network
- ❑ D. /bootlog
- ❑ E. /safeboot:minimal

43. Which of the following Boot.ini switches boots a Microsoft Windows XP computer into Safe mode?

Quick Answer: 143
Detailed Answer: 149

- ❑ A. /basevideo
- ❑ B. /noguiboot
- ❑ C. /sos
- ❑ D. /bootlog
- ❑ E. /safeboot:minimal

Quick Check

44. Which of the following Boot.ini switches boots a Microsoft Windows XP computer into Safe mode with networking support?

Quick Answer: 143
Detailed Answer: 149

- ❑ A. /basevideo
- ❑ B. /safeboot:network
- ❑ C. /sos
- ❑ D. /bootlog
- ❑ E. /safeboot:minimal

45. What does ARC stand for in terms of the ARC path located in the Boot.ini file of a Microsoft Windows XP computer?

Quick Answer: 143
Detailed Answer: 149

- ❑ A. Automatic Reboot Command
- ❑ B. Automatic Reboot Computing
- ❑ C. Asynchronous Relay Computing
- ❑ D. Advanced RISC Computing

46. What ARC path parameter located in the Boot.ini file of a Microsoft Windows XP computer specifies a non-SCSI hard disk controller or SCSI hard disk controller with the BIOS enabled?

Quick Answer: 143
Detailed Answer: 150

- ❑ A. multi(x)
- ❑ B. scsi(x)
- ❑ C. disk(x)
- ❑ D. rdisk(x)
- ❑ E. partition(x)

47. What ARC path parameter located in the Boot.ini file of a Microsoft Windows XP computer specifies a SCSI hard disk controller with the BIOS enabled?

Quick Answer: 143
Detailed Answer: 150

- ❑ A. multi(x)
- ❑ B. scsi(x)
- ❑ C. disk(x)
- ❑ D. rdisk(x)
- ❑ E. partition(x)

48. What ARC path parameter located in the Boot.ini file of a Microsoft Windows XP computer specifies the SCSI disk that the operating system resides on?

Quick Answer: 143
Detailed Answer: 150

- ❑ A. multi(x)
- ❑ B. scsi(x)
- ❑ C. disk(x)
- ❑ D. rdisk(x)
- ❑ E. partition(x)

Quick Check

49. What ARC path parameter located in the Boot.ini file of a Microsoft Windows XP computer specifies the EIDE disk that the operating system resides on?

Quick Answer: 143
Detailed Answer: 150

- ❑ A. multi(x)
- ❑ B. scsi(x)
- ❑ C. disk(x)
- ❑ D. rdisk(x)
- ❑ E. partition(x)

50. What ARC path parameter located in the Boot.ini file of a Microsoft Windows XP computer specifies the partition that the operating system resides on?

Quick Answer: 143
Detailed Answer: 150

- ❑ A. multi(x)
- ❑ B. scsi(x)
- ❑ C. disk(x)
- ❑ D. rdisk(x)
- ❑ E. partition(x)

51. What function key should you press while booting a Microsoft Windows XP computer in order to enter Safe mode?

Quick Answer: 143
Detailed Answer: 150

- ❑ A. F1
- ❑ B. F12
- ❑ C. F11
- ❑ D. F5
- ❑ E. F8

52. What Microsoft Windows XP Recovery Console command changes attributes of a selected file?

Quick Answer: 143
Detailed Answer: 150

- ❑ A. attrib
- ❑ B. change
- ❑ C. select
- ❑ D. attribute

53. What Microsoft Windows XP Recovery Console command adds, edits, or removes items from the boot.ini file?

Quick Answer: 143
Detailed Answer: 150

- ❑ A. bootconfig
- ❑ B. config
- ❑ C. bootcfg
- ❑ D. configboot

Quick Check

54. What Microsoft Windows XP Recovery Console command changes the current directory or displays the current directory?

Quick Answer: 143
Detailed Answer: 150

- ❑ A. display
- ❑ B. change
- ❑ C. dir
- ❑ D. cd

55. What Microsoft Windows XP Recovery Console command changes the current directory or displays the current directory?

Quick Answer: 143
Detailed Answer: 150

- ❑ A. chdir
- ❑ B. change
- ❑ C. changedir
- ❑ D. dirchange

56. What Microsoft Windows XP Recovery Console command runs CheckDisk in order to check your computer's hard drives?

Quick Answer: 143
Detailed Answer: 150

- ❑ A. check
- ❑ B. chkdsk
- ❑ C. checkdsk
- ❑ D. diskchecker

57. What Microsoft Windows XP Recovery Console command clears the screen?

Quick Answer: 143
Detailed Answer: 150

- ❑ A. screenclean
- ❑ B. clear
- ❑ C. wipe
- ❑ D. cls

58. What Microsoft Windows XP Recovery Console command copies files from removable media to your hard disk?

Quick Answer: 143
Detailed Answer: 150

- ❑ A. copy
- ❑ B. xcopy
- ❑ C. xcopy32
- ❑ D. filecopy

59. What Microsoft Windows XP Recovery Console command deletes a file, folder, or service?

Quick Answer: 143
Detailed Answer: 150

- ❑ A. delsrv
- ❑ B. erase
- ❑ C. del
- ❑ D. dserv

Quick Check

60. What Microsoft Windows XP Recovery Console command deletes a file, folder, or service?

Quick Answer: 143
Detailed Answer: 151

- ❑ A. delserv
- ❑ B. erase
- ❑ C. delete
- ❑ D. foldel

61. What Microsoft Windows XP Recovery Console command lists the contents of the currently selected directory on the system partition only?

Quick Answer: 143
Detailed Answer: 151

- ❑ A. list
- ❑ B. dirlist
- ❑ C. listdir
- ❑ D. dir

62. What Microsoft Windows XP Recovery Console command disables a driver or service?

Quick Answer: 143
Detailed Answer: 151

- ❑ A. stop
- ❑ B. enable
- ❑ C. halt
- ❑ D. disable

63. What Microsoft Windows XP Recovery Console command has the same effect as FDISK by creating or deleting partitions?

Quick Answer: 143
Detailed Answer: 151

- ❑ A. fdiskxp
- ❑ B. xpfdisk
- ❑ C. diskpart
- ❑ D. formatd

64. What Microsoft Windows XP Recovery Console command enables a driver or service?

Quick Answer: 143
Detailed Answer: 151

- ❑ A. disable
- ❑ B. enable
- ❑ C. start
- ❑ D. beginsrv

65. What Microsoft Windows XP Recovery Console command extracts a file or driver from a .CAB (cabinet) or compressed file?

Quick Answer: 143
Detailed Answer: 151

- ❑ A. extract
- ❑ B. expand
- ❑ C. unzip
- ❑ D. pkunzip

Quick Check

66. What Microsoft Windows XP Recovery Console command writes a new partition boot sector on the system partition only?

Quick Answer: 143
Detailed Answer: 151

- ❑ A. bootcfg
- ❑ B. bootsect
- ❑ C. fixboot
- ❑ D. fixmbr

67. What Microsoft Windows XP Recovery Console command writes a new MBR for the partition boot sector on the system partition only?

Quick Answer: 143
Detailed Answer: 151

- ❑ A. fixboot
- ❑ B. bootdisk
- ❑ C. bootfix
- ❑ D. fixmbr

68. What Microsoft Windows XP Recovery Console command formats the selected disk?

Quick Answer: 143
Detailed Answer: 151

- ❑ A. del
- ❑ B. fdisk
- ❑ C. delpart
- ❑ D. format

69. What Microsoft Windows XP Recovery Console command provides online help information about all the Recovery Console commands?

Quick Answer: 143
Detailed Answer: 151

- ❑ A. help
- ❑ B. RC /?
- ❑ C. /h
- ❑ D. F1

70. What Microsoft Windows XP Recovery Console command lists all the services running on a Microsoft Windows XP computer?

Quick Answer: 143
Detailed Answer: 151

- ❑ A. lstsrv
- ❑ B. listsrv
- ❑ C. listserv
- ❑ D. services

71. What Microsoft Windows XP Recovery Console command enables the user to choose which Microsoft Windows XP installation to log on to, if you have more than one?
    - ❑ A. log
    - ❑ B. login
    - ❑ C. logon
    - ❑ D. chooselog

Quick Answer: **143**
Detailed Answer: **151**

72. What Microsoft Windows XP Recovery Console command displays the current drive letter mappings?
    - ❑ A. mapd
    - ❑ B. mappings
    - ❑ C. dspmap
    - ❑ D. map

Quick Answer: **143**
Detailed Answer: **151**

73. What Microsoft Windows XP Recovery Console command creates a directory?
    - ❑ A. makedir
    - ❑ B. create
    - ❑ C. md
    - ❑ D. created

Quick Answer: **143**
Detailed Answer: **151**

74. What Microsoft Windows XP Recovery Console command creates a directory?
    - ❑ A. make
    - ❑ B. mkdir
    - ❑ C. maked
    - ❑ D. mdir

Quick Answer: **143**
Detailed Answer: **151**

75. What Microsoft Windows XP Recovery Console command displays the contents of a text file?
    - ❑ A. more
    - ❑ B. text
    - ❑ C. typem
    - ❑ D. typemore

Quick Answer: **143**
Detailed Answer: **151**

76. What Microsoft Windows XP Recovery Console command displays the contents of a text file?
    - ❑ A. texttype
    - ❑ B. text
    - ❑ C. list
    - ❑ D. type

Quick Answer: **143**
Detailed Answer: **152**

Quick Check

77. What Microsoft Windows XP Recovery Console command connects a network share to a drive letter?

Quick Answer: 143
Detailed Answer: 152

- ❑ A. use net
- ❑ B. net drive
- ❑ C. net use
- ❑ D. net send

78. What Microsoft Windows XP Recovery Console command removes a directory?

Quick Answer: 143
Detailed Answer: 152

- ❑ A. removed
- ❑ B. remove
- ❑ C. rd
- ❑ D. rdir

79. What Microsoft Windows XP Recovery Console command removes a directory?

Quick Answer: 143
Detailed Answer: 152

- ❑ A. delete
- ❑ B. rmdir
- ❑ C. remdir
- ❑ D. rem

80. What Microsoft Windows XP Recovery Console command renames a single file?

Quick Answer: 143
Detailed Answer: 152

- ❑ A. rfile
- ❑ B. ren
- ❑ C. rnme
- ❑ D. nameover

81. What Microsoft Windows XP Recovery Console command renames a single file?

Quick Answer: 143
Detailed Answer: 152

- ❑ A. rename
- ❑ B. replace
- ❑ C. replacename
- ❑ D. name

82. What Microsoft Windows XP Recovery Console command makes the current directory the system root of the drive you are logged in to?

Quick Answer: 144
Detailed Answer: 152

- ❑ A. systemroot
- ❑ B. system
- ❑ C. makeroot
- ❑ D. root

Quick Check

83. How do you access the Microsoft Windows XP Startup and Recovery settings?

Quick Answer: 144
Detailed Answer: 152

- ❑ A. Start, Settings, System, Advanced tab, Startup and Recovery
- ❑ B. Start, Settings, Control Panel, Startup and Recovery
- ❑ C. Start, Settings, Control Panel, System, Advanced tab, Startup and Recovery
- ❑ D. Start, Settings, Startup and Recovery

84. How large should the paging file on the system partition be in order to properly use the Write Debugging Information option of Startup and Recovery settings in Microsoft Windows XP?

Quick Answer: 144
Detailed Answer: 152

- ❑ A. At least one-and-a-half times the amount of RAM installed on the system
- ❑ B. At least 512KB larger than the amount of RAM installed on the system
- ❑ C. At least 16MB larger than the amount of RAM installed on the system
- ❑ D. At least 1MB larger than the amount of RAM installed on the system

85. How large is a small memory dump in Microsoft Windows XP?

Quick Answer: 144
Detailed Answer: 152

- ❑ A. 64KB
- ❑ B. 256KB
- ❑ C. 32KB
- ❑ D. 1MB

86. What is the name of the memory dump file in Microsoft Windows XP?

Quick Answer: 144
Detailed Answer: 152

- ❑ A. Mem.
- ❑ B. dmpMemory.dmp
- ❑ C. Memdump.txt
- ❑ D. Dumpmem.txt

87. What command-line tool is used to examine the contents of the memory dump file in Microsoft Windows XP?

Quick Answer: 144
Detailed Answer: 152

- ❑ A. Dumpchecker.exe
- ❑ B. Dumpcheck.exe
- ❑ C. Dumpchk.exe
- ❑ D. Checkdump.exe

Quick Check

88. What command-line tool from the Microsoft Windows XP CD is used to install the Recovery Console?

Quick Answer: 144
Detailed Answer: 152

- ❑ A. recover.exe
- ❑ B. command.com
- ❑ C. winnt32.exe /cmdcons
- ❑ D. console.exe
- ❑ E. winnt32.exe /console

89. After it has been installed, how do you run the Recovery Console in Microsoft Windows XP?

Quick Answer: 144
Detailed Answer: 152

- ❑ A. From the Please Select Operating System to Start menu during bootup
- ❑ B. From the Add/Remove Programs menu
- ❑ C. From the Administrative Tools menu
- ❑ D. From the Hardware Profiles menu during bootup

90. When starting the Recovery Console in Microsoft Windows XP, who must you log on as?

Quick Answer: 144
Detailed Answer: 153

- ❑ A. Administrator
- ❑ B. Power User
- ❑ C. User
- ❑ D. Server operator

91. Which option is needed during Microsoft Windows XP Setup to run the Recovery Console?

Quick Answer: 144
Detailed Answer: 153

- ❑ A. Repair
- ❑ B. Recover
- ❑ C. Replace
- ❑ D. Recovery

92. What feature of Microsoft Windows XP enables you to boot to a DOS prompt even when your hard disk is formatted with NTFS?

Quick Answer: 144
Detailed Answer: 153

- ❑ A. Disk Management
- ❑ B. Recovery Console
- ❑ C. Administrative Tools
- ❑ D. Restore Points

93. What feature of Microsoft Windows XP gathers information from your PC and then uploads data to a server to assist support providers in troubleshooting hardware and software issues?

    - ❑ A. Windows Report Tool
    - ❑ B. Recovery Console
    - ❑ C. Administrative Tools
    - ❑ D. Restore Points

Quick Answer: 144
Detailed Answer: 153

94. What file formats does the Windows Report Tool use to gather information from your PC and then upload data to a support provider server?

    - ❑ A. .CAB and .NFO
    - ❑ B. .COM and .SYS
    - ❑ C. .CAB and .SYS
    - ❑ D. .ZIP and .NFO

Quick Answer: 144
Detailed Answer: 153

95. What are the snapshots of critical system files and Registry settings you should take before making major changes to a Microsoft Windows XP PC called?

    - ❑ A. System Restore Points
    - ❑ B. System Points
    - ❑ C. System Snapshots
    - ❑ D. XPPoints
    - ❑ E. Recovery Console Points

Quick Answer: 144
Detailed Answer: 153

96. What percentage of disk space is allocated from each hard disk drive by default for System Restore Points in Microsoft Windows XP?

    - ❑ A. 12%
    - ❑ B. 10%
    - ❑ C. 8%
    - ❑ D. 16%
    - ❑ E. 32%

Quick Answer: 144
Detailed Answer: 153

Quick Check

97. What is true of System Restore Points in Microsoft Windows XP? (Select all that apply.)

- ❑ A. They are allocated 12% of each hard disk drive by default.
- ❑ B. They must be enabled to be used properly.
- ❑ C. A default restore point is created the first time System Restore is enabled.
- ❑ D. Right-click My Computer, select Properties, choose System Restore tab, and check the displayed check box.
- ❑ E. Right-click My Computer, select Properties, choose System Restore tab, and uncheck the displayed check box.

Quick Answer: **144**
Detailed Answer: **153**

98. What is true of System Restore Points in Microsoft Windows XP?

- ❑ A. They must be enabled while installing a program to be used properly.
- ❑ B. They must be enabled before installing a program to be used properly.
- ❑ C. They must be enabled after installing a program to be used properly.
- ❑ D. Right-click My Computer, select Properties, choose System Restore tab, and check the displayed check box.

Quick Answer: **144**
Detailed Answer: **153**

99. How would you roll back to a System Restore Point in Microsoft Windows XP?

- ❑ A. Start, Programs, Accessories, Systems Tools, System Restore
- ❑ B. Start, Programs, Accessories, Systems Tools, System Restore, Restore My Computer to an Earlier Time
- ❑ C. Start, Programs, Accessories, System Restore, Restore My Computer to an Earlier Time
- ❑ D. Start, Programs, Systems Tools, System Restore, Restore My Computer to an Earlier Time
- ❑ E. Start, Programs, Accessories, Systems Tools, System Restore, Restore My Computer

Quick Answer: **144**
Detailed Answer: **153**

100. What System Restore Point Registry setting in Microsoft Windows XP enables you to specify the amount of time an idle computer waits until it begins compressing restore point data in the background?

- ❑ A. CompressionBurst
- ❑ B. DiskPercent
- ❑ C. DSMax
- ❑ D. DSMin
- ❑ E. RestoreStatus

Quick Answer: **144**
Detailed Answer: **154**

Quick Check

101. What System Restore Point Registry setting in Microsoft Windows XP enables you to specify the percentage of disk space used for restore points, but cannot exceed the DSMax setting?

- ❑ A. CompressionBurst
- ❑ B. DiskPercent
- ❑ C. RPLifeInterval
- ❑ D. RPSessionInterval
- ❑ E. ThawInterval

Quick Answer: 144
Detailed Answer: 154

102. What System Restore Point Registry setting in Microsoft Windows XP enables you to specify the maximum amount of disk space that System Restore can use?

- ❑ A. RPSessionInterval
- ❑ B. ThawInterval
- ❑ C. DSMax
- ❑ D. RPGlobalInterval
- ❑ E. RPLifeInterval

Quick Answer: 144
Detailed Answer: 154

103. What System Restore Point Registry setting in Microsoft Windows XP enables you to specify the minimum amount of disk space that System Restore can use?

- ❑ A. CompressionBurst
- ❑ B. RPGlobalInterval
- ❑ C. DSMax
- ❑ D. DSMin
- ❑ E. RPLifeInterval
- ❑ F. RPSessionInterval

Quick Answer: 144
Detailed Answer: 154

104. What System Restore Point Registry setting in Microsoft Windows XP enables you to specify whether the last restore operation failed, succeeded, or was interrupted?

- ❑ A. RestoreStatus
- ❑ B. RPGlobalInterval
- ❑ C. RPLifeInterval
- ❑ D. RPSessionInterval
- ❑ E. ThawInterval

Quick Answer: 144
Detailed Answer: 154

Quick Check

105. What System Restore Point Registry setting in Microsoft Windows XP enables you to specify the time in seconds before creating an automatic restore point?

- ❑ A. CompressionBurst
- ❑ B. RPGlobalInterval
- ❑ C. RPLifeInterval
- ❑ D. RPSessionInterval

Quick Answer: 144
Detailed Answer: 154

106. What System Restore Point Registry setting in Microsoft Windows XP enables you to specify the time to live (TTL) seconds for restore points?

- ❑ A. RPGlobalInterval
- ❑ B. RPLifeInterval
- ❑ C. RPSessionInterval
- ❑ D. ThawInterval

Quick Answer: 144
Detailed Answer: 154

107. What System Restore Point Registry setting in Microsoft Windows XP enables you to specify the time in seconds before creating a restore point while the system is running?

- ❑ A. RestoreStatus
- ❑ B. RPGlobalInterval
- ❑ C. RPSessionInterval
- ❑ D. ThawInterval

Quick Answer: 144
Detailed Answer: 154

108. What System Restore Point Registry setting in Microsoft Windows XP enables you to specify the time in seconds that System Restore waits before waking itself from a disabled state?

- ❑ A. CompressionBurst
- ❑ B. DiskPercent
- ❑ C. DSMax
- ❑ D. DSMin
- ❑ E. ThawInterval

Quick Answer: 144
Detailed Answer: 154

109. What is the name of the new feature in Microsoft Windows XP that enables you to create an image of your system partition and burn it to a CD or write it to tape?

- ❑ A. System Restore Points
- ❑ B. Active Directory for Windows XP Recovery Wizard
- ❑ C. Recovery Console
- ❑ D. Automated System Recovery

Quick Answer: 144
Detailed Answer: 155

Quick Check

110. What is the name of the command-line tool in Microsoft Windows XP that enables you to create an image of your system partition and burn it to a CD or write it to tape?

- ❑ A. sysrestore
- ❑ B. imagexp
- ❑ C. rcon
- ❑ D. ntbackup
- ❑ E. rdisk

Quick Answer: **144**
Detailed Answer: **155**

111. What is the name of the command-line tool in Microsoft Windows XP that must be run to initiate the Automated System Recovery Wizard option?

- ❑ A. asr
- ❑ B. asrwizard
- ❑ C. console
- ❑ D. ntbackup

Quick Answer: **144**
Detailed Answer: **155**

112. You're the desktop administrator for your company. All employees have Windows XP Professional computers. Twenty programmers at the company use laptops. A programmer named Tom wants to install an external parallel port tape backup drive in order to use the removable storage features of Windows XP Professional. The tape drive is listed on the Hardware Compatibility List (HCL). Tom connects the tape drive to his laptop and then installs the manufacturer's software and drivers. When Tom attempts to create a media library for removable storage, the tape drive is not listed as an available library to select.

You need to give Tom the ability to install the driver for the tape drive. What should you do?

- ❑ A. Add Tom to the local Backup Operator group on his laptop.
- ❑ B. Run the Sigverif utility to verify the digital signature information for the print device driver.
- ❑ C. Disable EPP support in the system BIOS on Tom's laptop.
- ❑ D. Ensure that the driver signing options are set to Warn-Prompt me each time to choose an action.

Quick Answer: **144**
Detailed Answer: **155**

Quick Check

113. You're the desktop administrator for your company. All employees had used Windows 2000 Professional on their computers. You upgraded all computers to Windows XP Professional, and users experienced no problems after the upgrade was complete. A new employee has been issued a new client computer that is identical to all other client computers in the company. The new employee installs Windows XP Professional on this computer from a network server installation point. The new employee now reports that he cannot change his display settings from 640×480 screen resolution with only 16 colors.

You confirm that this computer has the same video hardware as all other clients. You also confirm that the hardware manufacturer does not have a video driver for Windows XP Professional. You need to enable the user to change his display settings to higher resolution and color quality. What should you do?

- ❑ A. Reboot the computer in Safe mode and select the standard VGA video driver.
- ❑ B. Install the older Windows 2000 Professional video drivers on the computer.
- ❑ C. In the Advanced Display settings on the Monitor tab, specify the correct driver for the monitor.
- ❑ D. In the Advanced Display settings on the Color Management tab, specify the appropriate color profile for the monitor.

Quick Answer: 144
Detailed Answer: 155

114. You're a desktop administrator for MovieTime Industries. You recently installed Windows XP Professional on a laptop that meets the minimum installation requirements for the operating system. After the install, you try to configure hibernation, but the option is unavailable. To be sure that the option becomes available, you update the BIOS on the laptop. After the BIOS update, the computer displays a STOP error every time you try to reboot the laptop.

You need to start the computer and enable hibernation. What should you do?

- ❑ A. Use the Recovery Console to add the correct Advanced Configuration and Power Interface (ACPI) HAL to the computer.
- ❑ B. Use the System Restore feature to restore the last restore point.
- ❑ C. Restart the computer with the last known good configuration.
- ❑ D. Reinstall Windows XP Professional to enable ACPI and power management support.

Quick Answer: 144
Detailed Answer: 155

115. You're a desktop administrator for the sales department at your company. All employees have Windows XP Professional laptops. Sales department users require dial-in access to the company network when they travel to customer locations. The same users also need to fax documents to customers from their laptops. You need to set up network dial-up access immediately for a user named Andrea.

You insert a 56Kbps PCMCIA fax modem card into Andrea's laptop. You restart the laptop and log on as a local administrator. After starting the Network Connection Wizard, the modem does not appear in the list of devices that you can select for a dial-up connection. You need to be able to install Andrea's modem. What should you do?

- ❑ A. Decrease the maximum port speed on the modem's COM port to 57600.
- ❑ B. Use the Add or Remove Windows Components Wizard to install the Fax service.
- ❑ C. Manually install the modem device driver provided by the manufacturer.
- ❑ D. Disable the laptop's built-in serial ports.

Quick Answer: **144**
Detailed Answer: **155**

116. You're the desktop administrator for your company. All employees use Windows XP Professional computers. An employee named Alex is issued a laptop. He successfully installs his printer and scanner hardware. A month later, Alex installs an updated printer driver. When he restarts his laptop, he receives this error message:

```
STOP.IRQL_NOT_LESS_OR_EQUAL
```

Alex restarts the laptop again, and he receives the same error message.

You need to ensure that Alex can successfully start Windows XP Professional. What should you do?

- ❑ A. Restart Alex's laptop in Safe mode. Log on as a local administrator and set the driver signing options to Ignore-Install the Software Anyway and Do Not Ask for My Approval.
- ❑ B. Restart Alex's laptop with the last known good configuration.
- ❑ C. Restart Alex's laptop in Safe mode. Create a local computer policy to enable Windows File Protection.
- ❑ D. Restart Alex's laptop in Recovery Console. Enable the new printer driver with the Service_system_start parameter.

Quick Answer: **144**
Detailed Answer: **155**

Quick Check

117. You're the desktop administrator for your company. A graphics designer name Mario installs a new application as well as an updated video driver on his Windows XP Professional computer. After the install, Mario restarts his computer and logs on. However, when he moves windows and dialog boxes, the display becomes distorted.

You need to find the correct video driver for the new application. You also need to be sure that Mario can run other applications without video distortion. What should you do?

- ❑ A. Use the Add/Remove Hardware Wizard to scan for new hardware and install any found hardware.
- ❑ B. Restart the computer with the last known good configuration.
- ❑ C. Run the Msconfig utility, and select the /BASEVIDEO check box.
- ❑ D. Use Device Manager to roll back the video driver.

Quick Answer: 144
Detailed Answer: 155

118. You're a help desk administrator for your company. You're configuring Microsoft Windows XP Professional on all the laptops in the sales department. Users in this department bring their laptops from their offices to the board room for a biweekly sales meeting.

Users need an easy way to put their laptops into a low-power state without using the Start button. They also need their laptops to restart as quickly as possible. You need to configure the power options on the laptops to meet these requirements. What should you do?

- ❑ A. Configure the laptops to enable standby when the lid is closed.
- ❑ B. Configure the power button on each laptop to enable hibernation.
- ❑ C. Configure all the laptops to use the Portable/Laptop power scheme.
- ❑ D. Configure the Critical Battery alarm on the laptops to hibernate when battery charge capacity drops to 10%.

Quick Answer: 144
Detailed Answer: 155

Quick Check

119. You're the desktop administrator for your company. All employees have Microsoft Windows XP Professional laptops. A salesperson named Robert has a local user account on his laptop. He is given a portable USB print device for his needs. You log on to his laptop and disable the restrictions on loading unsigned drivers. All other local computer policies are configured with the default settings. You restart Robert's computer. Robert connects the USB print device, but the printer does not appear inside the Printers folder and Robert cannot print any documents.

You need to be sure that Robert can install the printer and be able to print successfully. What should you do?

- ❑ A. Add the /fastdetect switch in the Boot.ini file on Robert's laptop.
- ❑ B. Add Robert to the local Print Operators group on his laptop.
- ❑ C. Modify the driver signing options on Robert's laptop, selecting the Make This Action the System Default check box.
- ❑ D. Disable the Prevent Users from Installing Printer Drivers local security policy setting.

Quick Answer: **144**
Detailed Answer: **156**

120. You're a desktop administrator for your organization. All users have Windows XP Professional computers. Users in the sales department have laptops. The laptops are used to create visual presentations and enter online orders. Sales representatives want to be able to use large external monitors to display their presentations at customer sites. These users also want to use the displays on the laptops to show their speaker notes and any additional data nearby. You confirm that the video adapters in the laptops support multiple monitor and dual-view capabilities. The sales representatives now state that when they connect the external monitors to their laptops, there is no option to define separate desktop displays in the display settings.

You need to have the sales representatives be able to display multiple desktops. What should you do?

- ❑ A. Create a monitor hardware profile on the sales representatives' laptops for the external monitors at the customer sites.
- ❑ B. Have the sales representatives disable all hardware video acceleration during their presentations.
- ❑ C. Configure the monitors on the sales representatives' laptops to use the Presentation power scheme.
- ❑ D. Install an updated driver from the video adapter's manufacturer.

Quick Answer: **144**
Detailed Answer: **156**

Quick Check

121. You're a desktop administrator for your company. All employees use Windows XP Professional computers. Employees in the research department use both desktop and laptop computers. All computers in the research department have four-port USB hubs attached. One user in the research department connects a portable USB hard disk to the USB hub attached to his laptop. However, the port on the USB hub shuts down and the hard disk does not function. The user experiences no problem when he attaches the same hard disk to his desktop computer's USB hub. A USB mouse and keyboard function normally when connected to the portable computer's USB hub. When the user attaches the hard disk directly to the USB port on his laptop, the device functions normally.

Quick Answer: 144
Detailed Answer: 156

You need to be sure that the USB hub on the user's laptop can use the USB hard disk. What should you do?

- ❑ A. Replace the portable hard disk's USB cable with a shorter USB cable.
- ❑ B. Enable the Assign IRQ to USB option in the computer's system BIOS.
- ❑ C. Disable all USB power management features for the USB root hub.
- ❑ D. Replace the portable computer's bus-powered USB hub with a self-powered USB hub.

122. You're a desktop administrator for your company. You install a new printer on your Microsoft Windows XP Professional computer. You share this printer with several users in your department. When you attempt to print to this printer, the output is several pages of unrecognizable characters. Other users complain of similar output.

Quick Answer: 144
Detailed Answer: 156

You need to be sure that the appropriate users can successfully print to this printer. What should you do?

- ❑ A. Run the Add Printer Driver Wizard to install the correct printer driver on your computer. Tell all the other users to disconnect and then reconnect to your shared printer.
- ❑ B. Configure the printer to print directly to the print device. Tell all the other users to make the same configuration.
- ❑ C. Configure the printer to use RAW as the default data type.
- ❑ D. Configure the printer to hold mismatched documents. Disable the advanced printing features.

123. You're a help desk technician for your company, which includes a main office and one branch office. All employees in the main office have Microsoft Windows XP Professional computers. All employees in the branch office have Microsoft Windows NT 4.0 Workstations.

Users in the branch office require access to a network printer shared on a Windows XP Professional computer in the main office. Branch office users access this printer by using their Web browser software, and cannot install the printer on their own computers. Branch office users complain that they are prompted to insert a manufacturer's disk whenever they try to use the printer by connecting to the company intranet Web site. Users in the main office have no problems using the printer.

You need to make the printer available to all the Branch office users. What should you do?

- ❑ A. Enable the basic authentication method on the Printers intranet site.
- ❑ B. Install the Windows NT 4.0 Workstation printer drivers on the Windows XP Professional print server in the main office.
- ❑ C. Enable support for ActiveX controls on the branch office computers.
- ❑ D. Disable the advanced printing features on the Windows XP Professional print server.

Quick Answer: **144**
Detailed Answer: **156**

124. You are the desktop administrator for MovieTime Productions. A user named Mary installs the Fax service with default options on her Microsoft Windows XP Professional computer. Her computer is currently configured to use an internal fax modem. Mary now states that she can send faxes properly from her computer. Mary complains, however, that her computer's fax monitor never answers any incoming calls.

How should you correct this problem?

- ❑ A. Reinstall the Fax service, selecting the option to receive faxes.
- ❑ B. Restart Mary's computer.
- ❑ C. Use the Fax console to redirect faxes to the My Faxes folder.
- ❑ D. Use the Fax Configuration Wizard to enable the fax modem to receive incoming faxes.

Quick Answer: **144**
Detailed Answer: **156**

Quick Check

125. You're a desktop administrator for your company. You install a new driver for the network adapter card on your Microsoft Windows XP Professional computer. When you restart the computer, the monitor displays a STOP error with no text before you are able to log on. Every time you restart the computer, a STOP error halts the start process.

You need to correct the error without affecting the user data on the computer. You also need to restore the original network adapter driver. What should you do?

- ❑ A. Restart the computer by using a Windows XP Professional CD, and select the option to perform an Automated System Recovery (ASR) restore when prompted.
- ❑ B. Restart the computer by using the Recovery Console, and stop the Network Connections service.
- ☑ C. Restart the computer with the last known good configuration.
- ❑ D. Restart the computer by using a Windows XP Professional bootable floppy disk and disable the network adapter. Restart the client computer and enable the network adapter.

Quick Answer: **144**
Detailed Answer: **156**

126. You're a desktop administrator for your company. All employees use Microsoft Windows XP Professional computers. Users in the sales department have laptop computers. Each of these users also has a portable USB hard disk and a company-issued digital camera. You install these devices on the laptops by using built-in Windows XP Professional drivers. One particular user installs an updated camera driver that he downloaded from the manufacturer, and then restarts his laptop. After the installation, he receives an error message indicating that a service or driver failed to start. When he logs on to his laptop, he discovers that he can no longer access his digital camera.

How should you correct this problem?

- ❑ A. Restart the user's laptop in Safe mode. In Device Manager, in the digital camera's properties, select the Roll Back Driver option.
- ☑ B. Restart the user's laptop with the last known good configuration.
- ❑ C. Restart the user's laptop in Safe mode. Log on as the local administrator. Set the driver signing options to Warn-Prompt Me Each Time to Choose an Action.
- ❑ D. Restart the user's laptop in the Recovery Console. Enable the new digital camera driver with the Service_system_auto parameter.

Quick Answer: **144**
Detailed Answer: **156**

127. You're a desktop administrator for your company. Your Microsoft Windows XP Professional computer is configured to use an external fax modem. The fax modem is set up to both send and receive faxes. You then install a new application that requires the computer to be restarted. After the computer restarts, you can no longer send and receive faxes. When you open the Fax console, you notice that options to send and receive faxes are now unavailable.

You need to reconfigure your computer to again be able to send and receive faxes. What should you do?

- ❑ A. Turn the fax modem off and then on again.
- ❑ B. Use the Fax Configuration Wizard to configure the fax modem to send and receive faxes.
- ❑ C. Configure the Fax service to start automatically, and then start the fax server.
- ❑ D. Log on as a local administrator and grant your user account the Allow, Full Control Permission on the fax printer driver.

Quick Answer: **144**
Detailed Answer: **156**

128. You're the desktop support technician for WorldCo Travel. Each day, a user named Kelly successfully faxes travel itineraries from her Microsoft Windows XP Professional computer. Kelly's computer is configured to use an external fax device. The fax device is configured to receive faxes, but the fax monitor apparently never answers any incoming calls.

You need to configure Kelly's computer to receive faxes. What should you do?

- ❑ A. Turn the external fax device off and then on again.
- ❑ B. Restart Kelly's computer.
- ❑ C. Configure the fax device to automatically answer incoming fax calls after the first ring.
- ❑ D. Use the fax monitor to manually answer the incoming fax.

Quick Answer: **144**
Detailed Answer: **156**

Quick Check

129. You're a desktop administrator for your company. The company's network consists of one Active Directory domain. All client computers run Microsoft Windows XP Professional. All client computers are Advanced Configuration and Power Interface (ACPI) compliant and use the Windows XP Professional power management features. You receive a flash BIOS update from the manufacturer of all the client computers. You update the BIOS on your own computer first. The BIOS seems to update correctly. When the computer restarts, however, you receive a STOP error message with some type of HAL mismatch.

Quick Answer: 144
Detailed Answer: 156

You manually restart the computer and receive the very same error message. You need to be able to fix your computer as fast as possible. What should you do?

- ❑ A. Restart the computer. Enter the BIOS setup, and re-enable ACPI power management support.
- ❑ B. Restart the computer by using the Recovery Console, and then copy the ACPI Hal.dll file from the original Microsoft Windows XP Professional CD-ROM to your computer.
- ❑ C. Restart the computer by using the last known good configuration.
- ❑ D. Restart the computer by using the original Microsoft Windows XP Professional CD-ROM, and then select the option to repair the installation.

Quick Check Answer Key

1. A, B, and C
2. A, B, and C
3. A, B, C, and D
4. A, B
5. A
6. A
7. B
8. C
9. D
10. E
11. B
12. A, B
13. A
14. B
15. C, D
16. C
17. D
18. A
19. B
20. B
21. A
22. B
23. C
24. D
25. E
26. A
27. D
28. C
29. A
30. C
31. D
32. D
33. D
34. D
35. A, C, and D
36. A, C, and D
37. A, B, and C
38. A, B, C, D, E, F, and G
39. A
40. B
41. C
42. D
43. E
44. B
45. D
46. A
47. B
48. C
49. D
50. E
51. E
52. A
53. C
54. D
55. A
56. B
57. D
58. A
59. C
60. C
61. D
62. D
63. C
64. B
65. B
66. C
67. D
68. D
69. A
70. B
71. C
72. D
73. C
74. B
75. A
76. D
77. C
78. C
79. B
80. B
81. A

Quick-Check Answer Key

82. A
83. C
84. D
85. A
86. B
87. C
88. C
89. A
90. A
91. A
92. B
93. A
94. A
95. A
96. A
97. A, B, C, and E
98. B
99. B
100. A
101. B
102. C
103. D
104. A
105. B
106. B
107. C
108. E
109. D
110. D
111. D
112. A
113. B
114. D
115. C
116. B
117. D
118. A
119. C
120. D
121. D
122. A
123. B
124. D
125. C
126. A
127. B
128. C
129. D

Answers and Explanations

1. **Answers: A, B, and C.**

   Explanation A. You can install a new display adapter in Microsoft Windows XP in Device Manager under Display Adapters.

   Explanation B. You can remove a display adapter in Microsoft Windows XP in Device Manager under Display Adapters.

   Explanation C. You can update drivers for a display adapter in Microsoft Windows XP in Device Manager under Display Adapters.

2. **Answers: A, B, and C.**

   Explanation A. You can install a new monitor in Microsoft Windows XP in Device Manager under Monitors.

   Explanation B. You can remove a monitor in Microsoft Windows XP in Device Manager under Monitors.

   Explanation C. You can update drivers for a monitor in Microsoft Windows XP in Device Manager under Monitors.

3. **Answers: A, B, C, and D.**

   Explanation A. PCMCIA (Personal Computer Memory Card International Association) cards are supported in Microsoft Windows XP for laptops.

   Explanation B. USB (universal serial bus) devices are supported in Microsoft Windows XP for laptops.

   Explanation C. The IEEE (Institute of Electrical and Electronics Engineers) standard 1394, also known as FireWire, is supported in Microsoft Windows XP for laptops.

   Explanation D. Infrared devices are supported in Microsoft Windows XP for laptops.

4. **Answers: A and B.**

   Explanation A. ACPI (advanced configuration and power interface) is supported in Microsoft Windows XP for laptops. ACPI allows the operating system to control the amount of power given to each peripheral. For example, a CD-ROM can be turned off when it is not in use.

   Explanation B. APM (advanced power management) is supported in Microsoft Windows XP for laptops. APM enables software developers to manipulate power management settings in a computer's BIOS (basic input/output system). APM can therefore help with controlling the display, keyboard, disk drives, and other devices.

5. **Answer: A.** You should create a new hardware profile to help conserve battery power. Use Device Manager to disable any unneeded devices, like modems or network adapter PCMCIA cards.

6. **Answer: A.** Constant power is maintained when plugged in or while running on batteries.

7. **Answer: B.** Constant power is maintained when plugged in.

8. **Answer: C.** Constant power is maintained when plugged in, but the system powers down within 1 minute of inactivity if running on batteries.

9. **Answer: D.** Constant power is maintained when plugged in, but the system powers down within 15 minutes of inactivity if running on batteries.

10. **Answer: E.** Everything shuts down within 30 minutes of inactivity when plugged in. Everything shuts down faster if running on batteries.

11. **Answer: B.** The monitor is always on, whether plugged in or running on batteries. The rest of the system is kept active while plugged in.

12. **Answers: A and B.**

    Explanation A. The Low Battery alarm is the first of the two alarms you will hear. It indicates that your batteries are getting low.

    Explanation B. The Critical Battery alarm is the second of the two alarms you will hear. It indicates your batteries are extremely low.

13. **Answer: A.** The Low Battery alarm is the first of the two alarms you will hear. It indicates your batteries are getting low.

14. **Answer: B.** The Critical Battery alarm is the second of the two alarms you will hear. It indicates your batteries are extremely low.

15. **Answers: C and D.**

    Explanation C. Standby is one of the two types of Advanced Power Options settings that can be configured in Microsoft Windows XP. Standby is the low power state that runs your computer using just minimal power.

    Explanation D. Hibernate is one of the two types of Advanced Power Options settings that can be configured in Microsoft Windows XP. Standby is the low power state that copies the contents of RAM, and therefore the entire current desktop, onto a hard drive. Then the computer is powered down. The next time you restart the computer, the desktop state is restored.

16. **Answer: C.** Standby is one of the two types of Advanced Power Options settings that can be configured in Microsoft Windows XP. Standby is the low power state that runs your computer using minimal power.

17. **Answer: D.** Hibernate is one of the two types of Advanced Power Options settings that can be configured in Microsoft Windows XP. Standby is the low power state that copies the contents of RAM, and therefore the entire current desktop, onto a hard drive. Then the computer is powered down. The next time you restart the computer, the desktop state is restored.
18. **Answer: A.** Keyboards are installed in Device Manager under Keyboards.
19. **Answer: B.** Mice, writing graphic tablets, and other pointing devices are installed in Device Manager under Mice and Other Pointing Devices.
20. **Answer: B.** Graphic tablets, mice, and other pointing devices are installed in Device Manager under Mice and Other Pointing Devices.
21. **Answer: A.** The sfc.exe /scannow command scans all protected system files immediately in Microsoft Windows XP.
22. **Answer: B.** The sfc.exe /scanonce command scans all protected system files at the very next reboot in Microsoft Windows XP.
23. **Answer: C.** The sfc.exe /scanboot command scans all protected system files at every reboot in Microsoft Windows XP.
24. **Answer: D.** The sfc.exe /cancel command cancels all pending scans of protected system files in Microsoft Windows XP.
25. **Answer: E.** The sfc.exe /quiet command replaces incorrect system files without prompting in Microsoft Windows XP.
26. **Answer: A.** The scf.exe /enable command sets system file protection back to default in Microsoft Windows XP.
27. **Answer: D.** The sfc.exe /purgecache command purges the file cache and then immediately rescans protected system files in Microsoft Windows XP.
28. **Answer: C.** The sfc.exe /cachesize=x command sets the file cache size for protected system files in Microsoft Windows XP.
29. **Answer: A.** A driver is a program that controls a device. Every device, whether it is a printer, disk drive, or keyboard, must have a driver program. Many drivers, such as the keyboard driver, come with the operating system. For other devices, you might need to load a new driver when you connect the device to your computer.
30. **Answer: C.** The Block option for configuring driver signing would halt the installation of all driver files. This would be a solution to the problem of end users connecting their own digital cameras to their work computers.
31. **Answer: D.** The Block option for configuring driver signing would stop the installation of any driver files. This would be a solution to the problem of end users connecting devices to their work computers.

32. **Answer: D.** The Driver.cab cabinet file on a Microsoft Windows XP CD contains all the original Microsoft Windows XP driver files.

33. **Answer: D.** The Verifier.exe command-line utility verifies all of a computer's digitally signed Microsoft Windows XP driver files.

34. **Answer: D.** The Driver Rollback feature in Microsoft Windows XP enables you to revert back to an older version of a driver that worked before any new driver you just tried to install failed.

35. **Answers: A, C, and D.**

    Explanation A. Allow the operating system to try to adjust itself automatically when installing new hardware. If you manually change a hardware setting, you could compound the problem.

    Explanation C. Microsoft Windows XP is capable of sharing resources (such as IRQs—interrupt requests) among several different hardware devices. This is normal on any given computer.

    Explanation D. You should avoid using the Registry Editor (regedit.exe command) except as a last resort to correct hardware conflicts.

36. **Answers: A, C, and D.**

    Explanation A. Microsoft Windows XP Professional can support up to two CPUs (central processing units).

    Explanation C. Adding a CPU to your system is actually called scaling.

    Explanation D. Microsoft Windows XP Professional supports SMP (symmetric multiprocessing), a computer architecture that provides fast performance by making multiple CPUs available to complete individual processes simultaneously.

37. **Answers: A, B, and C.**

    Explanation A. Network Adapters are installed using Add/Remove Hardware in Control Panel in Microsoft Windows XP.

    Explanation B. Each network adapter has its own icon under the Network and Dial-up Connection icon in Microsoft Windows XP.

    Explanation C. Network adapters in the same computer do not need to be identical in Microsoft Windows XP.

38. **Answers: A, B, C, D, E, F, and G.**

    Explanation A. The Boot.ini file is one of seven files that are used in the Microsoft Windows XP boot process. It is located in the system partition root, normally the C: drive.

Explanation B. The Bootsect.dos file is one of seven files that are used in the Microsoft Windows XP boot process. It is located in the system partition root, normally the C: drive.

Explanation C. The Hal.dll file is one of seven files that are used in the Microsoft Windows XP boot process. It is located in the %systemroot%\system32 subfolder.

Explanation D. The Ntdetect.com file is one of seven files that are used in the Microsoft Windows XP boot process. It is located in the system partition root, normally the C: drive.

Explanation E. The Ntldr file is one of seven files that are used in the Microsoft Windows XP boot process. It is located in the system partition root, normally the C: drive.

Explanation F. The Ntoskrnl.exe file is one of seven files that are used in the Microsoft Windows XP boot process. It is located in the %systemroot%\system32 subfolder.

Explanation G. The System file is one of seven files that are used in the Microsoft Windows XP boot process. It is located in the %systemroot%\system32\config subfolder.

39. **Answer: A.** The /basevideo switch of Boot.ini will boot a Microsoft Windows XP computer using a standard VGA driver.

40. **Answer: B.** The /noguiboot switch of Boot.ini will boot a Microsoft Windows XP computer without displaying the graphical startup screen.

41. **Answer: C.** The /sos switch of Boot.ini will display the device driver names of a Microsoft Windows XP computer as they are loaded.

42. **Answer: D.** The /bootlog switch of Boot.ini will enable boot logging on a Microsoft Windows XP computer. The resulting log file is created in text format, and is useful in troubleshooting the boot process to determine where a system boot process halted.

43. **Answer: E.** The /safeboot:minimal switch of Boot.ini boots a Microsoft Windows XP computer into Safe mode.

44. **Answer: B.** The /safeboot:network switch of Boot.ini will boot a Microsoft Windows XP computer into Safe mode with networking support. This means that network adapter driver files are loaded in Safe mode as well.

45. **Answer: D.** The term ARC stands for Advanced RISC (reduced instruction set computer) Computing. The ARC path is located in the Boot.ini file of a Microsoft Windows XP computer. The ARC path determines from which partition on which hard drive a computer will boot.

46. **Answer: A.** The multi(x) ARC path parameter located in the Boot.ini file of a Microsoft Windows XP computer specifies a non-SCSI hard disk controller or SCSI hard disk controller with the BIOS enabled.

47. **Answer: B.** The scsi(x) ARC path parameter located in the Boot.ini file of a Microsoft Windows XP computer specifies a SCSI hard disk controller with the BIOS enabled.

48. **Answer: C.** The disk(x) ARC path parameter located in the Boot.ini file of a Microsoft Windows XP computer specifies the SCSI disk that the operating system resides on. When multi(x) is also used in the ARC path, the x will always be 0 in the disk(0) parameter.

49. **Answer: D.** The rdisk(x) ARC path parameter located in the Boot.ini file of a Microsoft Windows XP computer specifies the EIDE disk that the operating system resides on. Note that rdisk(0) should be specified in the ARC path when used with a SCSI hard drive system.

50. **Answer: E.** The partition(x) ARC path parameter located in the Boot.ini file of a Microsoft Windows XP computer specifies the partition that the operating system resides on.

51. **Answer: E.** The F8 function key should be pressed while booting a Microsoft Windows XP computer in order to enter Safe mode.

52. **Answer: A.** The Microsoft Windows XP Recovery Console attrib command changes attributes of a selected file.

53. **Answer: C.** The Microsoft Windows XP Recovery Console bootcfg command adds, edits, or removes items from the boot.ini file.

54. **Answer: D.** The Microsoft Windows XP Recovery Console cd command changes the current directory or displays the current directory.

55. **Answer: A.** The Microsoft Windows XP Recovery Console chdir command changes the current directory or displays the current directory.

56. **Answer: B.** The Microsoft Windows XP Recovery Console chkdsk command runs CheckDisk to check your computer's hard drives.

57. **Answer: D.** The Microsoft Windows XP Recovery Console cls command clears the screen.

58. **Answer: A.** The Microsoft Windows XP Recovery Console copy command copies files from removable media to your hard disk.

59. **Answer: C.** The Microsoft Windows XP Recovery Console del command deletes a file, folder, or service.

60. **Answer: C.** The Microsoft Windows XP Recovery Console delete command deletes a file, folder, or service.

61. **Answer: D.** The Microsoft Windows XP Recovery Console dir command lists the contents of the currently selected directory on the system partition only.

62. **Answer: D.** The Microsoft Windows XP Recovery Console disable command disables a driver or service.

63. **Answer: C.** The Microsoft Windows XP Recovery Console diskpart command has the same effect as FDISK and creates or deletes partitions.

64. **Answer: B.** The Microsoft Windows XP Recovery Console enable command enables a driver or service.

65. **Answer: B.** The Microsoft Windows XP Recovery Console expand command extracts a file or driver from a .CAB (cabinet) or compressed file.

66. **Answer: C.** The Microsoft Windows XP Recovery Console fixboot command writes a new partition boot sector on the system partition only.

67. **Answer: D.** The Microsoft Windows XP Recovery Console fixmbr command writes a new MBR (master boot record) for the partition boot sector on the system partition only.

68. **Answer: D.** The Microsoft Windows XP Recovery Console format command formats the selected disk.

69. **Answer: A.** The Microsoft Windows XP Recovery Console help command provides online help information about all the Recovery Console commands.

70. **Answer: B.** The Microsoft Windows XP Recovery Console listsrv command lists all the services running on a Microsoft Windows XP computer.

71. **Answer: C.** The Microsoft Windows XP Recovery Console logon command enables the user to choose which Microsoft Windows XP installation to log on to, if you have more than one.

72. **Answer: D.** The Microsoft Windows XP Recovery Console map command displays the current drive letter mappings.

73. **Answer: C.** The Microsoft Windows XP Recovery Console md command creates a directory.

74. **Answer: B.** The Microsoft Windows XP Recovery Console mkdir command creates a directory.

75. **Answer: A.** The Microsoft Windows XP Recovery Console more command displays the contents of a text file.

76. **Answer: D.** The Microsoft Windows XP Recovery Console type command displays the contents of a text file.

77. **Answer: C.** The Microsoft Windows XP Recovery Console net use command connects a network share to a drive letter.

78. **Answer: C.** The Microsoft Windows XP Recovery Console rd command removes a directory.

79. **Answer: B.** The Microsoft Windows XP Recovery Console rmdir command removes a directory.

80. **Answer: B.** The Microsoft Windows XP Recovery Console ren command renames a single file.

81. **Answer: A.** The Microsoft Windows XP Recovery Console rename command renames a single file.

82. **Answer: A.** The Microsoft Windows XP Recovery Console systemroot command will make the current directory the system root of the drive you are logged in to.

83. **Answer: C.** The Microsoft Windows XP Startup and Recovery settings are accessed through Start, Settings, Control Panel, System, Advanced tab, Startup and Recovery. You can adjust the size and location of the paging file, as well as specify a small or large memory dump.

84. **Answer: D.** To properly use the Write Debugging Information option of Startup and Recovery settings in Microsoft Windows XP, the paging file on the system partition must be at least 1MB larger than the amount of RAM installed on the system.

85. **Answer: A.** A small memory dump in Microsoft Windows XP needs only 64KB of space. The small memory dump can be found in %systemroot%\minidump.

86. **Answer: B.** The name of the memory dump file in Microsoft Windows XP is memory.dmp. To examine the contents of the memory.dmp file, use the dumpchk.exe command.

87. **Answer: C.** The command-line tool dumpchk.exe is used to examine the contents of the memory dump file in Microsoft Windows XP.

88. **Answer: C.** The command-line tool Winnt32.exe /cmdcons from the Microsoft Windows XP CD is used to install the Recovery Console. It is located in the i386 folder on the original installation CD.

89. **Answer: A.** After it is installed, you run the Recovery Console in Microsoft Windows XP by choosing it from the Please Select Operating System to Start menu during bootup.

90. **Answer: A.** After it is installed, you must log on as Administrator to run the Recovery Console in Microsoft Windows XP.

91. **Answer: A.** The repair option is needed during Microsoft Windows XP Setup to run the Recovery Console.

92. **Answer: B.** The Recovery Console of Microsoft Windows XP enables you to boot to a DOS prompt even when your hard disk is formatted with NTFS.

93. **Answer: A.** The Windows Report Tool is the feature of Microsoft Windows XP that gathers information from your PC, and then uploads data to a server to assist support providers in troubleshooting hardware and software issues.

94. **Answer: A.** The file formats that the Windows Report Tool uses to gather information from your PC, and then uploads data to a support provider server are .CAB (compressed cabinet) and .NFO (Microsoft system information) file formats.

95. **Answer: A.** The snapshots of critical system files and Registry settings you should take before making major changes to a Microsoft Windows XP PC are called System Restore Points.

96. **Answer: A.** These snapshots of critical system files and Registry settings you should take before making major changes to a Microsoft Windows XP PC are called System Restore Points. They are allocated 12% of each hard disk drive by default.

97. **Answers: A, B, C, and E.**

    Explanation A. They are allocated 12% of each hard disk drive by default.

    Explanation B. These snapshots of critical system files and Registry settings must be enabled before making major changes to a Microsoft Windows XP PC.

    Explanation C. A default restore point is created the first time System Restore is enabled.

    Explanation E. A default restore point is created by right-clicking My Computer, selecting Properties, choosing the System Restore tab, and unchecking the displayed Turn Off System Restore on All Drives check box.

98. **Answer: B.** These snapshots of critical system files and Registry settings must be enabled before making major changes to a Microsoft Windows XP PC.

99. **Answer: B.** This is how you would roll back to a System Restore Point in Microsoft Windows XP: Start, Programs, Accessories, Systems Tools, System Restore, Restore My Computer to an Earlier Time.

100.**Answer: A.** The CompressionBurst System Restore Point Registry setting in Microsoft Windows XP enables you to specify the amount of time an idle computer waits until it begins compressing Restore Point data in the background. Always use extreme caution when editing the Registry.

101.**Answer: B.** The DiskPercent System Restore Point Registry setting in Microsoft Windows XP enables you to specify the percentage of disk space used for restore points, but cannot exceed the DSMax setting. Always use extreme caution when editing the Registry.

102.**Answer: C.** The DSMax System Restore Point Registry setting in Microsoft Windows XP enables you to specify the maximum amount of disk space that System Restore can use. Always use extreme caution when editing the Registry.

103.**Answer: D.** The DSMin System Restore Point Registry setting in Microsoft Windows XP enables you to specify the minimum amount of disk space that System Restore can use, but free disk space cannot fall below this value for System Restore to work. Always use extreme caution when editing the Registry.

104.**Answer: A.** The RestoreStatus System Restore Point Registry setting in Microsoft Windows XP holds a value of 0, 1, or 2, and specifies whether the last restore operation failed, succeeded, or was interrupted, respectively. Always use extreme caution when editing the Registry.

105.**Answer: B.** The RPGlobalInterval System Restore Point Registry setting in Microsoft Windows XP enables you to specify the time in seconds before creating an automatic restore point. The default setting is 86,400 (seconds), which equals 24 hours. Always use extreme caution when editing the Registry.

106.**Answer: B.** The RPLifeInterval System Restore Point Registry setting in Microsoft Windows XP enables you to specify the time to live (TTL) seconds for restore points. The default setting is 7,776,000 (seconds), which equals 90 days. Always use extreme caution when editing the Registry.

107.**Answer: C.** The RPSessionInterval System Restore Point Registry setting in Microsoft Windows XP enables you to specify the time in seconds before creating a restore point while the system is running. The default setting is turned off with a setting of 0 (seconds). Always use extreme caution when editing the Registry.

108.**Answer: E.** The ThawInterval System Restore Point Registry setting in Microsoft Windows XP enables you to specify the time in seconds that System Restore waits before waking itself from a disabled state. Always use extreme caution when editing the Registry.

109. **Answer: D.** Automated System Recovery is the name of the new feature in Microsoft Windows XP that enables you to create an image of your system partition and burn it to a CD or write it to tape. Then using a special floppy disk called the ASR (automated system recovery) disk, you can restore the computer from the image that was created.

110. **Answer: D.** Automated System Recovery is the name of the new feature in Microsoft Windows XP that enables you to create an image of your system partition and burn it to a CD or write it to tape. You must first use the command-line tool ntbackup to begin the Automated System Recovery Wizard.

111. **Answer: D.** Automated System Recovery is the name of the new feature in Microsoft Windows XP that enables you to create an image of your system partition and burn it to a CD or write it to tape. You must first use the command-line tool ntbackup to begin the Automated System Recovery Wizard.

112. **Answer: A.** You should add Tom to the local Backup Operators group on his laptop. The Backup Operators group gets permission to access storage devices such as the external parallel port tape backup drive.

113. **Answer: B.** You should install the older Windows 2000 Professional video drivers on the computer. They worked fine and were compatible on this particular hardware as all other users have them.

114. **Answer: D.** ACPI stands for advanced configuration and power interface. You should reinstall Windows XP Professional to enable ACPI and power management support. To change from non-ACPI to ACPI, you must first flash the BIOS and then reinstall the operating system.

115. **Answer: C.** You should manually install the modem device driver provided by the manufacturer. Use the Add/Remove Hardware Wizard under Start, Settings, Control Panel in Microsoft Windows XP.

116. **Answer: B.** You should restart Alex's laptop with the last known good configuration. This will start his laptop with the last known good Registry and hardware settings.

117. **Answer: D.** You should use Microsoft Windows XP's improved Device Manager to roll back the video driver. While in Device Manager, right-click the device, select Properties, Drivers tab, and click Roll Back Driver.

118. **Answer: A.** You should configure the laptops to enable standby when the lid is closed. Standby offers the quickest wake-up state. Although the screen and hard drives get powered off, RAM is kept running using very little battery power.

119.**Answer: C.** You should modify the driver signing options by selecting the Make This Action the System Default check box. Robert needs the capability to load unsigned drivers.

120.**Answer: D.** You should install an updated driver from the video adapter's manufacturer. The video adapter actually supports multiple monitors, so you need an updated device driver.

121.**Answer: D.** You should replace the portable computer's bus-powered USB hub with a self-powered USB hub. The bus-powered USB hub is not strong enough to support the power needs of the external hard drive.

122.**Answer: A.** You should run the Add Printer Driver Wizard to install the correct printer driver on your computer. Tell all the other users to disconnect and then reconnect to your shared printer.

123.**Answer: B.** You should install the Windows NT 4.0 Workstation printer drivers on the Windows XP Professional print server in the main office.

124.**Answer: D.** You should use the Fax Configuration Wizard to enable the fax modem to receive incoming faxes.

125.**Answer: C.** You should restart the computer with the last known good configuration. This is the classic situation where this response will work perfectly.

126.**Answer: A.** You should restart the user's laptop in Safe mode. In Device Manager, in the digital camera's properties, select the Roll Back Driver option.

127.**Answer: B.** You should use the Fax Configuration Wizard to configure the fax modem to send and receive faxes. You need to enable and configure the Fax service within Microsoft Windows XP.

128.**Answer: C.** You should configure the fax device to automatically answer incoming fax calls after the first ring.

129.**Answer: D.** You should restart the computer by using the original Microsoft Windows XP Professional CD-ROM, and then select the option to repair the installation.

Implementing, Managing, and Troubleshooting Disk Drives and Volumes

Quick Check

1. Which of the following are dynamic volume types? (Select all that apply.)

   ❑ A. Simple
   ❑ B. Spanned
   ❑ C. Striped Set
   ❑ D. Basic

Quick Answer: **166**
Detailed Answer: **167**

2. Which of the following is a dynamic volume type in Microsoft Windows XP that contains space from a single hard disk?

   ❑ A. Simple
   ❑ B. Spanned
   ❑ C. Mirrored
   ❑ D. Basic

Quick Answer: **166**
Detailed Answer: **167**

3. Which of the following is a dynamic volume type in Microsoft Windows XP that contains space from 2 to 32 hard disks, appearing as one logical drive, and is not fault tolerant?

   ❑ A. Simple
   ❑ B. Spanned
   ❑ C. Mirrored
   ❑ D. Basic

Quick Answer: **166**
Detailed Answer: **167**

Quick Check

4. You're using a laptop computer running Microsoft Windows XP and would like to covert the basic disk to a simple dynamic volume. You access Disk Management and try right-clicking on the disk. What happens when you try to convert the basic disk?

Quick Answer: 166
Detailed Answer: 167

- ❑ A. You won't see the option to covert the disk to dynamic.
- ❑ B. You'll be prompted to apply the latest service pack.
- ❑ C. You'll receive an error message stating invalid operation.
- ❑ D. You'll be prompted for your original source installation disk.
- ❑ E. The disk will be converted as if it were a desktop computer.

5. Which of the following is not a dynamic volume type in Microsoft Windows XP that contains space from a single disk, and is not fault tolerant?

Quick Answer: 166
Detailed Answer: 167

- ❑ A. Simple
- ❑ B. Spanned
- ❑ C. Striped Set
- ❑ D. Basic

6. Which dynamic volume condition (or state) in Microsoft Windows XP indicates that a volume is accessible and has no known problems?

Quick Answer: 166
Detailed Answer: 167

- ❑ A. Healthy
- ❑ B. Healthy (at risk)
- ❑ C. Initializing
- ❑ D. Failed
- ❑ E. Accessible

7. Which dynamic volume condition (or state) in Microsoft Windows XP indicates that a volume is accessible, but has I/O (input/output) errors?

Quick Answer: 166
Detailed Answer: 168

- ❑ A. Healthy
- ❑ B. Healthy (at risk)
- ❑ C. Initializing
- ❑ D. Failed
- ❑ E. Accessible (with I/O errors)

8. Which dynamic volume condition (or state) in Microsoft Windows XP indicates that a volume is being initialized?

Quick Answer: 166
Detailed Answer: 168

- ❑ A. Healthy
- ❑ B. Healthy (at risk)
- ❑ C. Initializing
- ❑ D. Failed
- ❑ E. Initialized

Quick Check

9. Which dynamic volume condition (or state) in Microsoft Windows XP indicates that a volume needs to be repaired or replaced?

   ❑ A. Healthy
   ❑ B. Healthy (at risk)
   ❑ C. Initializing
   ❑ D. Failed
   ❑ E. Failing

Quick Answer: 166
Detailed Answer: 168

10. You're the desktop administrator for your company. You upgrade all computers in the company from Microsoft Windows 98 to Windows XP Professional. Aaron, a user in the marketing department, works with large graphics and desktop publishing files. He wants to be able to save his files in a folder named MKTG on drive C of his computer. Unfortunately, Aaron does not have enough free disk space on the drive. You install a new hard disk on Aaron's computer, and create an NTFS volume named NewVol. You attempt to mount NewVol to MKTG, but the option to mount the volume to a folder is unavailable.

    You need to mount the new volume to the MKTG folder. Which command should you run on Andrew's computer?

    ❑ A. Convert c: /fs:ntfs
    ❑ B. Convert d: /fs:ntfs
    ❑ C. Convert c: /fs:fat32
    ❑ D. Convert d: /fs:fat32

Quick Answer: 166
Detailed Answer: 168

11. You have a home computer that originally had Windows NT 4.0 installed. You configured the two disks you had installed on the system as a stripe set. Later, you upgraded your machine to Windows 2000 Professional. Now you want to upgrade the machine to Windows XP Professional. What do you have to do first?

    ❑ A. Upgrade the computer to Windows XP Professional and run Diskpart to convert the stripe to a striped volume.
    ❑ B. Upgrade the computer to Windows XP Professional and run FTOnline to mount the stripe set and copy the data to a backup device.
    ❑ C. Back up the information from the stripe set, delete the stripe sets, re-create the disk as dynamic with a simple volume, and reload the data.
    ❑ D. Convert the disk to dynamic and continue with the upgrade.

Quick Answer: 166
Detailed Answer: 168

Quick Check

12. You're responsible for maintaining online copies of graphical images used by an application program. These images need to be available all the time; however, you have no idea how much storage space will be needed. How should you configure storage on your computer?

    Quick Answer: 166
    Detailed Answer: 168

    - ❑ A. Connect a tape drive to your computer and save the image files to tape when your disk fills.
    - ❑ B. Add additional disks to your computer when storage space runs low and use Disk Management to create a spanned volume.
    - ❑ C. Compress the images and place them in Zip files.
    - ❑ D. Create a RAID-5 disk structure on a Windows 2000 Server and store the images there.

13. You have an application that performs an analysis of statistical data captured by your engineering firm. To do this analysis, your application reads and writes large amounts of temporary files to disk. You want to provide the best throughput possible for this temporary information, but you do not need to provide any fault tolerance. What should you do?

    Quick Answer: 166
    Detailed Answer: 169

    - ❑ A. Create a spanned volume across two or more disks.
    - ❑ B. Create a striped volume across two or more disks.
    - ❑ C. Create a RAID-5 structure on a Windows 2000 Server and store the temporary files there.
    - ❑ D. Create a single large volume named \TEMP and direct your application to store its temporary files there.

14. As the system administrator, you set the policy on the configuration of new computer hardware purchased for the company. You decide that, for flexibility, you'll have all the disk storage devices for new Windows XP Professional computers configured as simple volumes. When you configure this on a new laptop, you find that the option to do the conversion from basic to dynamic disks is not present. What is your course of action?

    Quick Answer: 166
    Detailed Answer: 169

    - ❑ A. Make sure that you purchase disk drives that support being dynamic disks.
    - ❑ B. Amend your policy to allow laptops to remain configured with basic disks.
    - ❑ C. Manually fix the DMA, I/O, and IRQ resources used by the disk drive rather than letting Plug and Play choose them.
    - ❑ D. The disk drives cannot be made dynamic until a small partition is created at the end of the device.

Quick Check

15. You're in charge of the desktop deployments at a large telco. The company policy is to evergreen the users' desktop every three years. That means that you can expect a steady stream of new systems to be coming to you to be configured. You already have a standard image to apply to new machines, but you would also like to convert the disks to dynamic before sending them to users' offices. You would like to have an automatic way to do this during the imaging or Sysprep phase of the installation.

    What action should you take?

    ❑ A. You create a script that runs FSUTIL with the /Dynamic switch and run it after Sysprep.

    ❑ B. You create a script with Diskpart to convert the disks after Sysprep.

    ❑ C. You create a script that calls Convert with a [Dynamic] modifier after the drive letter and run this script after Sysprep.

    ❑ D. You include a script that will reformat the new drive. All new drives in Windows XP Professional are dynamic disks with simple volumes.

Quick Answer: **166**
Detailed Answer: **169**

16. While working with disk partitions, you notice your disk administrator showing that you have a basic disk. What features are not supported by a basic disk? (Select three answers.)

    ❑ A. Create simple, spanned, striped, mirrored, and RAID-5 volumes.

    ❑ B. Delete spanned volumes, striped volumes, mirrored volumes, and RAID-5 volumes.

    ❑ C. Break a mirror from a mirrored volume.

    ❑ D. Extend volumes and volume sets.

    ❑ E. Add a mirror to a simple volume.

Quick Answer: **166**
Detailed Answer: **169**

17. Brendan wants to convert one of the hard drives connected to his Windows XP Professional desktop computer from a basic disk to a dynamic disk. In the Disk Management console, Brendan right-clicks the physical disk designated as disk 1, but the option to Convert to Dynamic Disk is unavailable. Why would the option to convert the drive to a dynamic disk be disabled?

    ❑ A. There are already drive volumes with data stored on that physical disk.

    ❑ B. The drive is an external drive connected via USB or IEEE 1394 bus connections.

    ❑ C. The drive is an external Fiber Channel device.

    ❑ D. The drive has a sector size of greater than 512 bytes.

Quick Answer: **166**
Detailed Answer: **169**

Quick Check

18. Alexis wants to convert physical hard disk number 2 on her Windows XP Professional desktop computer from a basic disk to a dynamic disk using only the command line. Is a command-line tool available to accomplish this task? If so, what is the name of this utility and does it differ from the Disk Management console?

Quick Answer: 166
Detailed Answer: 169

- ❑ A. The command-line tool is called Diskperf.exe. Only administrative users may use it.
- ❑ B. No command-line tool equivalent to the Disk Management MMC exists.
- ❑ C. The command-line tool is called Diskpart.exe. You must restart the computer for the conversion process to take effect.
- ❑ D. The command-line tool is called Convert.exe. You don't need to restart the computer for the conversion to take place unless you are converting the boot disk.

19. What are the three types of dynamic volumes that are supported by dynamic disks under Windows XP Professional? (Select all that apply.)

Quick Answer: 166
Detailed Answer: 170

- ❑ A. Spanned volumes
- ❑ B. Extended volumes
- ❑ C. RAID-5 volumes
- ❑ D. Simple volumes
- ❑ E. Striped volumes

20. Sue has a Windows XP Professional computer that has two physical hard drives installed—both disks have been converted to dynamic disks. The first disk (disk 0) has a capacity of 20GB with 11GB of unallocated free space, a drive C (system and boot) volume of 2GB, and a drive D volume of 7GB. The second disk (disk 1) has a capacity of 30GB with 20GB of unallocated free space. Sue needs to extend drive D: (a simple volume) on her computer so that the volume will have an increased amount of total disk space—from 7GB to 14GB. How can she accomplish this without deleting any existing data? (Select all that apply.)

Quick Answer: 166
Detailed Answer: 170

- ❑ A. Repartition and reformat drive C.
- ❑ B. Extend drive D to an area of free space on disk 1.
- ❑ C. Extend drive D to an area of free space on disk 0.
- ❑ D. Convert disk 1 to basic and extend the volume.

Quick Check

21. To make accessing several different hard drive volumes and removable drives easier on a local Windows XP computer, you want your users to be able to access each drive volume through different folder names located on the same drive letter. How can you accomplish this?

Quick Answer: 166
Detailed Answer: 170

- ❑ A. Use the Subst.exe command-line utility to specify each folder as a unique drive letter.
- ❑ B. Use the Disk Management console to create mount points for each hard drive volume letter through empty folders on the same FAT or FAT32 volume.
- ❑ C. Use Diskpart.exe to create mount points for each hard drive volume letter through empty folders on the same NTFS volume.
- ❑ D. Use Diskperf.exe to create mount points for each hard drive volume letter through empty folders on the same NTFS volume.

22. What is the easiest way to convert an NTFS drive volume configured as drive D to the FAT32 file system without losing any existing data? Assume that the volume is not the system or boot volume.

Quick Answer: 166
Detailed Answer: 170

- ❑ A. Use the command convert d: /fs:fat32.
- ❑ B. Use the command convert d: /fs:-ntfs.
- ❑ C. Use the Disk Management console to revert the volume back to FAT or FAT32.
- ❑ D. Back up all the data stored on the NTFS drive volume, use Diskpart.exe or the Disk Management console to delete the volume, create a new volume, format the volume as FAT32, and then restore the backed-up data.

Quick Check

23. How can you set disk quotas on NTFS drive volumes for the Power Users group and for the Administrators group?

Quick Answer: 166
Detailed Answer: 171

- ❑ A. Right-click the drive letter in My Computer, select Properties, click the Quota tab, and mark the check boxes for Enable Quota Management and Deny Disk Space to Users Exceeding Quota Limit. Click Apply and click the Quota Entries button. Configure quota entries for the Power Users group and for the Administrators group.
- ❑ B. Right-click the drive letter in My Computer, select Properties, click the Quota tab, and mark the check boxes for Enable Quota Management and Deny Disk Space to Users Exceeding Quota Limit. Click Apply and click the Quota Entries button. Configure quota entries for the Power Users group.
- ❑ C. Right-click the drive letter in My Computer, select Properties, click the Quota tab, and mark the check boxes for Enable Quota Management and Deny Disk Space to Users Exceeding Quota Limit. Click Apply and click the Quota Entries button. Configure quota entries for each member of the Power Users group.
- ❑ D. Create a new local group named Super Users and make all the members of the Power Users group and the Administrators group members of this new group. Right-click the drive letter in My Computer, select Properties, click the Quota tab, and mark the check boxes for Enable Quota Management and Deny Disk Space to Users Exceeding Quota Limit. Click Apply and click the Quota Entries button. Configure quota entries for the Super Users group.

24. Brandy wants to move an NTFS-compressed file from NTFS drive D to an uncompressed folder on NTFS drive F. What will happen to the file when she performs this operation?

Quick Answer: 166
Detailed Answer: 171

- ❑ A. The compressed file will become uncompressed when it is moved to drive F.
- ❑ B. The compressed file will remain compressed when it is moved to drive F.
- ❑ C. Windows XP will prompt the user as to whether the file should remain compressed or should be uncompressed after it has been moved.
- ❑ D. Brandy will receive an error message when she attempts to move the file to an uncompressed folder.

Quick Answer: 166

Detailed Answer: 171

25. Terry encrypts an NTFS folder named SECRET DOCS on the hard drive of a Windows XP Professional computer. Terry is the only user with access to all the encrypted files in the SECRET DOCS folder (except for the DRA). Terry shares the computer with her associate, Kim. Kim is not the DRA. Later, Kim logs on to the same computer and attempts to copy one of the files stored inside of the SECRET DOCS folder, named Salaries.xls, to a floppy disk in drive A. After that, Kim tries to move the same file to an unencrypted folder on the same NTFS drive volume named PUBLIC DOCS. What are the results of Kim's file operations?

- ❑ A. Kim will receive an error message for trying to copy the encrypted file to a floppy disk, but he will successfully be able to move the encrypted file to the PUBLIC DOCS unencrypted NTFS folder, where the file will remain encrypted.
- ❑ B. Kim will receive an error message for trying to copy the encrypted file to a floppy disk, and he will also receive an error message for attempting to move the encrypted file to the PUBLIC DOCS unencrypted NTFS folder.
- ❑ C. Kim will receive an error message for trying to copy the encrypted file to a floppy disk, but he will be able to successfully move the encrypted file to the PUBLIC DOCS unencrypted NTFS folder, where it will lose its encryption attribute.
- ❑ D. Kim will successfully copy the encrypted file to a floppy disk, where it will remain encrypted, and he will successfully be able to move the encrypted file to the PUBLIC DOCS unencrypted NTFS folder.

Quick Check Answer Key

1. A, B, and C
2. A
3. B
4. A
5. D
6. A
7. B
8. C
9. D
10. A
11. D
12. B
13. B
14. B
15. B
16. A, D, and E
17. B
18. C
19. A, D, and E
20. B, C
21. C
22. D
23. C
24. A
25. A

Answers and Explanations

1. **Answers: A, B, and C.**

   Explanation A. A simple volume is a dynamic volume type in Microsoft Windows XP. A simple volume contains space from a single hard disk.

   Explanation B. A spanned volume is a dynamic volume type in Microsoft Windows XP. A spanned volume contains space from up to 32 hard disks, appearing as one logical drive. A spanned volume fills up the data storage area of one disk before going onto the next, and so on. Data read operations are slow because of the sequential nature of this process. Finally, there is no built-in fault tolerance in a spanned volume.

   Explanation C. A striped set is a dynamic volume type in Microsoft Windows XP. A striped set contains space from up to 32 hard disks, appearing as one logical drive. A striped set fills up the data storage areas of all disks evenly in "stripes." Data read/write operations are fastest because of the simultaneous nature of this process. Finally, there is built-in fault tolerance in a striped set.

2. **Answer: A.** A simple volume is a dynamic volume type in Microsoft Windows XP. A simple volume contains space from a single hard disk.

3. **Answer: B.** A spanned volume is a dynamic volume type in Microsoft Windows XP. A spanned volume contains space from 2 to 32 hard disks, appearing as one logical drive. A spanned volume fills up the data storage area of one disk before going onto the next, and so on. Data read operations are slow because of the sequential nature of this process. Finally, there is no built-in fault tolerance in a spanned volume.

4. **Answer: A.** The ability to convert a basic disk to a dynamic volume is not available on portable computers. Answer B is incorrect, although it is good practice to stay current with the latest service packs of operating system software. Answer C is incorrect because no such message will be displayed. Answer D is incorrect because the original source installation disk is not needed and could not be done. Answer E is incorrect because portable computers are currently limited by current technology to have only one internal hard drive.

5. **Answer: D.** Although a basic disk contains space from a single hard drive, basic disks are not a dynamic volume type. Basic disks are the opposite of dynamic disks. Basic disks are limited in their functionality with Microsoft Windows XP.

6. **Answer: A.** The dynamic volume condition (or state) in Microsoft Windows XP that indicates a volume is accessible and has no known problems is *Healthy*.

7. **Answer: B.** The dynamic volume condition (or state) in Microsoft Windows XP that indicates a volume is accessible, but has I/O errors is *Healthy (at risk)*. The individual disk that has problems will appear in the Disk Management snap-in of the Microsoft Management Console as Online (Errors).

8. **Answer: C.** As simple as it seems, the status message says *Initializing* during this period. No action is required, as the status will automatically change to Healthy when the initialization process is complete.

9. **Answer: D.** The dynamic volume condition (or state) in Microsoft Windows XP that indicates a volume needs to be repaired or replaced is *Failed*. The individual disk appears in the Disk Management snap-in of the Microsoft Management Console as Failed.

10. **Answer: A.** You need to run Convert c: /fs:ntfs on Aaron's computer. This is the only form of the convert command that NTFS allows the mounting of a new volume to a folder.

11. **Answer: D.** A stripe set was available in NT 4.0 on basic disks, and maintained for backward compatibility in Windows 2000. Because you upgraded your machine from NT 4.0 to Windows 2000, you were able to continue to use the stripe set. In Windows XP Professional, stripe sets on basic disks are not supported. You must upgrade the disks to dynamic disks, which will make the stripe set a striped volume before you can continue with the operating system upgrade.

    You cannot run Diskpart because the upgrade to Windows XP Professional will not continue with the stripe set configured. FTOnline was created to allow temporary access to legacy disk volumes; however, you will not be able to run FTOnline until the operating system upgrade completes. You can certainly back up your data, delete and re-create the disk volume, and then restore your data, but a procedure this complicated is not necessary.

12. **Answer: B.** The solution calls for online storage, but no performance requirement is mentioned. The application that uses the image files will not be able to find them if the images are rolled out to tape. Although this solution provides for all the images to be available, manual intervention would be required to load needed images back to disk. Likewise, most applications would not be able to extract a file from a Zip library and creating a RAID-5 structure provides more fault tolerance and I/O performance than is requested. The most efficient solution is to create a dynamic disk with a simple volume and span that volume to additional disk devices when space runs low. This allows the images to appear to be available from one location even though that might span several disks.

13. **Answer: B.** The problem requires better throughput on disk for data that is not going to be stored. There is no requirement for a fault-redundant RAID-5 configuration. Likewise, providing a single large volume or a spanned volume would not give the same performance as a striped volume. A striped volume will write 64KB blocks to each disk in rotation. This will have the effect of spreading the I/O load across all drives evenly.

14. **Answer: B.** Windows XP does not support dynamic disks on laptops, so your policy must be changed to reflect that. Neither Plug and Play nor the type of disk defines whether it can be dynamic. The *dynamic* part of dynamic disks refers to the storage structures created on the device, not the device itself. Finally, the Disk Management application will automatically reserve space at the end of the disk for its database when converting a basic disk to dynamic.

15. **Answer: B.** Diskpart is a command-line utility that enables administrators to perform many disk-management tasks. You can create a script that uses Diskpart to convert the basic disks in a new system to dynamic. That script can be run automatically during the post-Sysprep stage of an image installation (the GUIRUNONCE section of Sysprep.inf).

    The FSUtil utility will mount, dismount, or extend file systems but it will not convert basic disks to dynamic. In addition, there is no /Dynamic switch on FSUtil. Convert is used to convert FAT or FAT32 to NTFS but not to convert basic disks to dynamic. In addition, there is no [Dynamic] modifier in Convert. Format will still create only a basic disk.

16. **Answers: A, D, and E.** Basic disks are supported for backward compatibility. They cannot be used to create mirrors or volumes.

17. **Answer: B.** Hard disks connected via USB or FireWire (IEEE 1394) buses are not supported for dynamic disks. Answer A is incorrect because you are allowed to convert disks with existing drive volumes and data to dynamic disks—you cannot convert back to a basic disk without deleting all existing volumes (and therefore the data on those volumes), however. Answer C is incorrect because dynamic disks do support Fiber Channel drives. Answer D is incorrect because only disks that have a sector size of less than 512 bytes are not supported by dynamic disks.

18. **Answer: C.** Diskpart.exe is the command-line equivalent of Disk Management. You must restart the computer for the conversion to take effect. Answer A is incorrect because Diskperf.exe enables and disables hard disk performance counters on earlier versions of Windows; it does nothing for converting basic disks to dynamic disks. Answer B is incorrect because a command-line utility functionally equivalent to Disk Management exists: Diskpart.exe. Answer D is incorrect because the Convert.exe command-line tool is used to convert a FAT or FAT32 volume to NTFS.

19. **Answers: A, D, and E.** Spanned volumes enable you to store data sequentially over two or more physical disks, but Windows XP displays the disks as one logical drive volume. Simple volumes are the most fundamental dynamic volumes, with each simple volume residing on only one physical disk. Striped volumes are also supported under Windows XP, enabling you to store data in stripes across two or more physical disks, but Windows XP displays the disks as one logical drive volume. Answer B is incorrect because there is no such volume as an extended volume on a dynamic disk. Answer C is incorrect because Windows XP Professional does not support the fault-tolerant RAID-5 volume configuration.

20. **Answers: B, C.** A simple volume on a dynamic disk can be extended onto unallocated free space of additional dynamic disks up to a maximum of 32 dynamic disks—this automatically turns the volume into a spanned volume. A simple volume on a dynamic disk can also be extended onto an area of unallocated free space on the same dynamic disk. Answer A is incorrect because repartitioning and reformatting a disk deletes any data stored on the disk. Answer D is incorrect because converting a disk from dynamic to basic deletes any data stored on the disk.

21. **Answer: C.** You may use either Diskpart.exe or the Disk Management MMC snap-in to create mount points for a drive letter through empty NTFS folders. Answer A is incorrect because the Subst.exe command associates a specific drive letter path with a different drive letter root folder. Answer B is incorrect because you can create mount points only on empty NTFS folders. Answer D is incorrect because Diskperf.exe enables and disables hard disk performance counters on earlier versions of Windows.

22. **Answer: D.** Windows XP does not offer a conversion tool for converting an existing NTFS volume to FAT, FAT32, or any other file system. You must back up all the data on the volume, create a new volume, format it, and restore the data. Answer A is incorrect because the Convert.exe command does not support the conversion to the FAT or FAT32 file system. Answer B is incorrect because the Convert.exe command-line tool supports only a conversion to NTFS—prepending a minus sign (–) to the NTFS parameter is not supported. Answer C is incorrect because the Disk Management console only supports reformatting an existing NTFS drive volume to convert it to the FAT or FAT32 file system.

23. **Answer: C.** Windows XP Professional supports disk quotas on NTFS drive volumes only for individual users, not for groups. Therefore, you would have to create a quota entry for each member of the Power Users group—you cannot assign a quota limit to a group. All members of the Administrators group inherit a no-limit disk quota by default, so you cannot set quotas on members of this group. Answer A is incorrect for the reasons just cited. Answer B is incorrect because you cannot set quotas on groups. Answer D is incorrect for the same reason.

24. **Answer: A.** When you move a compressed file from one NTFS volume to a different NTFS volume, the file inherits the compression attribute from the target location. Answer B is incorrect because an NTFS compressed folder or file retains its compression attribute only when it is moved to another folder on the same NTFS volume. Answer C is incorrect because Windows XP never prompts the user as to whether a folder or file should remain compressed or uncompressed. Answer D is incorrect because Windows XP does not generate error messages for moving compressed files to an uncompressed folder.

25. **Answer: A.** Only the user who originally encrypted the file (or any users given shared access to the encrypted file) may copy the file to a non-NTFS drive volume or to any type of removable media. In addition, only the user who originally encrypted the file (or any users given shared access to the encrypted file) may copy the file or move it to a folder located on a different NTFS volume. A user without shared access to an encrypted file is permitted to move the file only to another folder located on the same NTFS volume, where the file remains encrypted. Answer B is incorrect because although Kim will receive an error message when he attempts to copy the file to a floppy disk, he will not receive an error message when he attempts to move the encrypted file to an unencrypted NTFS folder located on the same NTFS volume. Answer C is incorrect because although Kim will receive an error message when he attempts to copy the file to a floppy disk, he will be allowed to move the encrypted file to an unencrypted NTFS folder located on the same NTFS volume, but the file will not lose its encryption attribute. Answer D is incorrect because Kim will receive an error message when he attempts to copy the encrypted file to a floppy disk.

Implementing, Managing, and Troubleshooting Network Protocols and Services

Quick Check

1. What is used to resolve a computer hostname to an IP address?

   - ❑ A. DNS
   - ❑ B. WINS
   - ❑ C. Subnet mask
   - ❑ D. Default gateway

Quick Answer: **191**
Detailed Answer: **192**

2. What is used to resolve a NetBIOS name to an IP address?

   - ❑ A. DNS
   - ❑ B. WINS
   - ❑ C. Subnet mask
   - ❑ D. Default gateway

Quick Answer: **191**
Detailed Answer: **192**

3. What is a value that is used to help distinguish the network ID portion of an IP address from the host portion of an IP address?

   - ❑ A. DNS
   - ❑ B. WINS
   - ❑ C. Subnet mask
   - ❑ D. Default gateway

Quick Answer: **191**
Detailed Answer: **192**

4. What is typically a router's IP address for a host to send data packets to if an IP address is not available on the local network?

   - ❑ A. DNS
   - ❑ B. WINS
   - ❑ C. Subnet mask
   - ❑ D. Default gateway

Quick Answer: **191**
Detailed Answer: **192**

Quick Check

5. What protocol is a computer industry standard suite of protocols?
   - ❑ A. TCP/IP
   - ❑ B. NetBEUI
   - ❑ C. IPX/SPX
   - ❑ D. AppleTalk

Quick Answer: 191
Detailed Answer: 192

6. What is the most popular routable protocol?
   - ❑ A. NetBEUI
   - ❑ B. TCP/IP
   - ❑ C. IPX/SPX
   - ❑ D. AppleTalk

Quick Answer: 191
Detailed Answer: 192

7. What protocol is at the basis of the Internet?
   - ❑ A. AppleTalk
   - ❑ B. NetBEUI
   - ❑ C. IPX/SPX
   - ❑ D. TCP/IP

Quick Answer: 191
Detailed Answer: 192

8. What protocol is installed by default in Microsoft Windows XP?
   - ❑ A. IPX/SPX
   - ❑ B. NetBEUI
   - ❑ C. TCP/IP
   - ❑ D. AppleTalk

Quick Answer: 191
Detailed Answer: 192

9. What protocol uses Winsock in Microsoft Windows XP?
   - ❑ A. AppleTalk
   - ❑ B. NetBEUI
   - ❑ C. IPX/SPX
   - ❑ D. TCP/IP

Quick Answer: 191
Detailed Answer: 192

10. What protocol is used extensively to connect dissimilar systems?
    - ❑ A. IPX/SPX
    - ❑ B. NetBEUI
    - ❑ C. TCP/IP
    - ❑ D. AppleTalk

Quick Answer: 191
Detailed Answer: 192

11. What protocol uses addresses that can either be entered manually, or with the help of a DHCP Server?
    - ❑ A. TCP/IP
    - ❑ B. NetBEUI
    - ❑ C. IPX/SPX
    - ❑ D. AppleTalk

Quick Answer: 191
Detailed Answer: 193

12. What IP addresses are used by Microsoft Windows XP during APIPA?

Quick Answer: 191
Detailed Answer: 193

- ❑ A. 127.0.0.1
- ❑ B. 169.254.0.0 to 169.254.255.255
- ❑ C. 1.0.0.1 to 126.255.255.254
- ❑ D. 128.0.0.1 to 191.255.255.254

13. What IP address, or range of addresses, is used by Microsoft Windows XP for loopback testing?

Quick Answer: 191
Detailed Answer: 193

- ❑ A. 169.254.0.0 to 169.254.255.255
- ❑ B. 127.0.0.1
- ❑ C. 1.0.0.1 to 126.255.255.254
- ❑ D. 128.0.0.1 to 191.255.255.254

14. What does APIPA stand for in regard to Microsoft Windows XP networking?

Quick Answer: 191
Detailed Answer: 193

- ❑ A. Automatic Private Internet Protocol Addressing
- ❑ B. Automatic Private Internet Protocol Assignment
- ❑ C. Automatic Public Internet Protocol Advertising
- ❑ D. Automatic Public Internet Protocol Addressing

15. What does APIPA do in regard to Microsoft Windows XP networking?

Quick Answer: 191
Detailed Answer: 193

- ❑ A. Automatically assigns IP addresses without DHCP
- ❑ B. Automatically assigns IP addresses with DHCP
- ❑ C. Manually assigns IP addresses without DHCP
- ❑ D. Manually assigns IP addresses with DHCP

16. What versions of Microsoft Windows support APIPA? (Choose all that apply.)

Quick Answer: 191
Detailed Answer: 193

- ❑ A. Microsoft Windows XP
- ❑ B. Microsoft Windows 2000
- ❑ C. Microsoft Windows Me
- ❑ D. Microsoft Windows 98
- ❑ E. Microsoft Windows 95
- ❑ F. Microsoft Windows 3.11

17. What subnet mask is used by Microsoft Windows XP with APIPA?

Quick Answer: 191
Detailed Answer: 193

- ❑ A. 127.0.0.1
- ❑ B. 255.255.0.0
- ❑ C. 255.0.0.0
- ❑ D. 255.255.255.0

Quick Check

18. What version of Internet Explorer is included with Microsoft Windows XP?

Quick Answer: 191
Detailed Answer: 193

- ❑ A. Microsoft Internet Explorer 5.5
- ❑ B. Microsoft Windows XP does not come with Internet Explorer
- ❑ C. Microsoft Internet Explorer 6.0
- ❑ D. Microsoft Internet Explorer 7.0

19. What default cipher strength is the version of Internet Explorer that is included with Microsoft Windows XP?

Quick Answer: 191
Detailed Answer: 194

- ❑ A. 128-bit
- ❑ B. 256-bit
- ❑ C. 64-bit
- ❑ D. 56-bit

20. What full-featured text and videoconferencing client, formerly called MSN Messenger, is now fully integrated into Microsoft Windows XP?

Quick Answer: 191
Detailed Answer: 194

- ❑ A. Text Windows .NET Messenger
- ❑ B. MSNBC Messenger
- ❑ C. XP Messenger
- ❑ D. Windows Messenger

21. What feature of Microsoft Windows XP allows it to share an Internet connection with other computers on the private network?

Quick Answer: 191
Detailed Answer: 194

- ❑ A. Proxy 2002
- ❑ B. NAT
- ❑ C. Proxy 2.0
- ❑ D. ICS

Quick Check

22. You're a help desk technician for your company. Steve and Iris are software developers for your company. Steve is developing a Web application on his Windows XP Professional computer. The computer is named Steve29.

    Quick Answer: **191**
    Detailed Answer: **194**

    When Irene types http://Steve29 in the address bar of her Web browser, she cannot access the Web application by typing http://localhost or http://Steve29 in the address bar of her Web browser. She can access other resources on the company network. When you run the ping command from your computer, you cannot connect to Steve's computer. When you attempt to access http://Steve29 from your computer, Internet Explorer displays DNS or Server error.

    You need to ensure that Iris can access the Web application on Steve's computer. First, you establish a Remote Assistance connection to Steve's computer. What should you do next on Steve's computer?

    ❑ A. Stop and then restart the WWW Publishing service
    ❑ B. IPCONFIG /renew
    ❑ C. Under Local Area Connection properties, clear the Internet Connection Firewall check box
    ❑ D. Give the Everyone group Allow - Full Control permission on Inetpub

23. You're a help desk technician for your organization. Helen is a user in the research department who works from home. She reports a problem on her Windows XP Professional computer.

    Quick Answer: **191**
    Detailed Answer: **194**

    You instruct Helen to send you a Remote Assistance invitation, and then disconnect from the ISP. You receive the invitation on your Windows XP Professional computer and instruct Helen to then reconnect to her ISP. After you accept the invitation, you cannot connect to Helen's computer.

    You need to establish a Remote Assistance connection with Helen's computer. What should you do?

    ❑ A. Run the Remote Assistance Wizard from your organization's PC.
    ❑ B. Issue the command IPCONFIG /flush both computers.
    ❑ C. Instruct Helen to send a new Remote Assistance invitation and remain connected to her ISP. From your PC, accept the new invitation.
    ❑ D. Disable Internet Connection Firewall from Helen's PC, and then re-accept the invitation.

Quick Check

24. You're a help desk technician for your corporation. The network consists of a single Active Directory domain. The network includes Windows 2000 Advanced Server computers, and both Windows XP Professional and Windows 2000 Professional client computers. Except for all the domain controllers, computers on the network use DHCP to obtain their TCP/IP configuration. During the business day, the network administrators performed emergency maintenance on a file server named FileSrvA. FileSrvA was then restarted and seemed to experience no further problems.

    Employees begin reporting that when they try to access resources on FileSrvA, they receive the following error message: Network path not found. You confirm that FileSrvA is functional. You need to ensure that all employees can access FileSrvA. What command should you now instruct all employees to run?

    - ❑ A. IPCONFIG /flushdns
    - ❑ B. IPCONFIG /registerdns
    - ❑ C. NBTSTAT
    - ❑ D. IPCONFIG /all

Quick Answer: **191**
Detailed Answer: **194**

25. You're the desktop administrator for your company. Your company's software developers use Windows XP Professional and IIS on their client computers to develop Web-based applications. One developer reports that he can no longer access the Web-based application on his desktop by using his Web browser. When you attempt to access the application by using your Web browser, you also receive an error message: Cannot find server or DNS Error.

    You confirm the World Wide Web Publishing service is started on the developer's computer. You also verify that you're using the correct URL to access the developer's computer using your Web browser. You need to ensure that the developer can access the Web application by using his Web browser. How should you configure the developer's computer?

    - ❑ A. Start the IIS (Internet Information Service) Admin service
    - ❑ B. Start the default Web site
    - ❑ C. IPCONFIG /registerdns
    - ❑ D. Disable any stray host header entries

Quick Answer: **191**
Detailed Answer: **194**

Quick Answer: **191**
Detailed Answer: **194**

26. You're the desktop administrator for your company. Your company has offices in San Francisco and Boston. Both offices are connected by a wide area network (WAN) connection. The networks at both offices include Windows XP Professional computers. The company uses a single Active Directory domain that includes a Microsoft Exchange 2000 Server computer. Neither office is connected to the Internet. Paul is a member of the sales department in the Boston office. Paul needs to use Remote Assistance to obtain help from another sales employee in San Francisco. However, when Paul attempts to send a Remote Assistance invitation by using Windows Messenger, an error message reports that he does not have a .NET Passport.

    You need to ensure that Paul can send a Remote Assistance invitation by using Windows Messenger. How should you configure Paul's computer?

    - ❑ A. Install MSN Explorer. Configure to log on using a valid .NET Passport.
    - ❑ B. Configure Windows Messenger to log on by using an Exchange account.
    - ❑ C. Configure Windows Messenger to log on using a valid .NET Passport username and password.
    - ❑ D. Install a 56Kbps modem. Configure the modem to dial up to an ISP when an Internet connection is required.

Quick Check

27. You're a help desk technician for your company. Alice is a salesperson who works remotely. Alice uses a Windows XP Professional portable computer. She connects to the company network by dialing in to a company remote access server and logging on to the company Active Directory domain. Alice dials in to several different branch offices, depending on where she is located. Alice's user account is a member of the local Administrators group on her computer. She reports that she cannot enable Internet Connection Firewall on a new dial-up connection that she created. In the past, she enabled Internet Connection Firewall on other dial-up connections that she created.

    Quick Answer: **191**
    Detailed Answer: **194**

    You need to ensure that Alice can enable Internet Connection Firewall on new dial-up connections that she creates. What should you do?

    - ❑ A. Ask Alice to disable ICS Discovery and Control on her computer. Tell Alice to delete and re-create the new dial-up connection.
    - ❑ B. Remove Alice's user account from the local Administrators group. Add her user account to the Power Users group.
    - ❑ C. Ask a domain administrator to remove the Prohibit Use of Internet Connection Firewall on Your DNS Domain group policy in the domain. Instruct Alice to connect to the company network and to log on to the domain.
    - ❑ D. Tell Alice to delete and then re-create a new dial-up connection. Ask Alice to share her new dial-up connection by using ICS.

Quick Answer: **191**

Detailed Answer: **194**

28. You're a help desk technician for your company. Your Windows XP Professional computer is connected to the company's network, which is connected to the Internet via a T3 line. Your computer hosts a Web site that is accessed by other help desk technicians. You set up a new Windows XP Professional computer at home. That home computer is connected to the Internet by a broadband cable modem that's always on. It's configured to use a static IP address assigned by your ISP.

    You want to use a remote desktop connection to control your home computer while you are at work. You also want to prevent any other Internet traffic from reaching the home computer. You verify that your company's Internet firewall permits remote desktop connection traffic.

    Which further actions should you take? (Select all that apply.)

    ❑ A. On your home computer, enable Internet Connection Firewall.

    ❑ B. On your home computer, enable the Remote Desktop option in the Internet Connection Firewall services.

    ❑ C. On your office computer, enable Internet Connection Firewall.

    ❑ D. On your office computer, enable the Remote Desktop option in the Internet Connection Firewall services.

Quick Check

29. You're the administrator of all the Windows XP Professional portable computers for your company. All computers are members of a Windows 2000 domain. During the day, users connect their portable computers to the company network. While at home in the evening, users use their portable computers to access the Internet. Users report that when they connect their portable computers to the company network, they're able to access network resources. Users on the network are not able to connect to any shared folders that are defined on the portable computers.

    You confirm that users have the necessary permissions to connect to the shared folders on the portable computers. You want to ensure that the portable computers are protected when they are connected to the Internet during evening hours. You also want to ensure that users can access shared folders on the portable computers during daytime. What should you do?

    - ❑ A. Configure the Network TCP/IP settings on the Windows XP Professional portable computers to use DHCP. Configure the Alternate Configuration feature to use user-configured addresses.
    - ❑ B. On the Windows XP Professional portable computers, enable Internet Connection Sharing (ICS) Discovery and Control.
    - ❑ C. Link a Group Policy Object (GPO) to the company network sites. Configure the GPO to enable the Guest-only sharing and security model for local accounts.
    - ❑ D. On the Windows XP Professional portable computers, enable Internet Connection Firewall. Configure the local Group Policy Object to enable Prohibit the Use of ICF on Your DNS Domain Network.

Quick Answer: 191
Detailed Answer: 195

30. You're the desktop administrator for NWTraders, Inc. Peter is a user in the payroll department. Peter reports that he is not able to download a file from an FTP server by using Internet Explorer on his Windows XP Professional computer. When Peter attempts to access the FTP server by using the URL ftp://ftp.nwtraders.com, Internet Explorer displays the following error message: The password was rejected. Peter informs you that he has a username and password for the FTP server, but that Internet Explorer does not prompt him to type the username and password.

    You need to ensure that Peter can access the FTP server by using Internet Explorer on his own computer. Which URL should you tell Peter to use?

    - ❑ A. ftp://Peter:password@ftp.nwtraders.com
    - ❑ B. ftp://ftp.nwtraders.com@Peter:password
    - ❑ C. ftp://Peter@ftp.nwtraders.com
    - ❑ D. ftp://ftp.nwtraders.com/Peter

Quick Answer: **191**
Detailed Answer: **195**

31. What is the name of the new feature in Microsoft Windows XP that enables you to combine several different NICs for different networks into a single bridged NIC that behaves as a single network?

    - ❑ A. Single Bridging
    - ❑ B. Spanning Tree Bridging
    - ❑ C. Network Bridging
    - ❑ D. NIC Bridging

Quick Answer: **191**
Detailed Answer: **195**

32. What is the name of the new feature that acts like a limited version of Terminal Services that enables others to remotely administer Microsoft Windows XP Professional?

    - ❑ A. PCAnywhere
    - ❑ B. Remote Desktop Connection
    - ❑ C. GoToMyPC
    - ❑ D. NetMeeting

Quick Answer: **191**
Detailed Answer: **195**

33. How many remote desktop connections are supported at one time when allowing others to remotely administer a Microsoft Windows XP Professional computer?

    - ❑ A. None
    - ❑ B. One
    - ❑ C. Two
    - ❑ D. Three

Quick Answer: **191**
Detailed Answer: **195**

Quick Check

34. When troubleshooting network protocols and services on a Microsoft Windows XP Professional computer, which command will display current TCP/IP information in short format?

Quick Answer: 191
Detailed Answer: 195

- ❑ A. IPCONFIG
- ❑ B. IPCONFIG /all
- ❑ C. NBTSTAT
- ❑ D. NETSTAT
- ❑ E. PING

35. When troubleshooting network protocols and services on a Microsoft Windows XP Professional computer, which command will display current TCP/IP information in a long form with full details?

Quick Answer: 191
Detailed Answer: 195

- ❑ A. TRACERT
- ❑ B. IPCONFIG /all
- ❑ C. NBTSTAT
- ❑ D. Default gateway
- ❑ E. Subnet mask

36. When troubleshooting network protocols and services on a Microsoft Windows XP Professional computer, which command displays statistics for connections using NetBIOS over TCP/IP?

Quick Answer: 191
Detailed Answer: 195

- ❑ A. TRACERT
- ❑ B. IPCONFIG /all
- ❑ C. NBTSTAT
- ❑ D. NETSTAT
- ❑ E. Subnet mask

37. When troubleshooting network protocols and services on a Microsoft Windows XP Professional computer, which command displays statistics and connections for the TCP/IP (Transmission Control Protocol/Internet Protocol) only?

Quick Answer: 191
Detailed Answer: 195

- ❑ A. IPCONFIG
- ❑ B. Default gateway
- ❑ C. NBTSTAT
- ❑ D. NETSTAT
- ❑ E. Subnet mask

Quick Check

38. When troubleshooting network protocols and services on a Microsoft Windows XP Professional computer, which command tests network connections?

Quick Answer: 191
Detailed Answer: 195

- ❑ A. IPCONFIG
- ❑ B. IPCONFIG /all
- ❑ C. NBTSTAT
- ❑ D. NETSTAT
- ❑ E. PING

39. When troubleshooting network protocols and services on a Microsoft Windows XP Professional computer, which command checks a route to a remote system?

Quick Answer: 191
Detailed Answer: 195

- ❑ A. IPCONFIG
- ❑ B. TRACERT
- ❑ C. NBTSTAT
- ❑ D. NETSTAT
- ❑ E. PING

40. When troubleshooting network protocols and services on a Microsoft Windows XP Professional computer, what is the setting of a TCP/IP address that defines a subnet portion and a host portion of an IP address?

Quick Answer: 191
Detailed Answer: 195

- ❑ A. IPCONFIG
- ❑ B. IPCONFIG /all
- ❑ C. NBTSTAT
- ❑ D. Subnet mask
- ❑ E. PING

41. When troubleshooting network protocols and services on a Microsoft Windows XP Professional computer, what IP address does a computer network transmission default to when a packet is not local to the subnet?

Quick Answer: 191
Detailed Answer: 196

- ❑ A. IPCONFIG
- ❑ B. IPCONFIG /all
- ❑ C. Default gateway
- ❑ D. NETSTAT
- ❑ E. PING

42. What protocol is used by Microsoft Windows XP to allow Novell NetWare systems to access its resources?

Quick Answer: 191
Detailed Answer: 196

- ❑ A. NWLink
- ❑ B. DLC
- ❑ C. NetBEUI
- ❑ D. AppleTalk

Quick Check

43. What is a nonroutable protocol used by Microsoft Windows XP to communicate with IBM mainframes and AS/400s, and HP (Hewlett-Packard) JetDirect printers?

Quick Answer: 191
Detailed Answer: 196

- ❑ A. NWLink
- ❑ B. DLC
- ❑ C. NetBEUI
- ❑ D. AppleTalk

44. What protocol was originally designed by IBM for its LAN Manager server and later extended by Microsoft and Novell?

Quick Answer: 191
Detailed Answer: 196

- ❑ A. NWLink
- ❑ B. DLC
- ❑ C. NetBEUI
- ❑ D. AppleTalk

45. What protocol is not supported by Microsoft Windows XP, and is removed if found during an upgrade?

Quick Answer: 191
Detailed Answer: 196

- ❑ A. NWLink
- ❑ B. DLC
- ❑ C. NetBEUI
- ❑ D. AppleTalk

46. When working with Remote Access Services in Microsoft Windows XP, what authentication protocol is primarily used with Smart Cards and digital certificates?

Quick Answer: 191
Detailed Answer: 196

- ❑ A. EAP-TLS
- ❑ B. MD5-CHAP
- ❑ C. RADIUS
- ❑ D. MS-CHAP
- ❑ E. SPAP

47. When working with Remote Access Services in Microsoft Windows XP, what authentication protocol encrypts usernames and passwords with an MD5 security hashing algorithm?

Quick Answer: 191
Detailed Answer: 196

- ❑ A. CHAP
- ❑ B. MD5-CHAP
- ❑ C. PAP
- ❑ D. MS-CHAP
- ❑ E. SPAP

Quick Check

48. When working with Remote Access Services in Microsoft Windows XP, what authentication protocol is a vendor-independent authentication protocol where Windows XP can only act as a client?

    - ❑ A. CHAP
    - ❑ B. MD5-CHAP
    - ❑ C. RADIUS
    - ❑ D. MS-CHAP
    - ❑ E. PAP

Quick Answer: **191**
Detailed Answer: **196**

49. When working with Remote Access Services in Microsoft Windows XP, what authentication protocol encrypts the entire session, and is also supported using Microsoft Windows 2000 and Windows NT 4.0?

    - ❑ A. EAP-TLS
    - ❑ B. MD5-CHAP
    - ❑ C. RADIUS
    - ❑ D. MS-CHAP
    - ❑ E. SPAP

Quick Answer: **191**
Detailed Answer: **196**

50. When working with Remote Access Services in Microsoft Windows XP, what authentication protocol encrypts only the password and is used by Shiva LAN Rover clients?

    - ❑ A. EAP-TLS
    - ❑ B. MD5-CHAP
    - ❑ C. RADIUS
    - ❑ D. MS-CHAP
    - ❑ E. SPAP

Quick Answer: **191**
Detailed Answer: **196**

51. When working with Remote Access Services in Microsoft Windows XP, what authentication protocol encrypts only the username and password, and works well with several non-Microsoft clients?

    - ❑ A. EAP-TLS
    - ❑ B. MD5-CHAP
    - ❑ C. CHAP
    - ❑ D. MS-CHAP
    - ❑ E. SPAP

Quick Answer: **191**
Detailed Answer: **196**

Quick Check

52. When working with Remote Access Services in Microsoft Windows XP, what authentication protocol sends both the username and password in clear text, and is therefore not secure?

Quick Answer: 191
Detailed Answer: 197

❑ A. EAP-TLS
❑ B. MD5-CHAP
❑ C. RADIUS
❑ D. MS-CHAP
❑ E. PAP

53. Your company decides to use Smart Cards for authentication. What protocol must you use on your Microsoft Windows XP computer?

Quick Answer: 191
Detailed Answer: 197

❑ A. EAP-TLS
❑ B. MD5-CHAP
❑ C. RADIUS
❑ D. MS-CHAP
❑ E. SPAP

54. When speaking with another network technician named Michelle at your company, she mentions the authentication protocol in use encrypts usernames and passwords with a security hashing algorithm. Michelle also states this authentication protocol was developed in 1991 after an earlier version had been broken.

Which authentication protocol is Michelle talking about?

Quick Answer: 191
Detailed Answer: 197

❑ A. EAP-TLS
❑ B. MD5-CHAP
❑ C. PAP
❑ D. MS-CHAP
❑ E. SPAP

55. In what manner can a Microsoft Windows XP computer function when working with the vender-independent RADIUS authentication protocol?

Quick Answer: 191
Detailed Answer: 197

❑ A. Both server and client
❑ B. Server only
❑ C. Client only
❑ D. Neither server nor client

Quick Check

56. You're the network administrator at your company. Your network consists of both Microsoft Windows 2000 Professional and Windows XP Professional computers. You need to establish an authentication protocol.

    When working with Remote Access Services on your network, what authentication protocol should you use to provide the strongest encryption possible?

    - ❑ A. PAP
    - ❑ B. MD5-CHAP
    - ❑ C. RADIUS
    - ❑ D. MS-CHAP
    - ❑ E. SPAP

Quick Answer: 191
Detailed Answer: 197

57. You're the new network administrator for your organization. Some of the users on your network still use Shiva LAN Rover.

    What authentication protocol must be in use on your organization's network in order to accommodate those clients?

    - ❑ A. EAP-TLS
    - ❑ B. MD5-CHAP
    - ❑ C. CHAP
    - ❑ D. MS-CHAP
    - ❑ E. SPAP

Quick Answer: 191
Detailed Answer: 197

58. You are the help desk technician for your company. A newly hired vice president of finance needs you to set up a way for her to authenticate from the road with her laptop, which is running Novell NetWare 6.0. Other laptop users at your company use Microsoft Windows XP Professional.

    What authentication protocol will encrypt her username and password and work with her non-Microsoft laptop?

    - ❑ A. EAP-TLS
    - ❑ B. MD5-CHAP
    - ❑ C. RADIUS
    - ❑ D. CHAP
    - ❑ E. SPAP

Quick Answer: 191
Detailed Answer: 197

Quick Check

59. When working in the IT department at your company, another employee states that there is a nonsecure authentication protocol that sends both the username and password in clear text.

    What authentication protocol is the employee talking about?

    - ❑ A. EAP-TLS
    - ❑ B. PAP
    - ❑ C. RADIUS
    - ❑ D. MS-CHAP
    - ❑ E. SPAP

    Quick Answer: 191
    Detailed Answer: 197

60. When working in the IT department at your company, another employee states that the company uses PPTP (*Point-to-Point Tunneling Protocol*) for its Microsoft Windows XP computers in a VPN (*virtual private network*).

    What features are included in PPTP? (Select all that apply.)

    - ❑ A. Header compression
    - ❑ B. Tunnel authentication
    - ❑ C. Built-in encryption
    - ❑ D. Transmits over IP-based internetworks
    - ❑ E. Transmits over ATM, Frame Relay, UDP, or X.25

    Quick Answer: 191
    Detailed Answer: 197

61. When working in the IT department at your company, another employee states that the company uses L2TP (*Layer Two Tunneling Protocol*) for its Microsoft Windows XP computers in a VPN (*virtual private network*).

    What features are included in L2TP? (Select all that apply.)

    - ❑ A. Header compression
    - ❑ B. Tunnel authentication
    - ❑ C. Built-in encryption
    - ❑ D. Transmits over IP-based internetworks
    - ❑ E. Transmits over ATM, Frame Relay, UDP, or X.25

    Quick Answer: 191
    Detailed Answer: 197

62. What feature(s) of VPN connections do Microsoft Windows XP computers support? (Select all that apply.)

    - ❑ A. Single inbound connection
    - ❑ B. Tunneling protocols
    - ❑ C. Setting callback security
    - ❑ D. Multilink support

    Quick Answer: 191
    Detailed Answer: 198

Quick Check Answer Key

1. A
2. B
3. C
4. D
5. A
6. B
7. D
8. C
9. D
10. C
11. A
12. B
13. B
14. A
15. A
16. A, B, C, and D
17. B
18. C
19. A
20. D
21. D
22. C
23. C
24. A
25. B
26. B
27. C
28. A and B
29. D
30. A
31. C
32. B
33. B
34. A
35. B
36. C
37. D
38. E
39. B
40. D
41. C
42. A
43. B
44. C
45. D
46. A
47. B
48. C
49. D
50. E
51. C
52. E
53. A
54. B
55. C
56. D
57. E
58. D
59. B
60. C and D
61. A, B, D, and E
62. A, B, C, and D

Answers and Explanations

1. **Answer: A.** DNS (Domain Naming System) is used to resolve a computer hostname to an IP (Internet Protocol) address.
2. **Answer: B.** WINS (Windows Internet Naming Service) is used to resolve a NetBIOS name to an IP (Internet Protocol) address.
3. **Answer: C.** A subnet mask is a value that gets used to help distinguish the network ID portion of an IP (Internet Protocol) address from the host portion of an IP address.
4. **Answer: D.** A default gateway is typically a router's IP (Internet Protocol) address for a host to send data packets to if an IP address is not available on the local network.
5. **Answer: A.** TCP/IP (Transmission Control Protocol/Internet Protocol) is a computer industry standard suite of protocols (or *language*). It is able to pass over most networks, so it is considered *routable*. TCP/IP is the protocol at the basis of the Internet, and is installed by default in Microsoft Windows XP.
6. **Answer: B.** TCP/IP (Transmission Control Protocol/Internet Protocol) is a computer industry standard suite of protocols (or *language*). It is able to pass over most networks, so it is considered *routable*. TCP/IP is the protocol at the basis of the Internet, and is installed by default in Microsoft Windows XP.
7. **Answer: D.** TCP/IP (Transmission Control Protocol/Internet Protocol) is a computer industry standard suite of protocols (or *language*). It is able to pass over most networks, so it is considered *routable*. TCP/IP is the protocol at the basis of the Internet, and is installed by default in Microsoft Windows XP.
8. **Answer: C.** TCP/IP (Transmission Control Protocol/Internet Protocol) is a computer industry standard suite of protocols (or *language*). It is able to pass over most networks, so it is considered *routable*. TCP/IP is the protocol at the basis of the Internet, and is installed by default in Microsoft Windows XP.
9. **Answer: D.** TCP/IP (Transmission Control Protocol/Internet Protocol) uses Winsock (Microsoft Windows sockets interface). TCP/IP is used extensively to connect dissimilar systems, such as Novell to Microsoft. IP (Internet Protocol) addresses can either be entered manually, or with the help of a DHCP (Dynamic Host Configuration Protocol) server.
10. **Answer: C.** TCP/IP (Transmission Control Protocol/Internet Protocol) uses Winsock (Microsoft Windows sockets interface). TCP/IP is used extensively to connect dissimilar systems, such as Novell to Microsoft. IP (Internet Protocol) addresses can either be entered manually, or with the help of a DHCP (Dynamic Host Configuration Protocol) server.

11. **Answer: A.** TCP/IP (Transmission Control Protocol/Internet Protocol) uses Winsock (Microsoft Windows Sockets Interface). TCP/IP is used extensively to connect dissimilar systems, such as Novell to Microsoft. IP (Internet Protocol) addresses can either be entered manually, or with the help of a DHCP (Dynamic Host Configuration Protocol) server.

12. **Answer: B.** The IP (Internet Protocol) addresses used by Microsoft Windows XP during APIPA (Automatic Private Internet Protocol Addressing) are 169.254.0.0 to 169.254.255.255.

13. **Answer: B.** The single IP (Internet Protocol) address 127.0.0.1 is also called the *loopback address* and is used for testing.

14. **Answer: A.** The abbreviation APIPA stands for *Automatic Private Internet Protocol Addressing*. The addresses used by Microsoft Windows XP during APIPA are 169.254.0.0 to 169.254.255.255.

15. **Answer: A.** The abbreviation APIPA stands for *Automatic Private Internet Protocol Addressing*. The IP (Internet Protocol) address of a Microsoft Windows XP client computer gets automatically assigned when DHCP (Dynamic Host Configuration Protocol) is unavailable.

16. **Answers: A, B, C, and D.**

    Explanation A. The abbreviation APIPA stands for *Automatic Private Internet Protocol Addressing*. The IP (Internet Protocol) address of a Microsoft Windows XP client computer can be automatically assigned when a DHCP (Dynamic Host Configuration Protocol) server is unavailable.

    Explanation B. The IP (Internet Protocol) address of a Microsoft Windows 2000 client computer can be automatically assigned when a DHCP (Dynamic Host Configuration Protocol) server is unavailable.

    Explanation C. The IP (Internet Protocol) address of a Microsoft Windows Me client computer can be automatically assigned when a DHCP (Dynamic Host Configuration Protocol) server is unavailable.

    Explanation D. The IP (Internet Protocol) address of a Microsoft Windows 98 client computer can be automatically assigned when a DHCP (Dynamic Host Configuration Protocol) server is unavailable.

17. **Answer: B.** The subnet mask used with APIPA (Automatic Private Internet Protocol Addressing) is 255.255.0.0. The IP (Internet Protocol) addresses used by Microsoft Windows XP during APIPA are 169.254.0.0 to 169.254.255.255.

18. **Answer: C.** The version of Internet Explorer that is included with Microsoft Windows XP is 6.0.

19. **Answer: A.** The default cipher strength of 128 bits is used in Internet Explorer 6.0 that is included with Microsoft Windows XP.

20. **Answer: D.** The full-featured text and videoconferencing client that is now fully integrated into Microsoft Windows XP is called Windows Messenger. It was formerly called MSN Messenger.

21. **Answer: D.** ICS stands for *Internet Connection Sharing*. It is a feature of Microsoft Windows XP that allows it to share an Internet connection with other computers on the private network.

22. **Answer: C.** To ensure that Iris can access the Web application on Steve's computer, you first establish a Remote Assistance connection to Steve's computer. Then on Steve's computer under Local Area Connection properties, clear the Internet Connection Firewall check box.

23. **Answer: C.** To establish a Remote Assistance connection with Helen's computer, she needs to remain connected to her ISP (Internet service provider). You should instruct Helen to send a new Remote Assistance invitation and remain connected to her ISP. Then from your PC, accept the new invitation.

24. **Answer: A.** The IPCONFIG /flushdns command will clear any locally cached DNS (Domain Naming System) entries on each employee's computer. Then the computers will each re-query the DNS server to obtain the correct new IP (Internet Protocol) address of FileSrvA.

25. **Answer: B.** You should configure the developer's computer by starting the default Web site. This ensures that the developer can access the Web application by using his Web browser.

26. **Answer: B.** You should configure Windows Messenger to log on by using an Exchange account. There is no need to configure a .NET Passport.

27. **Answer: C.** You must ask a domain administrator to remove the Prohibit Use of Internet Connection Firewall on your DNS Domain group policy in the domain. Instruct Alice to connect to the company network and to log on to the domain.

28. **Answers: A and B.**

    Explanation A. On your home computer, enable the Internet Connection Firewall.

    Explanation B. On your home computer, enable the Remote Desktop option in the Internet Connection Firewall services.

29. **Answer: D.** On Windows XP Professional portable computers, enable Internet Connection Firewall (ICF) for evening use. Configure the local Group Policy Object (GPO) to enable Prohibit the Use of ICF on Your Company's DNS Domain Network.

30. **Answer: A.** Proper syntax is very important in establishing an FTP connection. You should tell Peter to use this URL (Universal Resource Locator): `ftp://Peter:password@ftp.nwtraders.com`.

31. **Answer: C.** Network Bridging is the new feature in Microsoft Windows XP that enables you to combine several different NICs (network interface cards) for different networks into a single bridged NIC that behaves as a single network.

32. **Answer: B.** Remote Desktop Connection is the name of the new feature that acts like a limited version of Terminal Services that enables others to remotely administer Microsoft Windows XP Professional.

33. **Answer: B.** The Remote Desktop Connections feature supports only one connection at a time when enabling others to remotely administer a Microsoft Windows XP Professional computer.

34. **Answer: A.** The IPCONFIG command will display current TCP/IP (Transmission Control Protocol/Internet Protocol) information in shortened format.

35. **Answer: B.** The IPCONFIG /all command will display current TCP/IP (Transmission Control Protocol/Internet Protocol) information in a long form with full details.

36. **Answer: C.** The NBTSTAT command displays statistics for connections using NetBIOS over TCP/IP (Transmission Control Protocol/Internet Protocol).

37. **Answer: D.** The NETSTAT command displays statistics and connections for the TCP/IP (Transmission Control Protocol/Internet Protocol) only.

38. **Answer: E.** The PING command tests network connections. It is often believed that Ping is an abbreviation for Packet Internet Groper, but PING's author has stated that the name comes from the sound made by SONAR.

39. **Answer: B.** The TRACERT (or trace route) command checks a route to a remote system.

40. **Answer: D.** A subnet mask is the setting of a TCP/IP (Transmission Control Protocol/Internet Protocol) address that defines a subnet portion and a host portion of an IP address.

41. **Answer: C.** A default gateway is the IP (Internet Protocol) address that a computer network transmission will default to when a packet is not local to the subnet.

42. **Answer: A.** NWLink is used by Microsoft Windows XP to allow Novell NetWare systems to access its resources. NWLink is Microsoft's version of the IPX/SPX (Internetwork Packet Exchange/Sequenced Packet Exchange) protocol.

43. **Answer: B.** DLC stands for *Data Link Control Protocol.* DLC is a special-purpose, nonroutable protocol used by Microsoft Windows XP to communicate with IBM mainframes and AS/400s (Application System 400s), and HP (Hewlett-Packard) JetDirect printers.

44. **Answer: C.** NetBEUI stands for *NetBIOS* (Basic Input/Output System) *Enhanced User Interface*. NetBEUI was originally designed by IBM for its LAN Manager server and later extended by Microsoft and Novell.

45. **Answer: D.** AppleTalk is not supported by Microsoft Windows XP, and is removed if found during an upgrade.

46. **Answer: A.** EAP-TLS stands for *Extensible Authentication Protocol-Transport Level Security*. EAP-TLS is primarily used with Smart Cards and digital certificates.

47. **Answer: B.** MD5-CHAP stands for *Message Digest 5 Challenge Handshake Authentication Protocol.* MD5-CHAP encrypts usernames and passwords with an MD5 security hashing algorithm.

48. **Answer: C.** RADIUS stands for *Remote Authentication Dial-In User Service*. RADIUS is a vendor-independent authentication protocol. Microsoft Windows XP can only act as a RADIUS client.

49. **Answer: D.** MS-CHAP stands for *Microsoft Challenge Handshake Authentication Protocol.* MS-CHAP encrypts the entire session and not just the username and password. MS-CHAP is supported using Microsoft Windows XP, Windows 2000, and Windows NT 4.0.

50. **Answer: E.** SPAP stands for *Shiva Password Authentication Protocol.* SPAP encrypts the password, but not data. SPAP is used only by Shiva LAN Rover clients.

51. **Answer: C.** CHAP stands for *Challenge Handshake Authentication Protocol.* CHAP encrypts only the username and password, but not session data. CHAP works with non-Microsoft clients.

52. **Answer: E.** PAP stands for *Password Authentication Protocol.* PAP sends both the username and password in clear text, and is therefore not secure.

53. **Answer: A.** EAP-TLS stands for *Extensible Authentication Protocol-Transport Level Security*. EAP-TLS is primarily used with Smart Cards and digital certificates.

54. **Answer: B.** MD5-CHAP stands for *Message Digest 5 Challenge Handshake Authentication Protocol.* MD5-CHAP encrypts usernames and passwords with an MD5 security hashing algorithm.

55. **Answer: C.** RADIUS stands for *Remote Authentication Dial-In User Service.* RADIUS is a vendor-independent authentication protocol. Microsoft Windows XP can only act as a RADIUS client.

56. **Answer: D.** MS-CHAP stands for *Microsoft Challenge Handshake Authentication Protocol.* MS-CHAP encrypts the entire session and not just the username and password. MS-CHAP is supported using Microsoft Windows XP, Windows 2000, and Windows NT 4.0.

57. **Answer: E.** SPAP stands for *Shiva Password Authentication Protocol.* SPAP encrypts the password, but not data. SPAP is used only by Shiva LAN Rover clients.

58. **Answer: D.** CHAP stands for *Challenge Handshake Authentication Protocol.* CHAP encrypts only the username and password, but not session data. CHAP works with non-Microsoft clients.

59. **Answer: B.** PAP stands for *Password Authentication Protocol.* PAP sends both the username and password in clear text, and is therefore not secure.

60. **Answers: C and D.**

    Explanation C. PPTP has built-in encryption.

    Explanation D. PPTP can transmit over IP-based internetworks.

61. **Answers: A, B, D, and E.**

    Explanation A. L2TP cannot use NAT (Network Address Translation) because of this, however.

    Explanation B. L2TP can provide full tunnel authentication.

    Explanation D. PPTP can transmit over IP-based internetworks.

    Explanation E. L2TP (Layer Two Tunneling Protocol) can use these advanced technologies.

62. **Answers: A, B, C, and D.**

 Explanation A. Microsoft Windows XP computers support only a single inbound connection.

 Explanation B. Microsoft Windows XP computers support either PPTP (Point-to-Point Tunneling Protocol) or L2TP (Layer Two Tunneling Protocol) for each VPN (virtual private network).

 Explanation C. Microsoft Windows XP computers support setting callback security, which enables you to have the bill charged to your company's phone number. This also forces the server machine to call back the client at a predefined number for extra security.

 Explanation D. Microsoft Windows XP computers support multilinking, which enables you to combine two or more modems into one logical link with increased bandwidth.

System Monitoring, Performance Optimization, and Recovery Features

Quick Check

1. Which of the following are true of the Task Scheduler in Microsoft Windows XP? (Select all that apply.)

   Quick Answer: **215**
   Detailed Answer: **216**

   ❑ A. Task Scheduler is used to automate events.
   ❑ B. Scheduled tasks are stored under Start, Settings, Control Panel, Scheduled Tasks.
   ❑ C. Security on a scheduled task can be set by group.
   ❑ D. Security on a scheduled task can be set by user.

2. Which of the following are types of caching when using Offline Files in Microsoft Windows XP? (Select all that apply.)

   Quick Answer: **215**
   Detailed Answer: **216**

   ❑ A. Manual caching for programs
   ❑ B. Manual caching for documents
   ❑ C. Automatic caching for programs
   ❑ D. Automatic caching for documents

3. Which of the following counters in the Performance Console of Microsoft Windows XP measures the time that a CPU spends executing a nonidle thread?

   Quick Answer: **215**
   Detailed Answer: **216**

   ❑ A. Processor - % Processor Time
   ❑ B. Processor - Processor Queue Length
   ❑ C. Processor - % CPU DPC Time
   ❑ D. Processor - % CPU Interrupts/Sec
   ❑ E. Logical disk - Disk Queue Length

4. Which of the following counters in the Performance Console of Microsoft Windows XP shows how many threads are in the processor queue?

   Quick Answer: **215**
   Detailed Answer: **216**

   ❑ A. Processor - % Processor Time
   ❑ B. Processor - Processor Queue Length
   ❑ C. Processor - % CPU DPC Time
   ❑ D. Processor - % CPU Interrupts/Sec
   ❑ E. Logical disk - Disk Queue Length

Quick Check

5. Which of the following counters in the Performance Console of Microsoft Windows XP measures software interrupts?

Quick Answer: 215
Detailed Answer: 216

- ❑ A. Processor - % Processor Time
- ❑ B. Processor - Processor Queue Length
- ❑ C. Processor - % CPU DPC Time
- ❑ D. Processor - % CPU Interrupts/Sec
- ❑ E. Logical disk - Disk Queue Length

6. Which of the following counters in the Performance Console of Microsoft Windows XP measures hardware interrupts?

Quick Answer: 215
Detailed Answer: 216

- ❑ A. Processor - % Processor Time
- ❑ B. Processor - Processor Queue Length
- ❑ C. Processor - % CPU DPC Time
- ❑ D. Processor - % CPU Interrupts/Sec
- ❑ E. Logical disk - Disk Queue Length

7. Which of the following counters in the Performance Console of Microsoft Windows XP measures the number of Logical Disk Queue entries?

Quick Answer: 215
Detailed Answer: 216

- ❑ A. Processor - % Processor Time
- ❑ B. Processor - Processor Queue Length
- ❑ C. Processor - % CPU DPC Time
- ❑ D. Processor - % CPU Interrupts/Sec
- ❑ E. Logical disk - Disk Queue Length

8. Which of the following counters in the Performance Console of Microsoft Windows XP measures the number of Physical Disk Queue entries?

Quick Answer: 215
Detailed Answer: 217

- ❑ A. Logical disk - Disk Queue Length
- ❑ B. Physical disk - Disk Queue Length
- ❑ C. Physical disk - % Disk Time
- ❑ D. Memory - Pages/Sec
- ❑ E. Memory - Committed Bytes

9. Which of the following counters in the Performance Console of Microsoft Windows XP measures paging performance?

Quick Answer: 215
Detailed Answer: 217

- ❑ A. Processor - % Processor Time
- ❑ B. Processor - Processor Queue Length
- ❑ C. Processor - % CPU DPC Time
- ❑ D. Physical disk - % Disk Time
- ❑ E. Logical disk - Disk Queue Length
- ❑ F. Physical disk - Disk Queue Length
- ❑ G. Memory - Pages/Sec
- ❑ H. Memory - Committed Bytes

Quick Check

10. Which of the following counters in the Performance Console of Microsoft Windows XP measures how paging and RAM are doing in your system?

Quick Answer: 215
Detailed Answer: 217

- ❑ A. Physical disk - % Disk Time
- ❑ B. Processor - Processor Queue Length
- ❑ C. Memory - Committed Bytes
- ❑ D. Physical disk - % Disk Time
- ❑ E. Memory - Pages/Sec

11. Which of the following counters in the Performance Console of Microsoft Windows XP measures how many bytes of RAM are committed to current processes in your system?

Quick Answer: 215
Detailed Answer: 217

- ❑ A. Memory - Pages/Sec
- ❑ B. Processor - Processor Queue Length
- ❑ C. Memory - Committed Bytes
- ❑ D. Physical disk - Disk Queue Length
- ❑ E. Logical disk - Disk Queue Length

12. Which of the following are like trace logs in Microsoft Windows XP, but log an event, send a message, or run a program only when a preset, user-defined threshold has been exceeded?

Quick Answer: 215
Detailed Answer: 217

- ❑ A. Field logs
- ❑ B. Alert logs
- ❑ C. Counter logs
- ❑ D. Trace logs

13. Which of the following record data from a local or a remote system on hardware usage and system service activity in Microsoft Windows XP?

Quick Answer: 215
Detailed Answer: 217

- ❑ A. Remote logs
- ❑ B. Alert logs
- ❑ C. Counter logs
- ❑ D. Trace logs

14. Which of the following are event-driven logs that record monitored data, such as page faults or disk drive I/O, in Microsoft Windows XP?

Quick Answer: 215
Detailed Answer: 217

- ❑ A. Tracker logs
- ❑ B. Alert logs
- ❑ C. Counter logs
- ❑ D. Trace logs

Quick Check

15. Which of the following subfolders holds the log files in the system's boot partition in Microsoft Windows XP?

Quick Answer: **215**
Detailed Answer: **2217**

- ❑ A. \Logfiles
- ❑ B. \Loglist
- ❑ C. \i386
- ❑ D. \Perflogs

16. Which of the following log file formats are compatible for import into Microsoft Excel from Microsoft Windows XP? (Select all that apply.)

Quick Answer: **215**
Detailed Answer: **217**

- ❑ A. BLG
- ❑ B. CSV
- ❑ C. LOG
- ❑ D. TSV

17. Which of the following is the best reason to create log files in Microsoft Windows XP?

Quick Answer: **215**
Detailed Answer: **217**

- ❑ A. Create job security
- ❑ B. Create less hard drive space
- ❑ C. Create weekly work of clearing logs
- ❑ D. Create a baseline for future reference

18. Which of the following is the recommended minimum paging file size in Microsoft Windows XP?

Quick Answer: **215**
Detailed Answer: **217**

- ❑ A. The same size as physical installed RAM
- ❑ B. One-and-a-half times the size of physical installed RAM
- ❑ C. The size of physical installed RAM plus 1MB
- ❑ D. Double the size of physical installed RAM

19. Which of the following is the recommended maximum paging file size in Microsoft Windows XP?

Quick Answer: **215**
Detailed Answer: **217**

- ❑ A. The same size as physical installed RAM
- ❑ B. Two-and-a-half times the size of physical installed RAM
- ❑ C. One-and-a-half times the size of physical installed RAM
- ❑ D. Double the size of physical installed RAM

20. Which of the following is the recommended maximum paging file size for a system with 128MB RAM in Microsoft Windows XP?

Quick Answer: **215**
Detailed Answer: **218**

- ❑ A. 128MB
- ❑ B. 192MB
- ❑ C. 320MB
- ❑ D. 256MB

Quick Check

21. Which of the following is the recommended maximum paging file size for a system with 256MB RAM in Microsoft Windows XP?

Quick Answer: 215
Detailed Answer: 218

- ❑ A. 640MB
- ❑ B. 320MB
- ❑ C. 128MB
- ❑ D. 512MB

22. Which of the following is the recommended maximum paging file size for a system with 384MB RAM in Microsoft Windows XP?

Quick Answer: 215
Detailed Answer: 218

- ❑ A. 320MB
- ❑ B. 1,024MB
- ❑ C. 64MB
- ❑ D. 960MB

23. Which of the following is the recommended maximum paging file size for a system with 512MB RAM in Microsoft Windows XP?

Quick Answer: 215
Detailed Answer: 218

- ❑ A. 1,280MB
- ❑ B. 512MB
- ❑ C. 960MB
- ❑ D. 1,024MB

24. Which of the following is the recommended minimum paging file size for a system with 512MB RAM in Microsoft Windows XP?

Quick Answer: 215
Detailed Answer: 218

- ❑ A. 512MB
- ❑ B. 768MB
- ❑ C. 513MB
- ❑ D. 1,024MB

25. Which of the following is the recommended minimum paging file size for a system with 384MB RAM in Microsoft Windows XP?

Quick Answer: 215
Detailed Answer: 218

- ❑ A. 128MB
- ❑ B. 576MB
- ❑ C. 512MB
- ❑ D. 768MB

Quick Check

26. Which of the following is the recommended minimum paging file size for a system with 256MB RAM in Microsoft Windows XP?
    - ❑ A. 128MB
    - ❑ B. 384MB
    - ❑ C. 512MB
    - ❑ D. 960MB

Quick Answer: **215**
Detailed Answer: **218**

27. Which of the following is the recommended minimum paging file size for a system with 128MB RAM in Microsoft Windows XP?
    - ❑ A. 128MB
    - ❑ B. 512MB
    - ❑ C. 192MB
    - ❑ D. 256MB

Quick Answer: **215**
Detailed Answer: **218**

28. When should hardware profiles be used in Microsoft Windows XP?
    - ❑ A. To store different configuration settings, usually with desktop PCs
    - ❑ B. To allow for different backgrounds on a desktop
    - ❑ C. To store different configuration settings, usually with portable PCs
    - ❑ D. To allow for different screensavers on a desktop

Quick Answer: **215**
Detailed Answer: **218**

29. When should hardware profiles be selected when used in Microsoft Windows XP?
    - ❑ A. At login
    - ❑ B. At shutdown
    - ❑ C. At startup
    - ❑ D. At logoff

Quick Answer: **215**
Detailed Answer: **218**

30. What single feature of Microsoft Windows XP enables you to create different sets of configuration settings to meet a user's different needs?
    - ❑ A. Software profiles
    - ❑ B. Hardware profiles
    - ❑ C. Hardware settings
    - ❑ D. Software settings

Quick Answer: **215**
Detailed Answer: **218**

Quick Check

31. How do you create hardware profiles in Microsoft Windows XP?

Quick Answer: 215
Detailed Answer: 218

- ❑ A. Choose Start, System, Settings, Control Panel, Hardware tab, Hardware Profiles.
- ❑ B. Choose Start, Settings, Control Panel, System, Hardware Profiles.
- ❑ C. Choose Start, Settings, Control Panel, System, Hardware tab, Hardware Profiles.
- ❑ D. Choose Start, Settings, System, Control Panel, Hardware tab, Hardware Profiles.

32. When devices are enabled and disabled in particular profiles through their properties in the Device Manager snap-in of Microsoft Windows XP, what are you creating for different users?

Quick Answer: 215
Detailed Answer: 218

- ❑ A. System logs
- ❑ B. System Restore Points
- ❑ C. Registry backups
- ❑ D. Hardware profiles

33. What command-line tool should you run to launch Microsoft Windows XP backup?

Quick Answer: 215
Detailed Answer: 218

- ❑ A. backup
- ❑ B. xpbackup
- ❑ C. ntbackup
- ❑ D. backupxp

34. What command-line tool should you run to back up system state information in Microsoft Windows XP?

Quick Answer: 215
Detailed Answer: 218

- ❑ A. backupxp /systemstate
- ❑ B. xpbackup /ss
- ❑ C. backupss
- ❑ D. systemstate

35. What groups can back up and restore all files in Microsoft Windows XP regardless of permissions? (Select all that apply.)

Quick Answer: 215
Detailed Answer: 219

- ❑ A. Guests
- ❑ B. Administrators
- ❑ C. Backup Operators
- ❑ D. Modem Operators

Quick Check

36. What backup type backs up all selected files and folders, while not clearing the archive bit, and is fast for restoring data in Microsoft Windows XP?

Quick Answer: 215
Detailed Answer: 219

- ❑ A. Copy
- ❑ B. Daily
- ❑ C. Differential
- ❑ D. Incremental
- ❑ E. Normal

37. What backup type backs up all selected files and folders that have changed throughout the day, while not clearing the archive bit, and is fastest for backing up data each day in Microsoft Windows XP?

Quick Answer: 215
Detailed Answer: 219

- ❑ A. Copy
- ❑ B. Daily
- ❑ C. Differential
- ❑ D. Incremental
- ❑ E. Normal

38. What backup type backs up all selected files and folders that have their archive bit set (that is, files that have changed since the last normal backup), while not clearing the archive bit, and is faster for backing up data each day in Microsoft Windows XP?

Quick Answer: 215
Detailed Answer: 219

- ❑ A. Copy
- ❑ B. Daily
- ❑ C. Differential
- ❑ D. Incremental
- ❑ E. Normal

39. What backup type only backs up selected files and folders that have their archive attribute set, and then also clears the archive bit afterward? This backup type is fastest for backing up data in Microsoft Windows XP.

Quick Answer: 215
Detailed Answer: 219

- ❑ A. Copy
- ❑ B. Daily
- ❑ C. Differential
- ❑ D. Incremental
- ❑ E. Normal

Quick Check

40. What backup type backs up all selected files and folders, and then also clears the archive bit? This backup type is fast for restoring data, and is often referred to as a *full backup* in Microsoft Windows XP.

Quick Answer: **215**
Detailed Answer: **219**

- ❑ A. Copy
- ❑ B. Daily
- ❑ C. Differential
- ❑ D. Incremental
- ❑ E. Normal

41. What are the main Microsoft Windows XP Registry subtrees? (Select all that apply.)

Quick Answer: **215**
Detailed Answer: **219**

- ❑ A. HKEY_CLASSES_ROOT
- ❑ B. HKEY_CURRENT_CONFIG
- ❑ C. HKEY_CURRENT_USERS
- ❑ D. HKEY_LOCAL_MACHINE
- ❑ E. HKEY_USERS

42. What is the main Microsoft Windows XP Registry subtree that holds software configuration data, file associations, and OLE (object linking and embedding) data?

Quick Answer: **215**
Detailed Answer: **220**

- ❑ A. HKEY_CLASSES_ROOT
- ❑ B. HKEY_CURRENT_CONFIG
- ❑ C. HKEY_CURRENT_USERS
- ❑ D. HKEY_LOCAL_MACHINE
- ❑ E. HKEY_USERS

43. What is the main Microsoft Windows XP Registry subtree that holds data on the active hardware profile extracted from the Microsoft Windows XP Registry subtrees SOFTWARE and SYSTEM?

Quick Answer: **215**
Detailed Answer: **220**

- ❑ A. HKEY_CLASSES_ROOT
- ❑ B. HKEY_CURRENT_CONFIG
- ❑ C. HKEY_CURRENT_USERS
- ❑ D. HKEY_LOCAL_MACHINE
- ❑ E. HKEY_USERS

Quick Check

44. What is the main Microsoft Windows XP Registry subtree that holds data about the active current user extracted from the Microsoft Windows XP Registry subtree HKEY_USERS?

Quick Answer: 215
Detailed Answer: 220

- ❑ A. HKEY_CLASSES_ROOT
- ❑ B. HKEY_CURRENT_CONFIG
- ❑ C. HKEY_CURRENT_USERS
- ❑ D. HKEY_LOCAL_MACHINE
- ❑ E. HKEY_USERS

45. What is the main Microsoft Windows XP Registry subtree that holds data about all local computer hardware, software, device drivers, and startup information?

Quick Answer: 215
Detailed Answer: 220

- ❑ A. HKEY_CLASSES_ROOT
- ❑ B. HKEY_CURRENT_CONFIG
- ❑ C. HKEY_CURRENT_USERS
- ❑ D. HKEY_LOCAL_MACHINE
- ❑ E. HKEY_USERS

46. What is the main Microsoft Windows XP Registry subtree that holds data for user identities and environments, including custom settings?

Quick Answer: 215
Detailed Answer: 220

- ❑ A. HKEY_CLASSES_ROOT
- ❑ B. HKEY_CURRENT_CONFIG
- ❑ C. HKEY_CURRENT_USERS
- ❑ D. HKEY_LOCAL_MACHINE
- ❑ E. HKEY_USERS

47. What is another name for the secondary logon service in Microsoft Windows XP?

Quick Answer: 215
Detailed Answer: 220

- ❑ A. Run For
- ❑ B. Run With
- ❑ C. Run By
- ❑ D. Run As

48. How do you run an application using the secondary logon service, also known as *Run As*, in Microsoft Windows XP?

Quick Answer: 215
Detailed Answer: 220

- ❑ A. Left-click the selected application, hold down Ctrl, right-click the icon, and finally select Run As.
- ❑ B. Left-click the selected application, hold down Ctrl, left-click the icon, and finally select Run As.
- ❑ C. Left-click the selected application, hold down Shift, left-click the icon, and finally select Run As.
- ❑ D. Left-click the selected application, hold down Shift, right-click the icon, and finally select Run As.

Quick Check

49. What is another name for the Microsoft Windows XP secondary logon service that is similar to the Unix Super User command?

Quick Answer: 215
Detailed Answer: 220

- ❑ A. Run For
- ❑ B. Run With
- ❑ C. Run As
- ❑ D. Run By

50. What type of user profile in Microsoft Windows XP is created the very first time a user logs on to the computer?

Quick Answer: 215
Detailed Answer: 220

- ❑ A. Hardware user profile
- ❑ B. Local user profile
- ❑ C. Mandatory user profile
- ❑ D. Roaming user profile

51. You're the desktop administrator for your company. All employees use Windows 2000 Professional on their computers. You then upgrade all computers to Windows XP Professional, and users experience no problems after the upgrade has been completed. A new employee is issued a new client computer that's identical to all other client computers in the company. The new employee installs Windows XP Professional on this computer from a network server installation point. The new employee now reports that he cannot change his display settings from 640×480 screen resolution with only 16 colors.

Quick Answer: 215
Detailed Answer: 220

You confirm that this computer has the same video hardware as all other clients. You also confirm that the hardware manufacturer does not have a video driver for Windows XP Professional. You need to enable the user to change his display settings to higher resolution and color quality. What should you do?

- ❑ A. On the Color Management tab of the Advanced Display settings, specify the appropriate color profile for the monitor.
- ❑ B. Reboot the computer in Safe mode and select the standard VGA video driver.
- ❑ C. On the Monitor tab of the Advanced Display settings, specify the correct driver for the monitor.
- ❑ D. Install the older Windows 2000 Professional video drivers on the computer.

Quick Check

52. You're a desktop administrator for Marketing Plus Advertisers. You've just deployed new Windows XP Professional computers to all advertising designers. Each computer has a built-in tape drive for data backups. The advertising designers need to back up their work to the tape drive. You add all advertising designers' user accounts to the Backup Operators group on their individual computers. The advertising designers work day shifts Monday through Friday, and their data will not take a very long time to back up fully.

    The advertising designers need to back up all their data weekly. They also need to back up all changes since the last full backup. The advertising designers want to use a backup method that enables them to recover their data as quickly as possible.

    What should you tell the advertising designers to do?

    - ❑ A. Perform a copy backup every Monday. Create an incremental backup for Tuesday, Wednesday, Thursday, and Friday.
    - ❑ B. Perform a differential backup every Monday. Create an incremental backup for Tuesday, Wednesday, Thursday, and Friday.
    - ❑ C. Perform a daily backup every Monday. Create an incremental backup for Tuesday, Wednesday, Thursday, and Friday.
    - ❑ D. Perform a normal backup every Monday. Create an incremental backup for Tuesday, Wednesday, Thursday, and Friday.

Quick Answer: **215**
Detailed Answer: **221**

53. You're a desktop administrator for your nonprofit organization. All users have either Windows 2000 Professional or Windows XP Professional computers. Users in the finance department run an application that requires several hours to process accounts receivable data. They complain that when they run the accounts receivable application, the performance of other software applications gets noticeably slower.

    You need to allow the accounts receivable application to run with the least performance impact on any other software applications. How should you configure the finance users' accounts receivable application?

    - ❑ A. Configure all accounts receivable applications to have AboveNormal priority.
    - ❑ B. Configure all accounts receivable applications to have BelowNormal priority.
    - ❑ C. Configure all other business applications to have High priority.
    - ❑ D. Configure all other business applications to have Realtime priority.

Quick Answer: **215**
Detailed Answer: **221**

Quick Check

54. You're a desktop administrator for your company. Your network consists of a single Active Directory domain. All users have Windows XP Professional computers, with all users' data on file servers. No company or user data is stored locally on client computers. Users from the sales department have laptops. When they travel, they must be able to use company data files, even when their laptops are not connected to the network. Caching of offline files is enabled on all shared folders on the file servers. Offline files are configured on all laptops used by employees of the sales department. These users also select several folders to be made available offline. Sales department users complain that when they're out of the office, the offline files aren't available to them.

Quick Answer: 215
Detailed Answer: 221

You need to be sure that the offline files are available to the sales users, even when they aren't connected to the network. What should you do?

- ❑ A. Change the caching options for the shared folder to allow automatic caching of documents.
- ❑ B. Grant the sales users Allow-Full Control permission on the shared folders.
- ❑ C. In the Advanced properties for Offline Files, select the Notify Me and Begin Working Offline check box on each of the sales department clients' laptops.
- ❑ D. Add the servers containing the sales department files to the Exception list on the offline files configuration.

Quick Check

55. You're a help desk administrator for your company. Edward, an employee in the marketing department, uses a Windows XP Professional computer. Edward often works with a file named Plans.xls, which is stored in a folder named \\MktgFiles\Plans. Initially, he can work with the file when he is out of the office and offline without copying it to his local hard disk. Edward now states he cannot open the file when he is out of the office.

    You need to ensure that Edward can always access Plans.xls when he is out of the office and offline. What should you do?

    - ❑ A. Tell Edward to open Windows Explorer, select Folder Options from the Tools menu, and select the Enable Offline Files check box on the Offline Files tab.
    - ❑ B. Tell Edward to increase the amount of hard disk space used for offline files on his computer.
    - ❑ C. Tell Edward to right-click the \\MktgFiles\Plans\Plans.xls file and select Make Available Offline from the context menu.
    - ❑ D. Tell Edward to open Windows Explorer, select Folder Options from the Tools menu, and select the Synchronize All Offline Files Before Logging Off check box on the Offline Files tab.

Quick Answer: **215**
Detailed Answer: **221**

56. You're the desktop administrator for your company. An advertising designer named Elias installs a photo-editing application on his Windows XP Professional computer. After installation, the performance on his computer is significantly slower. In trying to fix the problem, Elias uninstalls the photo-editing application and restarts his computer, but performance does not improve.

    You want to be sure that you preserve Elias's data and computer settings while getting his computer back to its previous working condition as fast as possible. What should you do?

    - ❑ A. Restore Windows XP Professional by using the most current System Restore Point.
    - ❑ B. Restart the computer with the last known good configuration.
    - ❑ C. Use Disk Defragmenter on the computer's hard disk.
    - ❑ D. Restore Windows XP Professional by using an automated system recovery (ASR) backup.

Quick Answer: **215**
Detailed Answer: **221**

Quick Check

57. You're a desktop administrator for your company. All users on the network have Windows XP Professional computers. Users in the sales department have dual-processor computers. The sales users state that when they run 16-bit Windows programs, their computer performance surprisingly becomes very slow. You decide to use System Monitor to monitor the sales users' computers. You notice that when running 16-bit applications, one processor shows a continuous utilization of more than 90%, whereas the other processor uses less than 10%.

    You need to improve application performance for the users in the sales department. What should you do?

    - ❑ A. Configure each application to run in a separate memory space.
    - ❑ B. Configure each application to run in high priority class.
    - ❑ C. For each application, set the compatibility mode to Windows 95.
    - ❑ D. Configure processor affinity for each application to allow it to run on both processors.

Quick Answer: **215**
Detailed Answer: **221**

58. You're the desktop administrator for your company. You upgrade all client computers from Microsoft Windows 98 to Windows XP Professional. A user now complains that when she tries to restore her data from a backup tape created in Windows 98, Windows Backup cannot read or restore the data from the tape.

    You need to enable the user to restore her data. What should you do?

    - ❑ A. Grant the user Allow-Modify permission on Removable Storage.
    - ❑ B. Restore the data to a Windows 98 computer. Back up the data in noncompressed mode. Restore the data on the user's computer.
    - ❑ C. Import the tapes into an existing application media pool. Log on as a local administrator and perform the restoration.
    - ❑ D. Create a new system media pool in Removable Storage. Add the tapes to the media pool. Perform the restoration.

Quick Answer: **215**
Detailed Answer: **221**

Quick Check

59. You're the administrator of 24 Windows XP Professional computers. Each computer has a single hard disk that has three volumes named C, D, and E. Each volume is 4GB in size, but has only one 1GB available space. The total physical memory in each computer is 196MB in size. The paging file on each computer is located on drive D. A user named Ericka claims that each day, about an hour after starting her computer, she gets an error message saying the system is low on virtual memory. Her computer then performs very slowly for 15 seconds.

    You want to improve the performance of Ericka's computer. Your company does not approve of the expense of installing additional memory. What should you do?

    - ❑ A. Increase the Buffers setting in the Config.sys file.
    - ❑ B. Move the current paging file to the system drive.
    - ❑ C. Increase the initial size of the paging file.
    - ❑ D. Enable the Adjust for Best Performance of System Cache memory usage option.

Quick Answer: 215
Detailed Answer: 221

60. You're the administrator of 12 Microsoft Windows XP Professional laptops in the sales department of your company. The company network uses DHCP to configure the IP addresses of the laptops when they are used in the office. Company policy allows the company laptops to be connected to users' home networks. The sales department manager complains that users who use home networks that have manually configured IP addresses are unable to connect their laptops to their home networks.

    You want to be sure that users can connect their laptops to both their home network when they are at home and to the company network when they are in the office. You do not want to adjust any administrative privileges of the sales department users. What should you do?

    - ❑ A. Add a script to the users' desktops that changes the IP configuration between dynamic and manual.
    - ❑ B. Configure the network adapters of the portable computers to enable ICS.
    - ❑ C. Configure the network adapters of the portable computers to enable APIPA.
    - ❑ D. Configure the IP properties of the portable computers so that they have an alternative configuration.

Quick Answer: 215
Detailed Answer: 221

Quick Check Answer Key

1. A, B, C, and D
2. B, C, and D
3. A
4. B
5. C
6. D
7. E
8. B
9. D
10. E
11. C
12. B
13. C
14. D
15. D
16. B and D
17. D
18. B
19. B
20. C
21. A
22. D
23. A
24. B
25. B
26. B
27. C
28. C
29. C
30. B
31. C
32. D
33. C
34. D
35. B and C
36. A
37. B
38. C
39. D
40. E
41. A, B, C, D, and E
42. A
43. B
44. C
45. D
46. E
47. D
48. D
49. C
50. B
51. D
52. D
53. B
54. C
55. C
56. A
57. A
58. B
59. C
60. D

Answers and Explanations

1. **Answers: A, B, C, and D.**

   Explanation A. Task Scheduler is used to automate events such as performing system backups, batch files, and running scripts.

   Explanation B. Scheduled tasks are stored under Start, Settings, Control Panel, Scheduled Tasks.

   Explanation C. Security on a scheduled task can be set by group or user.

   Explanation D. Security on a scheduled task can be set by user or group.

2. **Answers: B, C, and D.**

   Explanation B. Manual caching for documents is one of three types of caching when using offline files in Microsoft Windows XP. It is the default setting. Users must further specify which documents they want available when working offline.

   Explanation C. Automatic caching for programs is one of three types of caching when using offline files in Microsoft Windows XP. All programs opened by a user are cached on his local hard disk for offline use, with older versions being replaced by newer versions when they exist.

   Explanation D. Automatic caching for documents is one of three types of caching when using offline files in Microsoft Windows XP. All documents opened by a user are cached on his local hard disk for offline use, with older versions being replaced by newer versions when they exist.

3. **Answer: A.** The Processor - % Processor Time measures the time a CPU spends executing a non-idle thread. If this counter consistently measures more than 80%, a CPU upgrade is indicated.

4. **Answer: B.** The Processor - Processor Queue Length counter shows how many threads are in the Processor queue. More than two threads in the queue indicates the CPU is a system bottleneck.

5. **Answer: C.** The Processor - % CPU DPC (deferred procedure call) Time counter measures software interrupts.

6. **Answer: D.** The Processor - % CPU Interrupts/Sec counter measures hardware interrupts. Very high counter numbers in this area could mean a poorly written hardware device driver.

7. **Answer: E.** The Logical Disk - Disk Queue Length counter measures the number of logical disk queue entries. If this counter averages more than 2, upgrade the hard drive or its controller, or implement a stripe set.

8. **Answer: B.** The Physical Disk - Disk Queue Length counter measures the number of physical disk queue entries. If this counter averages more than 2, upgrade the hard drive or its controller, or implement a stripe set.

9. **Answer: D.** The Physical Disk - % Disk Time counter measures paging performance. If this counter is more than 90%, move data and/or the pagefile to another hard drive or upgrade the hard drive.

10. **Answer: E.** The Memory - Pages/Sec counter measures how paging and RAM are doing in your system. If this counter indicates more than 20 pages per second, add more RAM. Adding more RAM is probably the best upgrade to any computer system.

11. **Answer: C.** The Memory - Committed Bytes counter measures how many bytes of RAM are committed to current processes in your system. It should always read less than the total amount of RAM in your system.

12. **Answer: B.** Alert logs are like trace logs in Microsoft Windows XP, but log an event, send a message, or run a program only when a preset, user-defined threshold has been exceeded.

13. **Answer: C.** Counter logs record data from a local or a remote system on hardware usage and system service activity.

14. **Answer: D.** Trace logs are event-driven logs. They record monitored data such as page faults or disk drive I/O (input/output).

15. **Answer: D.** The \Perflogs folder holds the log files in the system's boot partition in Microsoft Windows XP.

16. **Answers: B and D.**

    Explanation B. CSV stands for *comma-separated values*. CSV log file format and one other format type are compatible for import into Microsoft Excel from Microsoft Windows XP.

    Explanation D. TSV stands for *tab-separated values*. TSV log file format and one other format type are compatible for import into Microsoft Excel from Microsoft Windows XP.

17. **Answer: D.** The best reason to create log files in Microsoft Windows XP is to create a baseline for future reference.

18. **Answer: B.** One-and-a-half times the size of physical installed RAM is the recommended minimum paging file size in Microsoft Windows XP.

19. **Answer: B.** Two-and-a-half times the size of physical installed RAM is the best recommended maximum paging file size in Microsoft Windows XP.

20. **Answer: C.** Two and a half times the size of physical installed RAM is the best recommended maximum paging file size in Microsoft Windows XP.
21. **Answer: A.** Two-and-a-half times the size of physical installed RAM is the best recommended maximum paging file size in Microsoft Windows XP.
22. **Answer: D.** Two-and-a-half times the size of physical installed RAM is the best recommended maximum paging file size in Microsoft Windows XP.
23. **Answer: A.** Two-and-a-half times the size of physical installed RAM is the best recommended maximum paging file size in Microsoft Windows XP.
24. **Answer: B.** One-and-a-half times the size of physical installed RAM is the recommended minimum paging file size in Microsoft Windows XP.
25. **Answer: B.** One-and-a-half times the size of physical installed RAM is the recommended minimum paging file size in Microsoft Windows XP.
26. **Answer: B.** One-and-a-half times the size of physical installed RAM is the recommended minimum paging file size in Microsoft Windows XP.
27. **Answer: C.** One-and-a-half times the size of physical installed RAM is the recommended minimum paging file size in Microsoft Windows XP.
28. **Answer: C.** Hardware profiles should be used in Microsoft Windows XP to store different configuration settings, usually with portable PCs.
29. **Answer: C.** Hardware profiles should be selected at startup when used in Microsoft Windows XP to load different configuration settings, usually with portable PCs.
30. **Answer: B.** Hardware profiles are the feature of Microsoft Windows XP that enables you to create different sets of configuration settings to meet a user's different needs.
31. **Answer: C.** Hardware profiles are created in Microsoft Windows XP by choosing Start, Settings, Control Panel, System, Hardware tab, Hardware Profiles.
32. **Answer: D.** Hardware profiles are created when you enable and disable devices in particular profiles through their properties in the Device Manager snap-in of Microsoft Windows XP.
33. **Answer: C.** The command-line tool you should run to launch Microsoft Windows XP backup is ntbackup.
34. **Answer: D.** The command-line tool you should run to back up system state information in Microsoft Windows XP backup is systemstate. System state information includes the system registry and COM objects.

35. **Answers: B and C.**

    Explanation B. Administrators is one of two default groups that can back up and restore all files in Microsoft Windows XP regardless of permissions.

    Explanation C. Backup Operators is one of two default groups that can back up and restore all files in Microsoft Windows XP regardless of permissions.

36. **Answer: A.** The Copy backup type backs up all selected files and folders, while not clearing the archive bit. The Copy backup type is fast for restoring data.

37. **Answer: B.** The Daily backup type backs up all selected files and folders that have changed throughout the day, while not clearing the archive bit. The Daily backup type is fastest for backing up data each day.

38. **Answer: C.** The Differential backup type backs up all selected files and folders that have their archive bit set (that is, files that have changed since the last Normal backup), while not clearing the archive bit. The Differential backup type is faster for backing up data each day.

39. **Answer: D.** The Incremental backup type only backs up selected files and folders that have their archive attribute set, and also clears the archive bit afterward. The Incremental backup type is fastest for backing up data.

40. **Answer: E.** The Normal backup type backs up all selected files and folders, and then also clears the archive bit. The Normal backup type is fast for restoring data. The Normal backup type is often referred to as a *full backup*.

41. **Answers: A, B, C, D, and E.**

    Explanation A. HKEY_CLASSES_ROOT is one of the five main subtrees in the Microsoft Windows XP Registry. It holds software configuration data, file associations, and OLE (object linking and embedding) data.

    Explanation B. HKEY_CURRENT_CONFIG is one of the five main subtrees in the Microsoft Windows XP Registry. It holds data on the active hardware profile extracted from the Microsoft Windows XP Registry subtrees SOFTWARE and SYSTEM.

    Explanation C. HKEY_CURRENT_USERS is one of the five main subtrees in the Microsoft Windows XP Registry. It holds data about the active current user extracted from the Microsoft Windows XP Registry subtree HKEY_USERS.

    Explanation D. HKEY_LOCAL_MACHINE is one of the five main subtrees in the Microsoft Windows XP Registry. It holds data about all local computer hardware, software, device drivers, and startup information.

    Explanation E. HKEY_USERS is one of the five main subtrees in the Microsoft Windows XP Registry. It holds data for user identities and environments, including custom settings.

42. **Answer: A.** HKEY_CLASSES_ROOT is one of the five main subtrees in the Microsoft Windows XP Registry. It holds software configuration data, file associations, and OLE (object linking and embedding) data.

43. **Answer: B.** HKEY_CURRENT_CONFIG is one of the five main subtrees in the Microsoft Windows XP Registry. It holds data on the active hardware profile extracted from the Microsoft Windows XP Registry subtrees SOFTWARE and SYSTEM.

44. **Answer: C.** HKEY_CURRENT_USERS is one of the five main subtrees in the Microsoft Windows XP Registry. It holds data about the active current user extracted from the Microsoft Windows XP Registry subtree HKEY_USERS.

45. **Answer: D.** HKEY_LOCAL_MACHINE is one of the five main subtrees in the Microsoft Windows XP Registry. It holds data about all local computer hardware, software, device drivers, and startup information.

46. **Answer: E.** HKEY_USERS is one of the five main subtrees in the Microsoft Windows XP Registry. It holds data for user identities and environments, including custom settings.

47. **Answer: D.** Another name for the secondary logon service in Microsoft Windows XP is *Run As*. Run As is used to run programs as another user, while still maintaining your current logon session. Run As is also useful for testing settings of another user's account.

48. **Answer: D.** To run a selected application using the secondary logon service (also known as *Run As*) in Microsoft Windows XP, you must left-click the selected application, hold down Shift, right-click the icon, and finally select Run As. Run As is used to run programs as another user, while still maintaining your current logon session.

49. **Answer: C.** Another name for the secondary logon service in Microsoft Windows XP is called *Run As*. Run As is useful for testing settings of another user's account. Run As is also similar in functionality to the Unix Super User command.

50. **Answer: B.** Local user profiles are created the very first time a user logs on to the computer. Local user profiles are stored on the local hard drive, as are all future changes.

51. **Answer: D.** You should install the older Windows 2000 Professional video drivers on the computer. They worked fine and were compatible on this particular hardware, as all other users have them.

52. **Answer: D.** You should tell the advertising designers to perform a normal backup every Monday. A normal backup is also sometimes called a full backup. Tell them to do an incremental backup for Tuesday, Wednesday, Thursday, and Friday.

53. **Answer: B.** You should configure all accounts receivable applications to have BelowNormal priority.

54. **Answer: C.** You should adjust the Advanced properties for offline files, selecting the Notify Me and Begin Working Offline check box on each of the sales department client computers.

55. **Answer: C.** You should tell Edward to right-click the \\MktgFiles\Plans\Plans.xls file and select Make Available Offline from the context menu.

56. **Answer: A.** You should restore Windows XP Professional by using the most current System Restore Point. That will roll back the Registry settings to their former productive state.

57. **Answer: A.** You should configure each application to run in a separate memory space.

58. **Answer: B.** You should restore the data to a Windows 98 computer. Then you need to back up the data in noncompressed mode. Finally, restore the data on the user's computer.

59. **Answer: C.** You should increase the initial size of the paging file on Ericka's computer. Adding more memory would also help, but is not allowed in this scenario.

60. **Answer: D.** You should configure the IP properties of the portable computers so that they have an alternative configuration.

Installing, Administering, and Troubleshooting Remote Access Services

Quick Check

1. When working with Remote Access Services in Microsoft Windows XP, what authentication protocol is primarily used with Smart Cards and digital certificates?

   Quick Answer: **236**
   Detailed Answer: **237**

   - ❑ A. EAP-TLS
   - ❑ B. MD5-CHAP
   - ❑ C. RADIUS
   - ❑ D. MS-CHAP
   - ❑ E. SPAP

2. When working with Remote Access Services in Microsoft Windows XP, what authentication protocol encrypts usernames and passwords with an MD5 security hashing algorithm?

   Quick Answer: **236**
   Detailed Answer: **237**

   - ❑ A. EAP-TLS
   - ❑ B. MD5-CHAP
   - ❑ C. RADIUS
   - ❑ D. CHAP
   - ❑ E. PAP

3. When working with Remote Access Services in Microsoft Windows XP, what authentication protocol is a vendor-independent authentication protocol in which Windows XP can only act as a client?

   Quick Answer: **236**
   Detailed Answer: **237**

   - ❑ A. CHAP
   - ❑ B. MD5-CHAP
   - ❑ C. RADIUS
   - ❑ D. PAP
   - ❑ E. SPAP

Quick Check

4. When working with Remote Access Services in Microsoft Windows XP, what authentication protocol encrypts the entire session and is also supported using Microsoft Windows 2000 and Windows NT 4.0?

Quick Answer: 236
Detailed Answer: 237

- ❑ A. EAP-TLS
- ❑ B. MD5-CHAP
- ❑ C. RADIUS
- ❑ D. MS-CHAP
- ❑ E. CHAP

5. When working with Remote Access Services in Microsoft Windows XP, what authentication protocol encrypts the password only and is used by Shiva LAN Rover clients?

Quick Answer: 236
Detailed Answer: 237

- ❑ A. EAP-TLS
- ❑ B. MD5-CHAP
- ❑ C. RADIUS
- ❑ D. MS-CHAP
- ❑ E. SPAP

6. When working with Remote Access Services in Microsoft Windows XP, what authentication protocol encrypts only the username and password, and works well with several non-Microsoft clients?

Quick Answer: 236
Detailed Answer: 237

- ❑ A. CHAP
- ❑ B. PAP
- ❑ C. RADIUS
- ❑ D. MS-CHAP
- ❑ E. SPAP

7. When working with Remote Access Services in Microsoft Windows XP, what authentication protocol sends both the username and password in clear text, and is therefore not secure?

Quick Answer: 236
Detailed Answer: 237

- ❑ A. CHAP
- ❑ B. PAP
- ❑ C. RADIUS
- ❑ D. MS-CHAP
- ❑ E. SPAP

Quick Check

8. Your company decides to use Smart Cards for authentication. What protocol must you use on your Microsoft Windows XP computer?

   Quick Answer: 236
   Detailed Answer: 237

   - ❑ A. EAP-TLS
   - ❑ B. MD5-CHAP
   - ❑ C. RADIUS
   - ❑ D. MS-CHAP
   - ❑ E. SPAP

9. When speaking with another network technician named Michelle at your company, she mentions the authentication protocol in use encrypts usernames and passwords with a security hashing algorithm. Michelle also states that this authentication protocol was developed in 1991 after an earlier version had been broken.

   Quick Answer: 236
   Detailed Answer: 237

   Which authentication protocol is Michelle talking about?

   - ❑ A. PAP
   - ❑ B. MD5-CHAP
   - ❑ C. RADIUS
   - ❑ D. MS-CHAP
   - ❑ E. SPAP

10. In what manner can a Microsoft Windows XP computer function when working with the vendor-independent RADIUS authentication protocol?

    Quick Answer: 236
    Detailed Answer: 237

    - ❑ A. Both server and client
    - ❑ B. Server only
    - ❑ C. Client only
    - ❑ D. Neither server nor client

11. You're the network administrator at your company. Your network consists of both Microsoft Windows 2000 Professional and Windows XP Professional computers. You need to establish an authentication protocol.

    Quick Answer: 236
    Detailed Answer: 237

    When working with Remote Access Services on your network, what authentication protocol should you use to provide the strongest encryption possible?

    - ❑ A. PAP
    - ❑ B. MD5-CHAP
    - ❑ C. RADIUS
    - ❑ D. MS-CHAP
    - ❑ E. CHAP

Quick Check

12. You're the new network administrator for your organization. Some of the users on your network still use Shiva LAN Rover.

    What authentication protocol must be in use on your organization's network to accommodate those clients?

    - ❑ A. EAP-TLS
    - ❑ B. MD5-CHAP
    - ❑ C. RADIUS
    - ❑ D. MS-CHAP
    - ❑ E. SPAP

Quick Answer: 236
Detailed Answer: 237

13. You're the help desk technician for your company. A newly hired vice president of finance needs you to set up a way for her to authenticate from the road with her laptop, which is running Novell NetWare 6.0. Other laptop users at your company use Microsoft Windows XP Professional.

    What authentication protocol will encrypt her username and password, and work with her non-Microsoft laptop?

    - ❑ A. EAP-TLS
    - ❑ B. MD5-CHAP
    - ❑ C. RADIUS
    - ❑ D. MS-CHAP
    - ❑ E. CHAP

Quick Answer: 236
Detailed Answer: 237

14. When working in the IT department at your company, another employee states that there is a nonsecure authentication protocol that sends both the username and password in clear text.

    What authentication protocol is the employee talking about?

    - ❑ A. EAP-TLS
    - ❑ B. PAP
    - ❑ C. RADIUS
    - ❑ D. MS-CHAP
    - ❑ E. SPAP

Quick Answer: 236
Detailed Answer: 238

15. When working in the IT department at your company, another employee states that the company uses PPTP (Point-to-Point Tunneling Protocol) for its Microsoft Windows XP computers in a VPN (virtual private network).

    What features are included in PPTP? (Choose two.)

    ❑ A. Header compression
    ❑ B. Tunnel authentication
    ❑ C. Built-in encryption
    ❑ D. Transmits over IP-based internetworks
    ❑ E. Transmits over ATM, Frame Relay, UDP, or X.25

Quick Answer: 236
Detailed Answer: 238

16. When working in the IT department at your company, another employee states that the company uses L2TP (Layer Two Tunneling Protocol) for its Microsoft Windows XP computers in a VPN (virtual private network).

    What features are included in L2TP? (Choose all that apply.)

    ❑ A. Wireless networking privacy
    ❑ B. Tunnel authentication
    ❑ C. Built-in encryption
    ❑ D. Transmits over IP-based internetworks
    ❑ E. Transmits over ATM, Frame Relay, UDP, or X.25

Quick Answer: 236
Detailed Answer: 238

17. What feature(s) of VPN connections do Microsoft Windows XP computers support? (Choose all that apply.)

    ❑ A. Single inbound connection
    ❑ B. Tunneling protocols
    ❑ C. Setting callback security
    ❑ D. Multilink support

Quick Answer: 236
Detailed Answer: 238

Quick Check

18. You've set up a home office that connects to a cable modem. You want the other computers in your household to be able to access the Internet through this single connection.

    You add a new network card to your gateway computer and attach it to your home network. On the external connection, you enable ICS.

    One computer cannot find any Web sites on the Internet. You examine its network settings and find the following when you look at IPCONFIG:

    ```
    Ethernet adapter Wireless Network Connection:
    Connection-specific DNS Suffix  . : Barknet.ads
    IP Address. . . . . . . . . . . . : 192.168.1.6
    Subnet Mask . . . . . . . . . . . : 255.255.224.0
    Default Gateway . . . . . . . . . : 192.168.1.10
    ```

    What should you do to fix the problem and allow the computer access to the Internet?

    - ❑ A. Disable ICF from the connection that attaches to the Internet.
    - ❑ B. Disable all TCP/IP filters in the Options part of the ICS gateway network configuration.
    - ❑ C. Set the computer up for DHCP because it does not have the correct subnet mask and does not point to the ICS gateway.
    - ❑ D. Reset the subnet mask to 255.255.255.0.

Quick Answer: **236**
Detailed Answer: **238**

19. You've installed Windows XP Professional on your home computer. You use this machine to access the Internet as well as keep some home account information. You are concerned about being hacked, so you enable ICF and ICS on the Internet network connection.

    Later, you check the logs and find that a remote system is opening and closing port 80.

    What should you do to protect your system?

    - ❑ A. Disable the ICS service.
    - ❑ B. Block the SMTP service from within ICF.
    - ❑ C. Block the Web server (HTTP) service.
    - ❑ D. Define a new Web service that uses port 80 and then block it.

Quick Answer: **236**
Detailed Answer: **239**

Quick Check

20. You've just taken a new position at a manufacturing company that requires you to travel frequently. The company provides a high-speed cable modem connection to your home and also has RAS servers to enable you to dial in from hotels. You must use a virtual private network because of security concerns.

    You create a VPN network configuration, but when you try to connect to the corporate VPN server, you get a message box that says Error 781—No Valid Certificate Was Found.

    What should you do to configure the connection correctly?

    - ❑ A. Open port 443 on your ICF configuration.
    - ❑ B. Configure the connection to use PPTP VPN.
    - ❑ C. Configure the connection to use L2TP IPSec VPN.
    - ❑ D. Configure the connection to use a secure password but not encryption.

Quick Answer: **236**
Detailed Answer: **239**

21. You've just taken a new position at a manufacturing company that requires you to travel frequently. The company provides a high-speed cable modem connection to your home and also has RAS servers to enable you to dial in from hotels. You must use a virtual private network because of security concerns.

    You're making a presentation at a customer site and need to access your corporate Web site to find some information for the customer.

    You plug into the customer's network, but find that you cannot access anything on the Internet from your browser.

    What should you do to enable your laptop to access your corporate LAN?

    - ❑ A. Configure your default gateway address to be 192.168.0.1.
    - ❑ B. Issue an IPCONFIG /RENEW command to get the latest IP address from the customer's network.
    - ❑ C. Enable Detect Proxy Settings in Internet Explorer.
    - ❑ D. Have the customer's Network group allow VPN access to your corporate network.

Quick Answer: **236**
Detailed Answer: **239**

Quick Check

22. You're doing help-desk duty when a user from your HR department working at home dials in via RAS and sends you an email request for assistance to change a configuration parameter.

    You accept the connection, but find that you can't connect to the desktop. You verify that the user is online and is using ICF to protect the RAS connection.

    What should you instruct the user to do?

    ❑ A. Go to the Remote tab in the System applet and enable the box labeled Allow This Computer to Be Controlled Remotely.

    ❑ B. Instruct the user to reissue the request for assistance and you reaccept it.

    ❑ C. Go to the Offer Assistance link from the Help and Support Center and connect to the user's computer from that point.

    ❑ D. Instruct the user to open up port 3389 (Remote Desktop service) in ICF.

Quick Answer: **236**
Detailed Answer: **239**

23. You're the network administrator at a software design company. Occasionally, you use contractors to work on specific parts of code you're developing for your customers. For security reasons, you insist on using the strongest data encryption possible for all RAS sessions. What do you instruct your contractors to configure their RAS connections to use?

    ❑ A. PAP

    ❑ B. CHAP

    ❑ C. MS-CHAP v2

    ❑ D. SPAP

Quick Answer: **236**
Detailed Answer: **240**

24. You're the network administrator for a network that has 50 users who dial in from home. A help desk analyst has asked you to explain the differences between SLIP and PPP. Which of the following would you tell the analyst apply only to PPP? (Select two.)

    ❑ A. Supports TCP/IP, IPX, and NetBEUI

    ❑ B. Passwords are sent as clear text

    ❑ C. Usually needs scripting to complete log on

    ❑ D. Supports encryption for authentication

    ❑ E. No error detection

    ❑ F. Can be used only for dial out

Quick Answer: **236**
Detailed Answer: **240**

Quick Check

25. You're an administrator of a small office. There are 10 Windows XP Professional computers. To connect to the Internet, you have shared an Internet connection. One of the users in the office cannot connect to your computer to access the Internet. When you run IPCONFIG on his computer, you see that the address assigned to his computer is 10.1.54.232. Which of the following address ranges should his IP address fall between?

Quick Answer: **236**
Detailed Answer: **240**

- ❑ A. 1.0.0.1 and 1.255.255.254
- ❑ B. 192.168.0.1 and 192.168.255.254
- ❑ C. 191.191.0.1 and 191.194.255.254
- ❑ D. 224.224.244.1 and 224.224.244.254

26. You're the network administrator for a network that has 50 users who dial in from home. A help desk analyst has asked you to explain the differences between SLIP and PPP. Which of the following would you tell the analyst apply only to PPP? (Select two.)

Quick Answer: **236**
Detailed Answer: **240**

- ❑ A. Supports TCP/IP, IPX, and NetBEUI
- ❑ B. Passwords are sent as clear text
- ❑ C. Usually needs scripting to complete log on
- ❑ D. Supports encryption for authentication
- ❑ E. No error detection
- ❑ F. Can be used only for dial out

27. Bob is a consultant for an IT outsourcing company. He has a number of clients that have network infrastructures that enable him to access their internal networks via a virtual private network (VPN). One of his new clients, ACME Corp., needs Bob to check the status of its Exchange Server. Bob configures a VPN connection for ACME on his Windows XP Professional workstation to use a Smart Card. Bob tries to check Automatically Use My Windows Logon Name and Password, but the option is grayed out. What should Bob do to enable this option?

Quick Answer: **236**
Detailed Answer: **240**

- ❑ A. Change the Security option setting from Require Secured Password to Allow Unsecured Password.
- ❑ B. Change the Security option setting from Typical to Advanced.
- ❑ C. Change the Security option setting from Use Smart Card to Require Secured Password.
- ❑ D. Disable his Smart Card.

Quick Check

28. You want to host a family Web site from your home on your Windows XP Professional workstation. You want to enable your family to access the Web site and add content via FTP. You create the site, register its name, and enable Internet Connection Firewall. Later, you receive reports that your family can access the Web page without problem, but no one can upload their files. What can you do to resolve the issue?

Quick Answer: 236
Detailed Answer: 240

- ❑ A. Ensure that the HTTP box on the Services tab of the Advanced Settings page of the ICF VPN Properties dialog box is cleared.
- ❑ B. Ensure that the FTP box on the Services tab of the Advanced Settings page of the ICF VPN Properties dialog box is cleared.
- ❑ C. Ensure that the HTTP box on the Services tab of the Advanced Settings page of the ICF VPN Properties dialog box is checked.
- ❑ D. Ensure that the FTP box on the Services tab of the Advanced Settings page of the ICF VPN Properties dialog box is checked.

29. Your manager informs you that you need to set up dial-up networking for all the clients in your network. She's concerned about ensuring that the clients will use the appropriate authentication protocols as the remote users dial in to the network. You want to calm her fears. Which authentication protocols does Windows XP Professional install, by default, when dial-up networking is installed on the computer? (Check all correct answers.)

Quick Answer: 236
Detailed Answer: 240

- ❑ A. PAP
- ❑ B. SPAP
- ❑ C. MS-CHAP
- ❑ D. MS-CHAPv2
- ❑ E. CHAP

30. You're the administrator for a national bank and your current protocol requires that you use Smart Cards for both local and remote user logons. You want the remote users to be able to use the Internet while connected to the corporate LAN. You do the following:
    - Enable a Smart Card logon process for the domain.
    - Enable the Extensible Authentication Protocol (EAP) and configure the Smart Card or other certificate (TLS) EAP type on the remote access router computer.
    - Enable Smart Card authentication on the VPN connection on the remote access client computer.

    What else must you do to ensure the successful connection of your VPN clients? (Check all correct answers.)

    ❑ A. Install a computer certificate on the remote access router.
    ❑ B. Configure remote access on the remote access router.
    ❑ C. Ensure that the check box Use Default Gateway on Remote Network on the General tab of the TCP/IP Properties sheet is checked.
    ❑ D. Ensure that Internet Connection Firewall on the VPN connection is enabled.

Quick Answer: 236
Detailed Answer: 241

Quick Check

31. You're the network administrator of an international tar factory. You have 200 Windows 2000 servers and 4,500 Windows XP Professional workstations. Two hundred fifty of the Windows XP Professional workstations are for the remote sales force. This remote sales force will access the corporate LAN via Virtual Private Networking and connect to a Windows 2000 Advanced Server running RRAS. You instruct the remote users on how to configure their workstations to use the corporate network via VPN. A few days later, one of the remote users calls you, explaining that he cannot access the Internet when he is connected to the corporate LAN. How should you resolve the issue?

Quick Answer: 236
Detailed Answer: 241

- ❑ A. Ensure that the check box Use Default Gateway on Remote Network on the General tab of the TCP/IP dialog box is checked.
- ❑ B. Clear the check box Use Default Gateway on Remote Network on the General tab of the TCP/IP dialog box.
- ❑ C. Ensure that the check box Allow Other Network Users to Connect Through This Computer's Internet Connection on the Internet Connection Sharing section on the Advanced Dial-Up properties sheet is checked.
- ❑ D. Clear the check box Require Data Encryption (Disconnect If None) on the Security tab of the VPN Properties dialog box.

32. John is the network administrator for SofaKing, Inc., which has 15 print devices distributed throughout the enterprise. SofaKing uses Internet Connection Sharing in its company to provide Internet access to its users. The users' computers receive an address from the server that is sharing the Internet connection. The print devices must have static TCP/IP addresses. You want to ensure that the Dynamic Host Control Protocol (DHCP) service does not assign a conflicting IP address. How should you accomplish this?

Quick Answer: 236
Detailed Answer: 241

- ❑ A. Edit the Registry and change the STOP value to 192.168.0.200.
- ❑ B. Edit the Registry value, STOP, to 192.168.0.1.
- ❑ C. Exclude the print devices' IP address from the DHCP scope.
- ❑ D. Exclude the servers' IP address from the DHCP scope.

Quick Check

33. You have several clients that have installed Windows XP Professional on their corporate workstations. One of your clients calls, requesting that you connect to his machine using Remote Desktop. You have a direct Internet connection and Internet Connection Firewall (ICF) enabled. You attempt to connect to your client's network via VPN. You have problems connecting to the client's machine. What is the first thing you should do?

    - ❑ A. Check the Dial Another Connection First box on the General tab of the VPN Properties dialog box.
    - ❑ B. Ensure that Internet Connection Firewall on the VPN connection is enabled.
    - ❑ C. Disable Internet Connection Firewall on the VPN connection.
    - ❑ D. Disable your direct Internet connection and dial in to your client's network.

Quick Answer: **236**
Detailed Answer: **241**

34. You have 250 Windows XP Professional computers in various OUs in your domain. You have 100 remote Windows XP Professional computers that use VPN connections to connect to the corporate LAN. You want the connections to be encrypted, so you use L2TP with IPSec on the VPN connection. What type of authentication is being used by default during the negotiation of security settings?

    - ❑ A. Preshared key authentication
    - ❑ B. Certificate-based authentication
    - ❑ C. Pass-through authentication
    - ❑ D. Internet authentication service

Quick Answer: **236**
Detailed Answer: **242**

Quick Check Answer Key

1. A
2. B
3. C
4. D
5. E
6. A
7. B
8. A
9. B
10. C
11. D
12. E
13. E
14. B
15. C, D
16. B, D, and E
17. A, B, C, and D
18. C
19. C
20. B
21. C
22. D
23. C
24. A, D
25. B
26. A, D
27. C
28. D
29. All the answers are correct
30. A and B
31. B
32. A
33. C
34. B

Answers and Explanations

1. **Answer: A.** EAP authenticates in conjunction with another device, such as a Smart Card reader, or a biometric device, such as a retinal scanner.
2. **Answer: B.** MD5-CHAP stands for *Message Digest 5 Challenge Handshake Authentication Protocol*. MD5-CHAP encrypts usernames and passwords with an MD5 security hashing algorithm.
3. **Answer: C.** RADIUS stands for *Remote Authentication Dial-In User Service*. RADIUS is a vender-independent authentication protocol. Microsoft Windows XP can only act as a RADIUS client.
4. **Answer: D.** MS-CHAP stands for *Microsoft Challenge Handshake Authentication Protocol*. MS-CHAP encrypts the entire session and not just the username and password. MS-CHAP is supported using Microsoft Windows XP, Windows 2000, and Windows NT 4.0.
5. **Answer: E.** SPAP stands for *Shiva Password Authentication Protocol*. SPAP encrypts the password, but not data. Shiva LAN Rover clients only use SPAP.
6. **Answer: A.** CHAP stands for *Challenge Handshake Authentication Protocol*. CHAP encrypts only the username and password, but not session data. CHAP works with non-Microsoft clients.
7. **Answer: B.** PAP stands for *Password Authentication Protocol*. PAP sends both the username and password in clear text, and is therefore not secure.
8. **Answer: A.** EAP-TLS stands for *Extensible Authentication Protocol-Transport Level Security*. EAP-TLS is primarily used with Smart Cards and digital certificates.
9. **Answer: B.** MD5-CHAP stands for *Message Digest 5 Challenge Handshake Authentication Protocol*. MD5-CHAP encrypts usernames and passwords with an MD5 security hashing algorithm.
10. **Answer: C.** Microsoft Windows XP can only act as a RADIUS client.
11. **Answer: D.** MS-CHAP stands for *Microsoft Challenge Handshake Authentication Protocol*. MS-CHAP encrypts the entire session and not just the username and password. MS-CHAP is supported using Microsoft Windows XP, Windows 2000, and Windows NT 4.0.
12. **Answer: E.** SPAP stands for *Shiva Password Authentication Protocol*. SPAP encrypts the password, but not data. SPAP is used only by Shiva LAN Rover clients.
13. **Answer: E.** CHAP stands for *Challenge Handshake Authentication Protocol*. CHAP encrypts only the username and password, but not session data. CHAP works with non-Microsoft clients.

14. **Answer: B.** PAP stands for *Password Authentication Protocol.* PAP sends both the username and password in clear text, and is therefore not secure.

15. **Answers: C and D.**

    Explanation C. PPTP has built-in encryption.

    Explanation D. PPTP can transmit over IP-based internetworks.

16. **Answers: B, D, and E.**

    Explanation B. L2TP can provide full tunnel authentication.

    Explanation D. PPTP can transmit over IP-based internetworks.

    Explanation E. L2TP (Layer Two Tunneling Protocol) can use these advanced technologies.

17. **Answers: A, B, C, and D.**

    Explanation A. Microsoft Windows XP computers support only a single inbound connection.

    Explanation B. Microsoft Windows XP computers support either PPTP (Point-to-Point Tunneling Protocol) or L2TP (Layer Two Tunneling Protocol) for each VPN (virtual private network).

    Explanation C. Microsoft Windows XP computers support setting callback security, which enables you to have the bill charged to your company's phone number. This also forces the server machine to call back the client at a predefined number for extra security.

    Explanation D. Microsoft Windows XP computers support multilinking, which enables you to combine two or more modems into one logical link with increased bandwidth.

18. **Answer: C.** The computer is not using DHCP. The IP addresses leased by the DHCP service set up as part of ICS range from 192.168.0.2 to 192.168.0.254 with a subnet mask of 255.255.255.0. The second clue is the default gateway address, which is always 192.168.0.1 for an ICS gateway. ICF never blocks outgoing Web traffic and the IP filters are used to enable certain TCP, UDP, or protocols from reaching your system (you would have to enable everything but port 80 for your system to function correctly on your network). Just setting the subnet mask to the correct value will not provide access to the Internet because of the incorrect gateway address.

19. **Answer: C.** If you do not have a Web site on your system, you should not allow anyone to attempt to access the service. What you're seeing is a remote user attempting to open up a Web site on your machine. Blocking port 80 will halt this. The ICS service is used to share a single port with a small network of computers and is not used to block network attacks. The SMTP service will block or pass port 25 traffic. There is no need to define a new service for port 80 because it's a common port already described in ICF.

20. **Answer: B.** If you see a request for a certificate during a VPN connection setup, the connection has been configured to use IPSec under L2TP. IPSec uses certificates to establish machine identity. PPTP does not use certificates and therefore does not issue this error message. The problem is not related to encryption because under PPTP, the keys for MPPE encryption are set up automatically. Port 443 is used in Internet Explorer for SSL connections (HTTPS).

21. **Answer: C.** Many corporations use a proxy server to provide network security and performance enhancements to Web access on the Internet. There are group policies that would automatically download that information to your machine if you formally joined their network and had your machine added to an organizational unit (OU) that had that GP applied. Just plugging into their network would not be enough and your current proxy setting (if you have one at all) would probably prevent you from getting any access to your corporate intranet. Setting your IE browser to detect proxy servers and to download their setting information would enable you to get access to the customer's proxy gateway. Resetting your default gateway address is relevant only on ICS networks, which a large corporation would not have. Neither would asking for a new IP address lease obtain the needed information. You could VPN out of the customer's network into your corporate network and then use your existing configuration to access your Internet Web site, but that is certainly taking the long way around.

22. **Answer: D.** Remote Assistance and Remote Desktop both use Terminal Services technology and both use port 3389 for access. If the user is using RAS to access the Corporate Network and ICF is configured on that connection, the most likely problem is that the Remote Desktop service has not been enabled in ICF. The Remote Control option in the System applet controls the degree to which a desktop can be controlled but does not allow or block it. That is set at the network connection. The Offer Assistance approach to desktop assistance is a different path to the same conclusion and still relies on port 3389.

23. **Answer: C.** Only MS-CHAP V2 will provide data encryption as well as secure password authentication. MS-CHAP V2 automatically sets up data-encryption keys while authenticating your contractor's user ID and passwords. PAP does not encrypt passwords. SPAP will encrypt passwords while connecting to a Shiva LAN Rover. CHAP will also encrypt passwords; however, none of the protocols other than MS-CHAP V2 will encrypt data.

24. **Answers: A and D.** Only PPP supports IPX and NetBEUI as well as TCP/IP. PPP also supports encryption of logon information if configured.

25. **Answer: B.** When you share an Internet connection on a Windows XP computer, it automatically assigns DHCP addresses to clients. The addresses that it assigns are between 192.168.0.1 and 192.168.255.254.

26. **Answers: A and D.** Only PPP supports IPX and NetBEUI as well as TCP/IP. PPP also supports encryption of logon information if configured.

27. **Answer: C.** The Automatically Use My Windows Logon Name and Password option is available only when the Security option setting Require Secured Password is selected. When using a Smart Card for authorization, the logon name and password entry will be secured and there is no need to have the system require a secured password. Answer B is incorrect because selecting Advanced on the Security option setting will gray out the option, not make it available. Answer A is incorrect because the Allow Unsecured Password option is only available with dial-up clients. Answer D is incorrect because you cannot disable the Smart Card and allow Bob to log on.

28. **Answer: D.** Any service that you want to provide for remote clients must be enabled on the Services tab of the Advanced Settings page on the ICF VPN Properties dialog box. Answer A is incorrect because that would cause the users to not be able to connect to the Web site, which is not what you want.Answer B is incorrect because the FTP service option must be selected, not cleared. Answer C is incorrect because the scenario clearly indicates that users are able to connect to the Web site, so the option had to have been checked.

29. All the answers are correct. An *authentication protocol* is a set of standards for exchanging logon name and password information between the two network devices. Microsoft Windows XP supports the most common authentication protocols and includes their own version of CHAP. For a dial-up connection, all of these protocols are selected and are supported for the remote access client.

30. **Answers: A and B.** You must install a computer certificate on the remote access router because you're using Smart Cards. You must also configure remote access on the remote access router that remote clients can connect to. Answer C is incorrect because it would cause the remote clients to not be able to connect to the Internet. Answer D is incorrect because it would cause the remote clients to have connectivity problems if ICF is installed.

31. **Answer: B.** The check box applies when you are connected to a local network and a dial-up network simultaneously. When checked, data that cannot be sent on the local network is forwarded to the dial-up network. Answer A is incorrect because the browser is using the remote server as its gateway (which is incorrect) and will not be able to connect to the Internet. Answer C is incorrect because the issue is about connecting to remote computers, not computers connecting to the user's computer. You would check the box if you wanted others to access the Internet through your computer. Answer D is incorrect because it wouldn't affect whether the user could access the Internet.

32. **Answer: A.** To ensure that the Dynamic Host Control Protocol (DHCP) service does not assign a conflicting IP address, you must edit the Registry and change the STOP value to 192.168.0.200. You would then assign to the printers static IP addresses from the range above 192.168.0.200, including 192.168.0.201 through 254. Answer B is incorrect because the value expressed in the answer would not allow enough addresses for the clients on the network. Answer C is incorrect because the DHCP scope is hard-coded and cannot be modified. Answer D is incorrect because the server IP addresses would not be in the DHCP scope.

33. **Answer: C.** You should not enable ICF on VPN connections because it will interfere with the operation of file sharing and other VPN functions. Answer A is incorrect because you would have the same problems with ICF. Answer B is incorrect because, by default, the option is already enabled. Although it seems that answer D would work, nothing in the scenario suggests that it is possible to dial in to the network.

34. **Answer: B.** When you make an L2TP with IPSec connection, an IPSec policy is automatically created to specify that the Internet Key Exchange (IKE) will use certificate-based authentication during the negotiation of security settings for L2TP. This means that both the L2TP client and L2TP server must have a computer certificate (also known as a *machine certificate*) installed before a successful L2TP-over-IPSec connection can be established. Answer A is incorrect because Microsoft does not recommend frequent use of preshared key authentication; the authentication key is stored unprotected in the IPSec policy. Preshared key methodology is provided *only* for interoperability purposes and to adhere to the IPSec standards set forth by the Internet Engineering Task Force (IETF). Answer C is incorrect because pass-through authentication is for access to resources, not the negotiation of security settings. Answer D is incorrect because IAS performs centralized authentication, authorization, auditing, and accounting of connections for dial-up and VPN remote access and demand-dial connections; it does not negotiate security settings.

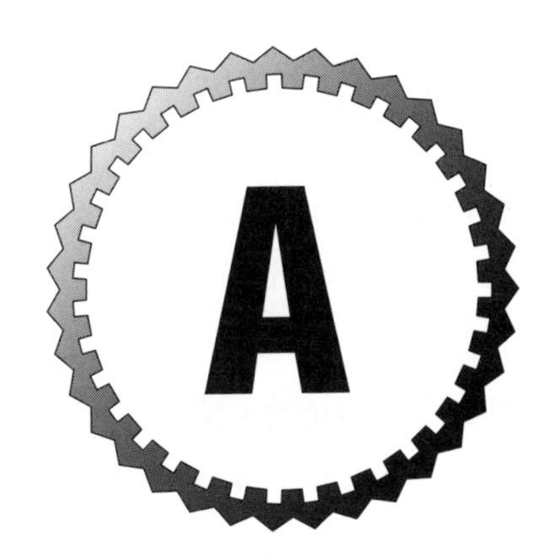

CD Contents and Installation Instructions

The CD features an innovative practice test engine powered by MeasureUp™, giving you yet another effective tool to assess your readiness for the exam.

Multiple Test Modes

MeasureUp practice tests are available in Study, Certification, Custom, Adaptive, Missed Question, and Non-Duplicate question modes.

Study Mode

Tests administered in Study Mode enable you to request the correct answer(s) and explanation to each question during the test. These tests are not timed. You can modify the testing environment *during* the test by selecting the Options button.

Certification Mode

Tests administered in Certification Mode closely simulate the actual testing environment you will encounter when taking a certification exam. These tests do not enable you to request the answer(s) and/or explanation to each question until after the exam.

Custom Mode

Custom Mode enables you to specify your preferred testing environment. Use this mode to specify the objectives you want to include in your test, the timer length, and other test properties. You can also modify the testing environment *during* the test by selecting the Options button.

Adaptive Mode

Tests administered in Adaptive Mode closely simulate the actual testing environment you will encounter taking an Adaptive exam. After answering a question, you are not allowed to go back—you are only allowed to move forward during the exam.

Missed Question Mode

Missed Question Mode enables you to take a test containing only the questions you have missed previously.

Non-Duplicate Mode

Non-Duplicate Mode enables you to take a test containing only questions not displayed previously.

Random Questions and Order of Answers

This feature helps you learn the material without memorizing questions and answers. Each time you take a practice test, the questions and answers appear in a different randomized order.

Detailed Explanations of Correct and Incorrect Answers

You'll receive automatic feedback on all correct and incorrect answers. The detailed answer explanations are a superb learning tool in their own right.

Attention to Exam Objectives

MeasureUp practice tests are designed to appropriately balance the questions over each technical area covered by a specific exam.

Installing the CD

The minimum system requirements for the CD-ROM are

- Windows 95, 98, Me, NT 4.0, 2000, or XP
- 7MB disk space for the testing engine
- An average of 1MB disk space for each test

To install the CD-ROM, follow these instructions:

If you need technical support, please contact MeasureUp at 678-356-5050 or email `support@measureup.com`. Additionally, you'll find Frequently Asked Questions (FAQs) at `www.measureup.com`.

1. Close all applications before beginning this installation.
2. Insert the CD into your CD-ROM drive. If the setup starts automatically, go to step 5. If the setup does not start automatically, continue with step 3.

3. From the Start menu, select Run.
4. In the Browse dialog box, double-click Setup.exe. In the Run dialog box, click OK to begin the installation.
5. On the Welcome screen, click Next.
6. To agree to the Software License Agreement, click Yes.
7. On the Choose Destination Location screen, click Next to install the software to `C:\Program Files\Certification Preparation`.
8. On the Setup Type screen, select Typical Setup. Click Next to continue.
9. After the installation is complete, verify that Yes, I Want to Restart My Computer Now is selected. If you select No, I Will Restart My Computer Later, you will not be able to use the program until you restart your computer.
10. Click Finish.
11. After restarting your computer, choose Start, Programs, MeasureUp Practice Tests.
12. Select the practice test you want to access and click Start Test.

Creating a Shortcut to the MeasureUp Practice Tests

To create a shortcut to the MeasureUp practice tests, follow these steps:

1. Right-click on your Desktop.
2. From the shortcut menu, select New, Shortcut.
3. Browse to `C:\Program Files\MeasureUp Practice Tests` and select the MeasureUpCertification.exe or Localware.exe file.
4. Click OK.
5. Click Next.
6. Rename the shortcut MeasureUp.
7. Click Finish.

After you have completed step 7, use the MeasureUp shortcut on your Desktop to access the MeasureUp practice test.

Technical Support

If you encounter problems with the MeasureUp test engine on the CD-ROM, please contact MeasureUp at 678-356-5050 or email support@measureup.com. Technical support hours are from 8:00 a.m. to 5:00 p.m. EST Monday through Friday. Additionally, you'll find Frequently Asked Questions (FAQs) at www.measureup.com.

If you'd like to purchase additional MeasureUp products, call 678-356-5050 or 800-649-1MUP (1687), or visit www.measureup.com.